THE ETHICS OF WELFARE

Human rights, dependency and responsibility

Edited by Hartley Dean

The POLICY

P~P

PRESS

First published in Great Britain in March 2004 by

The Policy Press
University of Bristol
Fourth Floor
Beacon House
Queen's Road
Bristol BS8 1QU
UK

Tel +44 (0)117 331 4054
Fax +44 (0)117 331 4093
e-mail tpp-info@bristol.ac.uk
www.policypress.org.uk

British Library Cataloguing in Publication Data
A catalogue record for this book is available from the British Library.

Library of Congress Cataloging-in-Publication Data
A catalog record for this book has been requested.

ISBN 1 86134 562 3 paperback

A hardcover version of this book is also available

Hartley Dean is a Lecturer in Social Policy at the London School of Economics and Political Science.

Cover design by Qube Design Associates, Bristol.
Front cover: photograph supplied by kind permission of Brenda Price, Photofusion.
Printed and bound in Great Britain by Hobbs the Printers Ltd, Southampton.

Contents

List of figures, tables and boxes

Figures

Tables

Boxes

Acknowledgements

Firstly, I most gratefully acknowledge the support of the Economic and Social Research Council (ESRC), which funded the research project that has informed much of this volume (Award Ref: R000239425). I should also acknowledge that that project would not have been possible without the cooperation of Luton Borough Council and the Department for Work and Pensions. Above all, the research depended upon the participation of the members of the public, the social workers and benefits administrators who agreed to be interviewed for the purposes of the project and to whom I am especially grateful. A word of appreciation is also due to the School of Sociology and Social Policy at the University of Nottingham, which provided a temporary 'home' for the project during its final stages. I am grateful, too, to the Department of Social Policy at the London School of Economics and Political Science for allowing me the time and space to put this book together while settling in to my present post.

An additional source of, and a testing ground for, some of the material in this book was the 'Dependency, Responsibility and Rights' stream at the European Social Policy Research Network conference at the University of Tilburg (the Netherlands) in August 2002, and I am extremely grateful to Wim van Oorschot, the organiser of the conference, for allowing me to convene that stream of papers.

I am especially grateful to the staff at The Policy Press, and Dawn Rushen in particular, for their efficiency and helpfulness.

Finally, my thanks must also go to all my fellow contributors, especially Kathryn Ellis, Ruth Rogers and Shane Doheny, who worked with me on the ESRC project; but also to Pete Dwyer and Michael Orton for their stimulating ideas and efficient execution.

Hartley Dean
London School of Economics and Political Science

Notes on contributors

Hartley Dean is Lecturer in Social Policy at the London School of Economics and Political Science.

Shane Doheny is a Research Assistant at the Management Research Centre, University of Bristol.

Peter Dwyer is Lecturer in Social Policy at the University of Leeds.

Kathryn Ellis is Senior Lecturer in the Applied Social Studies Department at the University of Luton.

Michael Orton is a Research Fellow at the University of Warwick.

Ruth Rogers is a Research Fellow at Canterbury Christ Church University College.

Introduction

Hartley Dean

An important part of this book's context has been the introduction to the UK of the 1998 Human Rights Act (which incorporates into UK law the provisions of the European Convention on Human Rights) and, in the global context, the new relevance attached to the language of human rights. At the same time that human rights have been moving up the political agenda, policy makers of the so-called 'third way' have been insisting, on the one hand, that we can have no rights without responsibilities, while implying, on the other, that we cannot be properly responsible if we allow ourselves to be dependent – and dependent on the state, especially. This paradox represents an ethical conundrum with significant consequences for the future of welfare provision.

This book explores and discusses, therefore, the relationship between concepts of responsibility and discourses of rights on the one hand, and the ways in which rights are to be understood in relation to human dependency and interdependency on the other. It investigates how emergent discourses of human rights may change the ways in which the welfare state and its future are envisaged. It also aims, however, to kick-start a new kind of debate about the moral foundations of social policy and welfare reform. Although a significant amount of scholarship has been devoted to the discussion of citizenship and welfare, it has not been directly concerned with the contested ethical nexus that links dependency, responsibility and rights.

The book is in substantial part an outcome from a UK-based research project funded by the Economic and Social Research Council (ESRC). That project centred upon an interview-based study that explored popular and welfare provider discourses as they impinge upon questions of dependency, responsibility and rights. Additionally, some chapters of this book draw upon analyses of policy and governmental documents or texts, analyses that were conducted or written up in direct conjunction with the interview study.

Additional material has been drawn from papers given at a conference of the European Social Policy Research Network entitled 'Social values, social policies: Normative foundations of changing social policies in European countries', held at the University of Tilburg (the Netherlands), 29-30 August 2002.

In this book, all of this material is placed in the context of a broader account of mutual dependency, social responsibility and human rights, and is used to develop a discussion of the ethics of welfare in a global context and, in particular, the potential tensions and synergies between the development of human rights, on the one hand, and the maintenance of social and welfare rights on the other. The book's chapters vary in some respects in their style and approach, but together they exhibit an overriding unity of purpose, insofar as they all address themselves to the need to rethink the ethical nexus that connects dependency, responsibility and rights.

The Economic and Social Research Council study

The research upon which Parts One and Two of this book draw, involving Kathryn Ellis, Ruth Rogers, Shane Doheny and myself, had focused primarily upon two areas of social policy: benefits provision for working-age people, and social care provision for older and disabled people. Our research objectives were:

- to explore the extent to which, in the British context, the emerging discourse of human rights may accommodate or permit either an enlarged or a more restricted understanding of social rights;
- to study the different ways in which dependency, on the one hand, and responsibility, on the other, are apprehended within prevailing political discourses, in the discourses of welfare providers/professionals and in popular discourse;
- to draw conclusions as to the extent to which contradictory social constructions of dependency and responsibility may shape or inhibit the future development of social rights;
- to contribute to the debate concerning the place of social rights in relation to human rights and to an understanding of the discursive repertoires that the debate is currently drawing upon;
- to inform policy makers and welfare providers/professionals as to the nature of popular preoccupations and understandings about dependency, responsibility and the rights of individuals as citizens of a welfare state.

There were two substantive components to the investigation which were conducted between November 2001 and May 2002:

1. A study of popular discourses around dependency, responsibility and rights, based on in-depth interviews with an achieved sample of 49 working-age adults with widely differing incomes. Parts of this sample were recruited for the project in Dover and Sheffield. The other substantial part was recruited from within the Luton Citizen's Panel with the agreement of Luton Borough Council. The sample was boosted (to include an additional high-income earner) with one extra interview conducted in London.
2. A study of professional/provider discourses around dependency, responsibility and rights. This was based on in-depth interviews with two groups of people: an achieved sample of nine benefits administrators employed within the Department for Work and Pensions (DWP), and an achieved sample of 14 local authority social workers and care workers. The first group was recruited with assistance from a DWP District Office, but because the timing of our fieldwork coincided with a period of major reorganisation within

the DWP the sample is smaller than had been hoped for. The second group was recruited with the assistance of three English local authorities.

A common and loosely structured interview schedule was used in both sets of interviews. The interviews explored with participants their perceptions of and attitudes towards dependency and responsibility; the meaning of dependency and responsibility in relation to welfare services and benefits; and, in this context, the scope and relevance of human rights. Respondents in both studies were guaranteed complete confidentiality, and this is reflected in the manner in which findings are reported. All interviews were fully transcribed and a preliminary analysis of the responses recorded in the transcripts was undertaken, followed by a more detailed discourse-based analysis. Clearly, the sample sizes in the second study were small and there are limits to the generalisations that may be based on our findings. Nonetheless, in spite of the significant caution that is called for, the richness of the data and the nature of the findings were such that they are of intrinsic interest and warranted our attention.

The Tilburg conference

Preliminary outputs from this research were presented at the European Social Policy Research Network conference in Tilburg, at which I convened a stream of papers around the general theme of 'Dependency, responsibility and rights', to which a range of other academics also contributed, two of whom – Peter Dwyer and Michael Orton – have kindly provided chapters for this book.

Outline of the book

The book is in four parts. **Part One** sets the theoretical scene by addressing dependency, responsibility and rights as ideological constructions. Chapter One discusses the extent to which social or welfare rights appear to have been marginalised within the global human rights agenda; it argues that this reflects a failure adequately to conceptualise human dependency and social responsibility. Chapter Two then discusses the nature of human interdependency and links this to recent demands for a political ethic of care. Chapter Three draws on an illustrative analysis of British government press releases as well as recent theoretical debates in order to develop a critical discussion of competing conceptions of responsibility.

Part Two presents the findings from the research described earlier on popular and welfare provider discourses. Chapter Four discusses the findings from the interviews with our core sample of working-age adults, while Chapter Five discusses the findings from our interviews with social workers and Chapter Six the findings from our interviews with benefits administrators.

Part Three of the book presents findings from other research and focuses more on the experiences of welfare service users and benefits recipients. Chapter Seven draws on recent qualitative studies conducted within the UK and Europe in order to explore different notions of agency and dependency and the ways these may legitimise or invalidate claims to welfare. Chapter Eight draws on an analysis of guidance issued by the UK government to the claimants of Jobseeker's Allowance and illustrates the ways in which the responsibilities and rights of unemployed people can be reconstituted through their dependency on the state. Chapter Nine draws on a UK-based qualitative study of people who have defaulted on their responsibilities to pay taxes towards the cost of local authority services and explores their wider notions of responsibility to family and community.

Part Four contains a single concluding chapter, Chapter Ten, which draws together themes developed in earlier chapters. The indications are that, whereas popular discourse can accommodate an appreciation of human interdependency and welfare providers remain committed to a public service ethos, 'third way' thinking – espoused inter alia by Britain's New Labour government – is associated with a narrowing of solidaristic responsibilities that fetters understandings of welfare rights. This book's concluding chapter examines the scope for a human rights approach to social welfare and proposes a way of conceptualising the connections between dependency, responsibility and rights.

It should emerge in the course of what follows that it is difficult, if not impossible, to consider dependency, responsibility and rights apart from each other. They are necessarily connected elements of our social humanity. As such, it will be argued, they are socially and ethically constructed. My own argument is that it is through rights that we may yet construct a social policy framework to accommodate and connect our dependencies and our responsibilities.

Part One
Ideological constructions

ONE

Human rights and welfare rights: contextualising dependency and responsibility

Hartley Dean

Human rights are an ideological fiction. This is not to diminish the concept; rather, it is to recognise that the notion of a universally definable set of rights that are inherent to human beings by virtue of their humanity is a socially constructed ideal. Human rights are an expression neither of eternal verities on the one hand, nor mere moral norms on the other, but of systemically derived ethical principles or social values.

The common wisdom that informs much current debate about welfare reform is that economic globalisation has signalled the end of the 'golden age' of the welfare state. More particularly, however, it has been argued that the concept of social or welfare rights – as a distinctive component of citizenship within capitalist welfare states – has been eclipsed and that the development of social welfare should now be conceptualised as the pursuit not of social *rights*, but of the minimum social *standards* appropriate to any particular stage of economic development (Mishra, 1999).

However, should we accept that globalisation (insofar that this contested concept does relate to palpable processes) has political and cultural as well as economic dimensions (for example, Held et al, 1999), then we should also acknowledge that one of its effects has been the ascendancy of a particular human rights discourse. Enthusiasts for human rights now speak of a 'third wave' in the development of human rights that is closely linked to globalisation (Klug, 2000). Even the fiercest theoretical critics of the substantive gap between law and justice around the globe acknowledge the prevailing concept of human rights as "the new ideal that has triumphed on the world stage" (Douzinas, 2000, p 2). There is a paradox here. The 1980s and 1990s witnessed a renaissance of interest in the concept of *citizenship*, not only within the academic subjects of Political Science and Sociology, but also within academic Social Policy (for example, Jordan, 1989; Roche, 1992; Twine, 1994; Lister, 1997; Dean, 1999), an interest that succeeded in pushing debate about rights and welfare beyond the bounds of the seminal theory of citizenship first espoused by T.H. Marshall in 1950. However, with the re-emergent preoccupation with human rights, the debate has entered a new and potentially quite different phase. The new ascendancy of human rights discourse may displace, rather than enhance, our understanding of citizenship; it may marginalise, rather than promote, the cause of social welfare.

Self-evidently, the concept of human rights is more global than that of citizenship, insofar that it encompasses notions of entitlement that transcend considerations of nationality (for example, Turner, 1993). During what Klug (2000) characterises as the 'second wave' of human rights development, the United Nations Declaration of Human Rights (UNDHR) of 1948 clearly envisaged that human rights should encompass not only civil and political rights, but social, economic and cultural rights as well. In practice, however, the realisation of substantive social rights has always taken second place to the support given by Western powers and international bodies to the promotion of civil liberties and democratic freedoms (see Bobbio, 1996, ch 4; Dean, 1996, 2002; Deacon, 1997). Taking as an example Britain's new Human Rights Act of 1998 (implemented in 2000), this incorporated directly into British constitutional law the provisions of the European Convention on Human Rights (ECHR), but, conspicuously, it did not incorporate the provisions of that convention's sister document, the Council of Europe's Social Charter. The ECHR does provide a right to education (or rather a right not to be denied education), but it does not provide a universal right to adequate subsistence, shelter, health or social care. Britain's Human Rights Act signals a shift in domestic political discourse and portends a changing context for the development of social policy. However, it has been enacted at the same time that the language of rights in relation to the provision of social security and collective provision is giving way to an emphasis on social responsibility and self-provisioning.

This chapter aims to examine the broader issues that flow from the distinctively liberal-individualist conception of human rights that is associated with globalisation. It briefly discusses the historical and conceptual background to human rights and human welfare before exploring the ways in which human rights discourse is entering current debates about global social development and European social protection. It draws out some alternative interpretations of human rights and uses the example of current 'workfare' policies in Europe to illustrate the ways in which social rights are compromised precisely because it is a particular interpretation of human rights that is ascendant. In so doing, I hope to set the context in which the rest of this book sets out to re-conceptualise the nature of human interdependency and the ethics of social responsibility, since it is these that furnish the basis for any understanding of welfare rights as a species of human right.

Human rights and social rights

Concepts of citizenship rights may be traced back, if not to antiquity and the Athenian city-state, then to the Western Enlightenment and the French and American Revolutions. The discourse of human rights, in contrast, is relatively new. It found its seminal statement during the post-Second World War period in the symbolically important UNDHR. Although human rights are often regarded as a class of natural or pre-legal rights, Clarke (1996, p 119) points out that 'human' is no less a social and political construct than 'citizen' and, historically speaking, it is a term of more recent provenance. Citizen rights, Clarke contends, provide the model for human rights – not the other way round. Any charter or declaration of rights assumes that its signatory states (whether local, national or supranational) are, or will at least *potentially* be, capable of guaranteeing such rights. Declarations of human rights characteristically contain a mixture of rights that actually exist, insofar that they are universally enforceable, and rights that should exist, but that are not yet universally enforceable (for example, Bobbio, 1996) – what Feinberg has called "manifesto rights" (cited in Campbell, 1983, p 19). As I have already noted, the UNDHR incorporates not only civil and political rights – to life, liberty, property, equality before the law, privacy, fair trial, religious freedom, free speech and assembly, to participate in government, to political asylum, and an absolute right not to be tortured – but also what it refers to as 'economic, social and cultural' rights. What are here referred to as economic and cultural rights might legitimately be encompassed within a broad concept of 'social' rights, and include rights to education, work and even leisure. Most particularly, article 25 states:

> Everyone has the right to a standard of living adequate for the health and well being of himself and his family, including food, clothing, housing and medical care and necessary social services, and the right to security in the event of unemployment, sickness, disability, widowhood, old age or other lack of livelihood in circumstances beyond his control.

It is widely supposed that during the negotiations that led up to the proclamation of the UNDHR, provision for social rights was included at the insistence of the Soviet bloc, reflecting the rights provisions of the Soviet constitution and a very different view of what freedom required (Goodwin, 1987, p 240; and see Bowring, 2002). In the event, it has to be noted not only that the Soviet bloc nations all abstained when the declaration was eventually adopted, but also that there were other ideological forces at work. US President Roosevelt (whose widow, Eleanor, went on to be the US delegate to the UN General Assembly and to be one of the principal architects of the UNDHR) had clearly signalled in an address in 1941 that 'freedom from want' was one of the freedoms to be achieved in any postwar international order and, famously, that "necessitous men are not free men" (see Eide, 1997). It is to the doctrine of social liberalism rather than that of socialism that we probably owe the social rights provisions of the UNDHR.

Nonetheless, the idea that social rights may properly be conceived as human rights has been vigorously challenged by neoliberals and legal positivists alike (for example, Nozick, 1974 for the former, and Cranston, 1973 for the latter).

In any event, although the international human rights regime provides for the monitoring and reporting of human rights abuses, it lacks effective means of enforcement (for example, Held et al, 1999). Most significantly, however, when in the 1960s it came to defining more specifically the substance of the principles outlined in the UNDHR, it is striking that the UN eventually adopted two quite separate covenants: one on Civil and Political Rights and the other on Economic, Social and Cultural Rights (van Genugten, 1997), implying at the very least that there was a fundamental difference between civil and political freedoms on the one hand and substantive rights to work and welfare upon the other. Similar distinctions have tended to emerge in the various regional human rights instruments that have developed around the world. In 1950, the Council of Europe adopted its own ECHR (relating only to civil and political rights), and over a decade later in 1961 a separate sister document, the Social Charter (relating to economic and social rights). Only the former provided a means of enforcing the rights it created through the European Court of Human Rights (although the revised Social Charter of 1996 – that came into force in 1999 – provides a right not of individual redress, but of collective complaint by trades unions and non-governmental organisations to a European Committee for Social Rights). The constitutional status of social rights as a species of human right remains weak, at best (Dean, 1996, 2002).

However ineffectual in terms of its substantive impact, the emergent human rights regime of the late 20th century had played nonetheless a significant role in the complex and contested process of 'globalisation' (for example, Held et al, 1999). It is not only the economic power of transnational capital that has diluted the power of nation states, but also the ideological challenge to national sovereignty represented by the ascendant discourse of human rights and its attendant apparatuses. Habermas (2001, p 119) goes so far as to argue that, in the transition from nation states to a cosmopolitan order, "human rights provide the sole recognised basis of legitimation for the politics of the international community". In this context, human rights discourse, when it is primarily construed in terms of the values of liberal democracy, may not so much promote the development of social rights as help to constrain the capacity of nation states to adopt protectionist welfare policies. It has contributed to the passing of the 'golden age' of state welfare (Esping-Andersen, 1996).

Optimistic (and some would say 'utopian') commentators have discussed the possibility that a form of 'global citizenship' might emerge, predicated on a global conception of human rights. Falk (1994), for example, has suggested that, quite apart from the consequences of economic globalisation, there are several other intimately interconnected grounds upon which it is possible to conceive or advocate forms of global citizenship: longstanding aspirational demands for global peace and justice; emergent modes of transnational political mobilisation arising both from regional movements and new social movements; and the emerging ecological crisis. From a more pessimistic (and some might say 'realistic') perspective, however, Soysal (1994) has argued that two institutionalised principles of the global system – national sovereignty and universal human rights – have collided (Turner, 1993). Soysal illustrates how one consequence of this is to be observed in the rights that are begrudgingly afforded by developed nations to migrant labour (Morris, 2001). Nonetheless, to the extent that it is the developed nation states that are accorded responsibility for maintaining human rights, paradoxically this can also fortify their authority and even justify humanitarian or military intervention in other parts of the world – as recent events, such as the US-led invasion of Iraq in 2003, all too plainly attest. Soysal implies that, as our concepts of rights become globalised, they become abstracted and detached from our sense of local belonging or identity; from our capacity to regulate our own lives. Human rights discourse tends to be abstract, totalising and 'top-down', rather than concrete, particular and 'bottom-up' in nature. This, I believe, is a critical insight so far as the maintenance and development of social or welfare rights are concerned, and one to which I shall return.

The new human rights discourse

First, however, I wish to draw attention to the new ways in which human rights are being invoked. For example, in its *Human Development Report 2000*, the United Nations Development Programme (UNDP) sought to concert demands for human development, with demands for human rights. Recognising that, in the past "the rhetoric of human rights was reduced to a weapon in the propaganda for geopolitical interests" (UNDP, 2000, p 3), the end of the Cold War, UNDP argues, has created a climate in which it is possible to realise the common vision and common purpose that informs the respective concepts of human rights and human development. The former is concerned with basic human freedoms, the latter with the enhancement of human capabilities. The language of the *Human Development Report* is clearly influenced by Amartya Sen, who is in fact the author of the report's first chapter. Sen's contribution to the report draws carefully upon Kant's distinction between perfect and imperfect duties, which he uses to underline the point that just because rights may not be fulfilled, this does not mean they do not exist. Sen's argument (as I read it) is that rights may be constituted through the aspirations and demands of the dispossessed even when the powerful repudiate or neglect the duties that such rights would impose upon them. This, however, is not quite the reading that the UNDP would seem to adopt in the rest of its report, in which Sen's notion of human capability is subtly appropriated as a malleable concept more akin to that of human or social *capital* (Coleman, 1988; Putnam, 2000). Development is assumed self-evidently to require economic growth and rights to require liberal democracy. Both require a pluralistic and apolitical social context in which NGOs and civil society groups can play a role as much as government (although, conspicuously, trade unions are never mentioned, in spite of the critical role that they can play in developing rights). The enforceability of rights, it is assumed, requires mechanisms akin to those by which global *trade* is governed and here, as it identifies the gaps that exist in the global order, the

UNDP begins to draw upon managerialist expressions: it speaks of the need for incentive structures, for regulatory jurisdiction and for adequate participation. It speaks of the need for poor countries to avail themselves of the *opportunities* that globalisation offers (UNDP, 2000, p 9), but it does not recognise that, while the powerful may interpret the risks of a globalised capitalist economy in terms of opportunity, the vulnerable may interpret them in terms of insecurity (Vail, 1999).

One can but welcome the UNDP's demand that, in the pursuit of human development, economic, social and cultural rights should be given as much attention as civil and political rights (UNDP, 2000, p 13). Nonetheless, the document contains many hallmarks of what has elsewhere been characterised as new managerialist doctrine (for example, Hood, 1991; Clarke and Newman, 1997): its demands for better use of information is couched in the language of depoliticised, evidence based, policy-making; the processes by which the achievement of human rights can be managed invoke such recognisable techniques as self-assessment, benchmarking, culture change – drawn from the repertoire of new managerialism. Human rights have in a sense become colonised in the cause of a managerialist approach to human development. There is a danger that the cause of welfare rights may be eclipsed by the liberal individualism that provides the unspoken ideological foundations of global managerial orthodoxy.

In the European context, there has been an attenuated process by which the rhetoric of human rights has been brought into the realm of governance, as distinct from that of jurisprudence. As the European Community evolved into the European Union (EU), it become increasingly concerned to promote what it called a 'social dimension' to the process of European economic integration and development (CEC, 1993). To this end the EU Charter of Fundamental Social Rights of 1989 and the Social Protocols (or 'Social Chapters') to the 1993 and 1997 Maastricht and Amsterdam treaties had sought to build upon earlier measures under the Treaty of Rome relating to freedom of movement, health and safety at work and the equal treatment of men and women. The constraints upon the process stemmed from the liberal traditions observed by UK governments, on the one hand, which consistently sought to resist or opt out from the notion that fundamental rights should have a social dimension, and from continental European/Catholic trade union traditions on the other, that interpreted social-solidaristic rights as workers' rights, rather than more broadly as citizens' rights. However, as the EU seeks both to widen and deepen its scope, it has now proclaimed a Charter of Fundamental Rights of the European Union (CEU, 2000) that draws explicitly on both the ECHR and the Council of Europe's Social Charter.

The preamble to the charter declares that "the Union is founded on the indivisible, universal values of human dignity, freedom, equality and solidarity" and that "it is necessary to strengthen the protection of fundamental rights in the light of changes in society, social progress and scientific and technological developments by making those rights more visible in a Charter" (CEU, 2000, p 11). The charter itself does not establish new powers for the EU, nor does it establish any justifiable rights; but its language is significant. The chapters relating to 'Dignity' (that is, concerned with the right to life and the integrity of the person), 'Freedoms' (concerned primarily with civil liberties), 'Equality' (formal equality and non-discrimination, not substantive social equality), 'Citizens' Rights' (in fact, concerned primarily with political rights) and 'Justice' (concerned with legal rights) are all squarely situated in the liberal-democratic civil and political rights tradition. Rights to education and work are proclaimed in the chapter entitled 'Freedoms', but they are framed in essence as permissive or negative rights. While reference is made to the 'possibility' of free compulsory education and the 'freedom to choose an occupation', there is no outright obligation upon member states to provide education or work. Only in the chapter entitled 'Solidarity' is reference made to substantive social rights. Most of the rights provided for relate to employment protection – not welfare provision. However, there is a right to health care. In respect of social security and social assistance, article 34 states only that "The Union recognises and respects the entitlement to social security benefits and social services [where these have been established by member states]". Several commentators have complained in the past that, insofar that the EU is concerned to address the social consequences of economic integration, it seeks to combat not social inequality in Europe, but social exclusion and risks to social cohesion (Townsend, 1992; Gold and Mayes, 1993; Room, 1995; Levitas, 1996). The EU has now framed a human rights document that is effectively consistent with that objective and that fails effectively to harness human rights to social protection, or does so only in the most equivocal terms.

Interpreting human rights

Just as the discourse of citizenship with which academic Social Policy has been preoccupied of late is fraught with contradiction, so too is the new discourse of human rights. I have sought elsewhere (Dean, 1999) to develop the conventional theoretical dichotomy between liberal and republican models of citizenship and to locate this within popular discourse. I have argued that the fundamental distinction lies between contractarian and solidaristic notions of citizenship, and that the inherent ambiguity of public opinion towards the welfare state stems from the way in which people draw on conflicting moral repertoires. At the heart of the dichotomy between contractarian and solidaristic notions of citizenship lie fundamentally different ideas about the nature of the human condition. At one extreme lies an essentially Hobbesian view that society is composed of self-interested and inherently competitive individuals whose mutually destructive propensities require a contractual arrangement by which certain individual freedoms must be 'traded' in return for social order achieved through state regulation. At the other extreme lies a view that the human subject is endemically vulnerable and to survive requires collectively organised mechanisms for mutual cooperation and support: in other words, what matters, as Richard Rorty has put it, "is our loyalty to other human beings clinging together against the dark" (cited in Doyal and Gough, 1991, p 19). Even if we translate a defence of welfare systems from the language of citizenship to a language of human rights, the same basic dichotomy is likely to apply (Habermas, 2001, p 116). The dichotomy is between a view that regards human rights as a reflection or incorporation of the duties or obligations that are necessary to the maintenance of order among wholly autonomous subjects, and a view that regards them as a response to or recognition of human inter-dependency. If one takes the defence of human dignity as an ideological commitment that characteristically features in human rights instruments, it is clear that the dominant interpretation of this – certainly in the Charter of Fundamental Rights of the European Union – stems from a notion of dignity that is synonymous with individual autonomy and the integrity of the self. However, this is not the only meaning of dignity: it can also refer to issues of social status and recognition as prerequisites for inclusion with diversity (Honneth, 1995).

Insofar that human rights discourse may be displacing social citizenship discourse, it is a particular interpretation of human rights that is ascendant and an interpretation to which the notion of individual responsibility is central. The New Right laid the ground for such a transition during the 1980s, but it has been fuelled by a variety of cultural and intellectual influences. Roche (1992), for example, has contended that, since the global crisis of the welfare state in the 1970s, the 'dominant paradigm' of social citizenship has come under attack from across the political spectrum as a 'discourse of duty', as well as rights, emerged. This discourse has taken several forms, ranging from New Right and neo-conservative claims that welfare rights undermine the 'traditional' obligations that people have to sustain themselves through work and to provide for each other through the family, through to the challenges to the administrative power of welfare states that were posed by new social movements. The emerging consensus required an abandonment of the priority once accorded to social rights and a reconsideration of "the moral and ideological claims of personal responsibility" (Roche, 1992, p 246). The powerful orthodoxy that has begun to emerge is one in which rights and responsibilities are seen to exist as part of a reciprocal calculus (for example, Jordan, 1998). Insofar that human rights might encompass rights to social protection, it would appear that they are seen as conditional on the acceptance of responsibilities.

Article 22 of the Universal Declaration of Human Rights had proclaimed a right to 'social security', but as Goodin (2001), Townsend (2002) and others have pointed out, the expression 'social security' has all but disappeared from contemporary political discourse. This is most clearly exemplified in Britain, where in 2001 the main central government department with responsibility for income maintenance, the Department of Social Security, was reconstituted under the title 'Department for Work and Pensions'. The welfare reforms introduced by Britain's New Labour government, promise "opportunity not dependence" (DSS, 1998, p 2) and the British Prime Minister now frequently elides references to rights in favour of the language of opportunities:

> the belief in the equal worth of all [is] the central belief that drives my politics.... Note: it is equal worth, not equality of income or outcome; or simply, equality of opportunity.... So: let us start applying this principle to modern Government.... We do so on the basis of building a community where citizens are of equal worth. Opportunity to all; responsibility from all.... I don't think you can make the case for Government, for spending tax payers' money on public services or social exclusion ... without this covenant of opportunities and responsibilities. (Blair, 2000, p 4)

This suggests that social rights are being reduced to labour market opportunities. Although it may not have been in Blair's mind, it could also mean that those who abjure the responsibility to rise to such opportunities (and who therefore succumb to dependence) are unworthy and, by implication, justifiably less equal. The 'worth' of citizens is measured by a social contract in which they surrender irresponsible freedoms (which are equated with dependency) in return for opportunities. It is this perception, or something rather close to it, that seems to inform the emergent human rights paradigm.

Of course, a more solidaristic conception of human rights would accept that dependence and responsibility are by no means incompatible. Turner (1993, p 507), for example, drawing on philosophical anthropology, has argued that "it is from a collectively held recognition of individual frailty that rights as a system of mutual protection gain their emotive force". This is another argument to which I shall return.

Workfare and the dilution of social rights

I should like briefly to illustrate my argument with a specific example of the way in which the ostensible commitment in Europe to universal human rights is belied by an approach to social rights that is highly selective.

The concept of 'workfare' has always been controversial. Although it is often presented as a new idea that originated in the late 20th century in the US, its fundamental tenets date back to an era when the relief of poverty across much of Western Europe was conditional upon the performance of forced labour (Piven and Cloward, 1974; Whiteside, 1995). However, one of the fundamental premises of modern human rights has been the prohibition of slavery and forced labour, albeit that under the terms of the ECHR, for example, forced labour does not include "any work which forms part of normal civic obligation" (article 4.3.d). As we enter the 21st century, most European nations are developing active labour market or 'welfare-to-work' policies in which social assistance for some social groups is, at least to some degree, conditional upon the performance of compulsory activities relating to work (whether subsidised or unsubsidised) or training (Lødemel and Trickey, 2000). Forced labour under the Poor Laws was an explicit deterrent to idleness. The ideological justifications for contemporary forms of workfare range, on the one hand, from the proposition that it discourages dependency, while promoting responsibility; and on the other, to the proposition that it prevents social exclusion by 'reinserting' those who have been marginalised from the labour market. Lødemel and Trickey's (2000) comparative study of workfare regimes helpfully demonstrates the extent to which both kinds of argument have combined to generate in several countries a kind of blue–red (or 'purple') coalition willing to support, if not the withdrawal of social rights, then the application of conditionality in relation to welfare provision. At the risk of oversimplifying the findings presented in Lødemel and Trickey's book, my own interpretation of them would be that:

- The US represents an extreme contractarian tradition in which the enforcement of civic obligation *overrides* rights; the function of workfare is to prevent dependency; the primary objective is labour market attachment (or 'work-first'); and the system is calculated to 'hassle' as much as help the citizen.
- France represents a republican tradition which seeks to *assert* a right to work in spite of the structural constraints imposed by economic globalisation; the function of workfare is to achieve social integration; the primary objective is to create labour market opportunities (although this is very seriously compromised by a desire to protect the rights enjoyed by existing workers); and the system is calculated to help rather than to hassle the citizen.
- There is an emergent 'European centralised' workfare model that is epitomised by the Dutch Jobseekers' Employment scheme, Danish activation and the UK New Deal policies which represent what might be termed a 'third way' consensus (Giddens, 1998) based on conditional rights; the function is to foster independence; the primary objective is human resource development; and the system is calculated – through individualised casework support on the one hand and sanctions for non-compliance based on the withdrawal of social assistance benefits on the other – to engender a kind of 'tough love' (see Jordan, 2000).

What is interesting here is that conventional welfare regime and path-dependency theory is of limited predictive value. On close examination, anglophone countries such as the US and UK may actually be diverging rather than converging, as indeed it would seem are Scandinavian countries such as Denmark and Norway. Although there are some similarities between continental European nations such as France and Germany, these are not especially strong. Part of this complexity stems from the different approaches to social assistance with which different countries have started out in the first place (Gough et al, 1997), the scale of the labour market problems they have faced, and the extent to which policy makers have sought selectively to target particular social groups. Significantly, however, one of the features that singles out the dominant European centralised model relates to the extent to which in the countries concerned the administration of social assistance and the specification of work and training schemes is highly centralised.

While there has been a certain amount of devolution in the UK in relation to the *delivery* of New Deal/workfare experiments and pilots, there has been no devolution of central *control*, not least because financial power continues to rest with central government rather than with any of the local authorities, commercial and voluntary-sector groups that have been drawn in as partners in the administration of New Deal schemes. Certainly, there has been no attempt to adapt schemes in response to particular local labour market conditions (Theodore and Peck, 1999). In Canada, where a similar pattern of centralised control is evident, one critic suggests that processes of global policy transfer and disjointed forms of local experimentation in relation to workfare, far from enhancing rational and democratically accountable policy making, is serving to sustain "an internationally restricted policy wisdom" (Herd, 2002, p 110). In terms of its impact on labour force participation and its popular acceptability, the introduction of the New Deals in the UK has been adjudged modestly successful (see Millar, 1999), but this does not detract from the fact that they have been premised on the imposition of a centrally driven policy prescription and a curtailment of rights.

The new 'policy wisdom' is consistent with a restrictive, top-down conception of human rights in which the subject is to be bolstered as an independent, competitive individual, rather than protected as an interdependent social being who may be vulnerable to exploitation. The UK's New Deal programme has achieved labour market and training opportunities of a higher quality than those provided under earlier schemes, which had been explicitly condemned by younger participants as no more than 'slave labour' (Coles, 1995). It is clear nonetheless that participants are still mindful that the labour market opportunities opened up by the New Deal entail what they describe as 'crap jobs', rather than 'career jobs' (Lloyd, 1999). (In Chapter Seven, Ruth Rogers addresses the fuller implications in terms of the way that unemployed claimants are 'constituted' by New Deal type processes.) It is widely acknowledged that participants have generally been appreciative of the casework role fulfilled by New Deal personal advisers, but critical because the choices offered to them have in practice been highly restricted (Legard et al, 1998). While the Charter of Fundamental Rights of the European Union (CEU, 2000, article 15) asserts the "freedom to choose an occupation and [the] right to engage in work", under the workfare regimes that are now developing across Europe a substantive choice of occupation for certain social groups may well be prescribed and a right to subsist without working will in most circumstances be denied.

Rights and reform

The dominant conception of human rights in Europe – certainly that which is accepted by the EU as opposed to the Council of Europe – is driven by particular assumptions about the nature of globalisation, and it is inadequate for any effective process of welfare reform. I argue this for three reasons:

1. In spite of the lip service that is often paid in EU instruments to notions of solidarity, the dominant conception of human rights fails to give sufficient weight to the idea that their purpose is social protection; and that human rights should afford the human subject material and ontological security, safety or 'asylum' (in the original meaning of that word). It neither recognises nor celebrates human interdependency. The compromise struck within the Charter of Fundamental Rights of the European Union marginalises several of the rights asserted, for example, in the revised Social Charter of the Council of Europe (which many EU members have still to ratify). A richer notion of fundamental rights is required than that permitted by the prevailing global-liberal hegemony. This would recognise that social security provision can offer asylum from the risks of an exploitative labour market. Social housing can offer asylum from the risks of homelessness. Social care can offer asylum from the risks accompanying the impairment and isolation that may be associated with disability or old age. If 'social inclusion' means anything, it means being admitted to dependency upon those around us.

2. In their insistence that rights and responsibilities go together, current discourses of responsibility — especially those in the emergent 'third way' tradition — tend to embrace a variety of specific responsibilities while conflating a number of concepts to do with duties, obligations and obedience (Dean, 2002, ch 10; this is further explored by Shane Doheny in Chapter Three of this book). For now, let us observe how responsibility may be reduced to:

   • civic duty, which is celebrated in terms of a system of expectations that are reciprocal and symmetrical, but in which the responsibility of the citizen (as a worker and consumer) is individualised;

   • or else a form of moral obligation that calls upon a closed system of communitarian norms and values based on collective loyalties and protectionist practices (Driver and Martell, 1997);

   • or, when neither duty nor obligation have any purchase, mere obedience which is elicited through penalties and sanctions and what amounts in effect to the governance of irresponsibility (Dwyer, 2000).

   However, none of these capture an ethical concept of responsibility from which a more solidaristic and systemic concept of human rights might flow. Such a notion would necessarily be essentially rational, reflexive and democratic. It would recognise that responsibilities are shared, as much as individual; that they may have to be asymmetrically distributed, rather than reciprocal; that they depend nonetheless on general assent.

3. The prevailing consensus on human rights is ethically deficient in a different sense, since it is constructed upon an ethic of work and a set of assumptions about the role of work in the maintenance of human society, while failing to accommodate any corresponding ethic of care. Work is seen — as much

in the republican as the liberal tradition – as the primary responsibility of the individual and the first bulwark against poverty or social exclusion. Care, on the other hand, is seen at best as something that must be accommodated to work. While Esping-Andersen (1999), for example, has acknowledged the impact that changes in the household economy may have on the future trajectory of welfare regimes, this falls short of the demand by feminist commentators that care "should be recognised as a central political and intellectual issue for social policy" (Williams, 2001, p 469). Sevenhuijsen (1998, 2000) has challenged the fundamental ethical premise that underpins welfare citizenship by arguing for a 'democratic ethic of care', that "starts from the idea that everybody needs care and is (in principle at least) capable of care giving" (2000, p 15). Inclusive relationships, it is argued, are achieved in the context of specific social networks of care and responsibility and cannot be created by ascribing rights and responsibilities. The citizen must first be understood not as an abstract individual or 'equal rights holder', but as a 'self-in-relationship'. Like Turner (see earlier in this chapter), Sevenhuijsen argues that "vulnerability is part and parcel of ordinary human subjectivity" (2000, p 19), and in this context care is as much a daily practice as work. A feminist ethic of care displaces the dominant discourse of human rights in favour of an understanding that human freedom is built upon interdependency: it is our need for, and capacity to, care that precede and shape our rights and responsibilities. (This is considered in greater depth by Kathryn Ellis in Chapter Two of this book.)

We may note that the new political ethics of care envisaged by Fiona Williams would entail tolerance of human limitations and frailties, and an acceptance of human diversity, but its task would be "less one of arguing against autonomy as a liberal concept than one of redefining the concept of autonomy to fit with a notion of interdependence" (Williams, 2001, p 481). It has been suggested that policy discourses that favour 'work–life balance', which may be found both in the revised Social Charter of the Council of Europe (article 27) and the Charter of Fundamental Rights of the European Union (article 34), offer a space in which to argue for an ethic of care, but these articles are framed in terms of 'equal opportunities' for workers with family responsibilities: they remain premised on an assumption that care must be accommodated with work (and that its place is within the ideologically constructed family).

Should human rights discourse have anything to offer the cause of welfare reform, it must be more broadly conceived in an ethical sense. But it must also be capable of engaging with the issue of the state.

Human rights and the ethical state

Although Bauman (1993) has argued that the postmodern epoch creates a space for entirely new and authentically ethical discourses, this idea is generally interpreted in terms of an individual ethical obligation to the self-governing self. Rose (1996), for example, contends that in a 'post-social' era, governments seek through workfare type policies to promote not only personal human capital and individual prudentialism, but also the ethical skills necessary to *self-management*. On these accounts, postmodern ethics will allow little scope for welfare rights.

Drawing inter alia upon the work of Hegel and the social psychologist, Mead, Axel Honneth (1995) offers a rather different approach, reinterpreting the development of human societies in terms of the struggle for recognition. His quest is for "a normative theory that is capable of depicting the hypothetical end-point of an expansion of relations of recognition" (Honneth, 1995, p 171), and that requires a formal concept of 'ethical life'. This normative theory rests on an empirical analysis of historical struggles that have progressed beyond conflicts between status groups to conflicts that bear upon individualised identity. Rights – together with love and solidarity – play a part in the formation of identity and the realisation of ethical life, since rights are concerned with the recognition of the capacity of an individual to assert claims and to participate as a legal and political subject. Honneth's contribution acknowledges the scope for a non-Hobbesian interpretation of human rights and is clearly important, but it does not address the future of the welfare state and the implications this has for achieving ethical life.

Insofar that the demise of the welfare state is widely predicted, there is an abundance of speculation as to what might lie beyond it (for example, Pierson, 1998), or of what indeed a postmodern 'welfare society' might look like (Rodger, 2000). Rodger's (2000, p 188) assertion is that "self-organised welfare in a civil society in which state control is at 'arm's length' may come to pass through sheer necessity". This notion of a 'welfare society' in which the state assumes at best a secondary role is altogether different from, say, Gramsci's powerful but elusive notion of an 'ethical state'. An ethical state might reasonably be supposed to be, if not the precondition, then the medium for achieving Honneth's ethical life. Gramsci equates the ethical state with a 'regulated society' in which coercion is superseded and law subsumed. The state is not some 'phantasmagorical entity', but a collective organism with a collective consciousness (Gramsci, 1988, p 244). Rights in a regulated society, as I understand it, would be no more and no less than human capacities that are consensually conferred and guaranteed (Hirst, 1980; and see Dean, 2002, ch 1).

What this might entail is a view of human rights that not only encompasses social or welfare rights, but also conceptualises these in terms of global responsibilities, on the one hand, and in terms of local needs on the other.

The philosopher Karl Otto Apel has addressed the question of global responsibilities. Apel (1980, 1991) argues that responsibility is the key normative feature in political discourse because, by addressing any problem in argument, we are implicitly acknowledging a responsibility – both at an individual and a collective level – for solving that problem. According to Apel, however, liberalism as the dominant ideological paradigm of modernity has effectively paralysed the possibility of an ethic of social responsibility since it separates the public sphere of scientific rationality from the private sphere of preferences and values. What is required is an ethical principle of 'co-responsibility'. This might become possible upon three conditions:

1. It would have to be rational and transcend tradition.
2. It would require a global communication community, something made possible by cultural, technological and economic globalisation such that already "we have become members of a real communication community" (Apel, 1991, p 269). This idea has obvious resonance with Habermas' (1987) counterfactual notion of the 'ideal speech situation'. The ideal speech situation is an abstract political objective through which it would become possible for human beings to engage in undistorted and uncoerced kinds of negotiation, although Apel, for his part, is actually taking account of the concrete possibilities for collaborative scientific interpretation that are opened up by information and communication technologies, for example.
3. A principle of co-responsibility would require that scientific and ethical claims to truth be taken equally seriously. This idea has an obvious resonance with Beck's (1992) demand for the de-monopolisation of science and a form of reflexivity based on negotiation between different epistemologies. The ethical fulcrum of such negotiation is human need:

> the members of the communication community (and this implies all thinking beings) are also committed to considering all the potential claims of all the potential members – and this means all human 'needs' in as much as they could be affected by norms and consequently make *claims* on their fellow human beings. As potential 'claims' that can be communicated interpersonally, all human needs are ethically *relevant*. They must be *acknowledged* if they can be justified interpersonally through arguments. (Apel, 1980, p 277)

Shane Doheny has more to say about Apel in Chapter Three of this book, but in the meantime, my own understanding is that Apel's concept of 'co-responsibility' implies that human needs may achieve universal definition through a global form of rights. His concept is a riposte to postmodernity's claim that "the foolproof – universal and unshakably founded – ethical code will never be found" (Bauman, 1993, p 10). It presupposes that there are certain basic human needs whose optimal satisfaction must precede the imposition of any social obligations (Doyal and Gough, 1991) and that it is possible to negotiate the empirical, ontological and normative consensus that is required to translate the particular demands of diverse social movements into universally recognisable human rights (Hewitt, 1993). The importance of this is that it implies a relationship between rights and responsibilities that goes far beyond the narrow contractarian calculus implied by the 'third way' motto – "no rights without responsibilities" (Giddens, 1998, p 65) – because responsibility is by nature cooperative and negotiated, not an inherent obligation or a priori doctrine.

It is hard nonetheless to articulate Apel's abstract reasoning about global responsibilities to concrete struggles over rights at the level of the state, but in some of the emerging 'anti-globalisation' literature, for example, we can see attempts to develop our understanding of human rights as a means to something other than the imposition a global liberal-democratic orthodoxy; as something more than a kind of postmodern folklore that 'compresses' moral issues to the right of individuals to be left alone (Bauman, 1993, p 243). De Sousa Santos (2001) has envisaged the possibility of a kind of counter-hegemonic globalisation process through what he calls 'native languages of emancipation'. Although it is not necessarily a prototype, the paradox of the so-called 'anti-globalisation' movement is that, through the power of the Internet, it has established a counter-hegemonic global communication community of sorts (for example, Yeates, 2002).

However, this does bring us back to the more concrete question of local needs and, I suggest, to Nancy Fraser's conception of a "politics of needs interpretation" (Fraser, 1989, Chapter Seven). It is precisely because we do not inhabit 'welfare societies' but welfare states that people must find ways on a day-to-day basis to reconcile their needs with rules prescribed by the state (see Chapter Seven of this book) or to define their responsibilities in spite of such rules (see Chapter Nine). A 'politics of needs interpretation' would enlarge the scope and reach of welfare rights guaranteed by the state. It would seek to define in specific contexts and for specific social groups what is required for personal autonomy; it would stretch beyond the essential or 'thin' definitions espoused by Doyal and Gough (1991) to encompass enlarged or 'thick' definitions (see Drover and Kerans, 1993). This would indeed entail demands for recognition as well as for redistribution (Honneth, 1995; and see Fraser, 1995); for rights that recognise specific needs stemming from social differences constituted by gender, ethnicity, age, disability and sexuality. It would entail not only demands for opportunities, but for safety or 'asylum' (see earlier in this chapter), including protection against exploitation and provision that ensures ontological as well as bare material security.

What this implies, in my view, is that conditionality and the commodification of essential services should be opposed. Conditionality in social protection relates, on the one hand, to the expanded application of means-tested safety nets and, on the other, to applications of 'work-testing' that turns the development of what economists now call 'human capital' into a compulsory, rather than an emancipatory, process. The commodification of public services is a process that will be accelerated as a result of the Multilateral Agreement on Investment being brokered by the World Trade Organisation (WTO), the final implication of which is that health and social services provided under governmental authority will no longer be exempt from free trade and competition requirements under the General Agreement on Trade and Services (see Deacon, 2000; Yeates, 2001). It is precisely this implication, amongst others, that has driven mass protests against the WTO and other international governmental organisations by the 'anti-globalisation' movement referred to above. It is a movement that has drawn together an extraordinary coalition of interests. The diversity of the street protesters has been characterised in the news media in terms of a contrast between the 'fluffy' and the 'spiky': between peaceful libertarians and aggressive anarchists (see Yeates, 2002, p 14). The question that I raise in conclusion is what significance these issues might have for the social values of those who are neither fluffy nor spiky, and whose focus is indeed upon *local* needs and preoccupations, rather than the global stage?

Conclusion

The thinking that informs this chapter has also informed the research project, whose findings are presented in Part Two of this book. Peter Taylor-Gooby (2002) has drawn upon social attitude data to suggest that the social values exhibited by the majority of Europe's citizens are opposed to the way in which substantive social protection is being marginalised in favour of a more restrictive and formalistic conception of individual rights and personal responsibility. Our study, it is hoped, will bring greater depth to this finding by illuminating the complex and contradictory discursive moral repertoires that underpin everyday attitudes (Dean, 1999). It may also provide clearer insights into how competing social interests may be mobilised to render hegemonic support to particular moral repertoires or social values and whether, indeed, it would be possible to re-conceptualise dependency and responsibility in a way that can more effectively encompass welfare rights as human rights. I return to this in Chapter Ten.

References

Apel, K. (1980) *Towards the transformation of philosophy*, London: Routledge.

Apel, K. (1991) 'A planetary macro-ethics for humankind', in E. Deutsch (ed) *Culture and modernity: East-West philosophical perspectives*, Honolulu: University of Hawaii Press.

Bauman, Z. (1993) *Postmodern ethics*, Oxford: Blackwell.

Beck, U. (1992) *Risk society: Towards a new modernity*, London: Sage Publications.

Blair, T. (2000) 'Values and the power of community', Speech to the Global Ethics Foundation, Tübigen, 30 June.

Bobbio, N. (1996) *The age of rights*, Cambridge: Polity.

Bowring, W. (2001) 'Forbidden relations? The UK's discourse of human rights and the struggle for social justice', Inaugural Professorial Lecture, University of North London, 30 January.

Campbell, T. (1983) *The Left and Rights*, London: Routledge and Kegan Paul.

CEC (Commission of the European Communities) (1993) *European social policy: Options for the Union*, Luxembourg: Office for Official Publications of the European Communities.

CEU (Council of the European Union) (2000) *Charter of Fundamental Rights of the European Union: Explanations relating to the complete text of the charter*, Luxembourg: Office for Official Publications of the European Communities.

Clarke, J. and Newman, J. (1997) *The managerial state*, London: Sage Publications.

Clarke, P.B. (1996) *Deep citizenship*, London: Pluto.

Coleman, J. (1988) 'Social capital in the creation of human capital', *American Journal of Sociology*, vol 94, pp 95-121.

Coles, B. (1995) *Youth and social policy*, London: UCL Press.

Cranston, M. (1973) *What are human rights?*, London: Bodley Head.

Deacon, B. with Hulse, M. and Stubbs, P. (1997) *Global social policy*, London: Sage Publications.

Deacon, B. (2000) 'Globalisation: a threat to equitable social provision', in H. Dean, R. Sykes and R. Woods (eds) *Social Policy Review*, vol 12, Newcastle: Social Policy Association.

Dean, H. (1996) *Welfare, law and citizenship*, Hemel Hempstead: Prentice Hall/ Harvester Wheatsheaf.

Dean, H. with Melrose, M. (1999) *Poverty, riches and social citizenship*, Basingstoke: Macmillan.

Dean, H. (2002) *Welfare rights and social policy*, Harlow: Prentice Hall.

De Sousa Santos, B. (2001) 'Towards a multicultural conception of human rights', *World Social Forum*, Library of alternatives, (www.worldsocialforum.org).

Douzinas, C. (2000) *The end of human rights*, Oxford: Hart Publishing.

Doyal, L. and Gough, I. (1991) *A theory of human need*, Basingstoke: Macmillan.

Driver, S. and Martell, L. (1997) 'New Labour's communitarianisms', *Critical Social Policy*, vol 17, no 3, pp 27-46.

Drover, G. and Kerans, P. (eds) (1993) *New approaches to welfare theory*, Aldershot: Edward Elgar.

DSS (Department of Social Security) (1998) *New ambitions for our country: A new contract for welfare*, Cm 3805, London: The Stationery Office.

Dwyer, P. (2000) *Welfare rights and responsibilities: Contesting social citizenship*, Bristol: The Policy Press.

Eide, A. (1997) 'Human rights and the elimination of poverty', in A. Kjonstad and J. Veit-Wilson (eds) *Law, power and poverty*, Bergen: CROP/ISSL.

Esping-Andersen, G. (ed.) (1996) *Welfare states in transition*, London: Sage Publications.

Esping-Andersen, G. (1999) *Social foundations of post-industrial economies*, Oxford: Oxford University Press.

Falk, R. (1994) 'The making of a global citizenship', in B. van Steenbergen (ed) *The condition of citizenship*, London: Sage Publications.

Fraser, N. (1989) *Unruly practices: Power, discourse and gender in contemporary social theory*, Cambridge: Polity.

Fraser, N. (1995) 'From redistribution to recognition: dilemmas of social justice in a "post-socialist" age', *New Left Review*, vol 212, pp 68-93.

Giddens, A. (1998) *The Third Way*, Cambridge: Polity.

Gold, M. and Mayes, D. (1993) 'Rethinking a social policy for Europe', in R. Simpson and R. Walker (eds) *Europe: For richer or poorer?*, London: Child Poverty Action Group.

Goodin, R.E. (2001) 'Perverse principles of welfare reform', Paper to the European Institute of Social Security conference 'European Social Security and Global Politics', Bergen, 27-29 September.

Goodwin, B. (1987) *Using political ideas* (2nd edn), Chichester: John Wiley & Sons.

Gough, I., Bradshaw, J., Ditch, J., Eardley, T. and Whiteford, P. (1997) 'Social assistance in OECD countries', *Journal of European Social Policy*, vol 7, no 1, pp 17-43.

Gramsci, A. (1988) *A Gramsci reader*, G. Forgacs (ed) London: Lawrence & Wishart.

Habermas, J. (1987) *The theory of communicative action. Vol 2: Lifeworld and system*, Cambridge: Polity.

Habermas, J. (2001) *The postnational constellation: Political essays*, Cambridge: Polity.

Held, D., McGrew, A., Goldblatt, D. and Perraton, J. (1999) *Global transformations*, Cambridge: Polity.

Herd, D. (2002) 'Rhetoric and retrenchment: "common sense" welfare reform in Ontario', *Benefits*, vol 10, no 2, pp 105-10.

Hewitt, M. (1993) 'Social movements and social need: problems with post-modern political theory', *Critical Social Policy*, vol 13, no 1, pp 52-74.

Hirst, P. (1980) 'Law, socialism and rights', in P. Carlen and M. Collison (eds) *Radical issues in criminology*, Oxford: Martin Robertson.

Honneth, A. (1995) *The struggle for recognition: The moral grammar of social conflicts*, Cambridge: Polity.

Hood, C. (1991) 'A public management for all seasons?', *Public Administration*, vol 69, no 1, pp 3-19.

Jordan, B. (1989) *The common good: Citizenship, morality and self-interest*, Oxford: Blackwell.

Jordan, B. (1998) *The new politics of welfare*, London: Sage Publications.

Jordan, B. with Jordan, C. (2000) *Social work and the Third Way: Tough love as social policy*, London: Sage Publications.

Klug, F. (2000) *Values for a Godless age: The story of the United Kingdom's new bill of rights*, Harmondsworth: Penguin.

Legard, R., Ritchie, J., Keegan, J. and Turner, T. (1998) *New deal for young unemployed people: The gateway*, Sheffield: Employment Service.

Levitas, R. (1996) 'The concept of social exclusion and the new Durkeimian hegemony', *Critical Social Policy*, vol 16, no 2, pp 5-20.

Lister, R. (1997) *Citizenship: Feminist perspectives*, Basingstoke: Macmillan.

Lloyd, T. (1999) *Young men, the job market and gendered work*, York: Joseph Rowntree Foundation.

Lødemel, I. and Trickey, H. (eds) (2000) *'An offer you can't refuse': Workfare in international perspective*, Bristol: The Policy Press.

Marshall, T.H. (1950) 'Citizenship and social class', in T. Marshall and T. Bottomore (1992) *Citizenship and social class*, London: Pluto.

Millar, J. (2000) *Keeping track of welfare reform: The New Deal programmes*, York: Joseph Rowntree Foundation.

Mishra, R. (1999) *Globalisation and the welfare state*, Aldershot: Edward Elgar.

Morris, L. (2001) 'Stratified rights and the management of migration', *European Societies*, vol 3, no 4, pp 387-411.

Nozick, R. (1974) *Anarchy, state and utopia*, Oxford: Blackwell.

Pierson, C. (1998) *Beyond the welfare state*, Cambridge: Polity.

Piven, F. and Cloward, R. (1974) *Regulating the poor*, London: Tavistock.

Putnam, R. (2000) *Bowling alone: The collapse and revival of American community*, New York, NY: Simon and Schuster.

Roche, M. (1992) *Rethinking citizenship: Welfare, ideology and change in modern society*, Cambridge: Polity.

Rodger, J. (2000) *From a welfare state to a welfare society*, Basingstoke: Macmillan.

Room, G. (ed.) (1995) *Beyond the threshold: The measurement and analysis of social exclusion*, Bristol: The Policy Press.

Rose, N. (1996) 'The death of the social?', *Economy and Society*, vol 25, no 3, pp 327-56.

Sevenhuijsen, S. (1998) *Citizenship and the ethics of care*, London: Routledge.

Sevenhuijsen, S. (2000) 'Caring in the Third Way: the relation between obligation, responsibility and care in Third Way discourse', *Critical Social Policy*, vol 20, no 1, pp 5-37.

Soysal, Y. (1994) *Limits of citizenship: Migrants and postnational membership in Europe*, Chicago, IL: Chicago University Press.

Taylor-Gooby, P. (2002) 'Open markets and welfare values: welfare values, inequality and social change in the Silver Age of the welfare state', Plenary paper to European Social Policy Research Network conference 'Social Policies, Social Values', University of Tilburg, 29-31 August.

Theodore, N. and Peck, J. (1999) 'Welfare-to-work: national problems, local solutions?', *Critical Social Policy*, vol 19, no 4, pp 485-510.

Townsend, P. (1992) *Hard times: The prospects for European social policy*, Eleanor Rathbone Memorial Lecture, Liverpool: Liverpool University Press.

Townsend, P. (2002) 'Human rights, transnational corporations and the World Bank', Paper to Social Policy Association conference 'Localities, Regeneration and Welfare', Teesside, 16-18 July.

Turner, B. (1993) 'Outline of a theory of human rights', *Sociology*, vol 27, no 3, pp 489-512.

Twine, F. (1994) *Citizenship and social rights: The interdependence of self and society*, London: Sage Publications.

UNDP (United Nations Development Programme) (2000) *Human Development Report 2000*, Oxford: Oxford University Press.

Vail, J. (1999) 'Insecure times: conceptualising insecurity and security', in J. Vail, J. Wheelock and M. Hill (eds) *Insecure times: Living with insecurity in contemporary society*, London: Routledge.

Van Genugten, W. (1997) 'The use of Human Rights instruments in the struggle against (extreme) poverty', in A. Kjonstad and J. Veit-Wilson (eds) *Law, power and poverty*, Bergen: CROP/ISSL.

Whiteside, N. (1995) 'Employment policy: a chronicle of decline?', in D. Gladstone (ed) *British social welfare: Past, present and future*, London: UCL Press.

Williams, F. (2001) 'In and beyond New Labour: towards a political ethics of care', *Critical Social Policy*, vol 21, no 4, pp 467-93.

Yeates, N. (2001) *Globalization and social policy*, London: Sage Publications.

Yeates, N. (2002) 'The "anti-globalisation" movement and its implications for social policy', in R. Sykes, C. Bochel and N. Ellison (eds) *Social Policy Review 14*, Bristol: The Policy Press/Social Policy Association.

TWO

Dependency, justice and the ethic of care

Kathryn Ellis

This chapter is based on the premise that an examination of the relationship between care and justice is useful both for exploring the key themes of dependency, responsibility and rights with which this book is primarily concerned and for imagining different welfare futures. The chapter is in three parts. The first reviews the development of a feminist ethic of care and the differing principles of justice on which it draws. In the second part, the principal ideas associated with a political ethic of care are used to throw further light on dependency, responsibility and rights as they relate to recent policy developments in care in the UK. In the final section, the debate is extended to consider what lessons might be drawn from a discussion of care and justice as the basis for developing a more socially just set of arrangements for care.

The ethical framework of care

Justice and care

When Carol Gilligan (1982) took issue with Lawrence Kohlberg's (1981) psychological theory of children's moral development by claiming to have uncovered a 'different voice' among the women she interviewed, she sparked a long-running debate about the existence of masculine and feminine modes of moral reasoning (see Larabee, 1993). Gilligan maintained that a feminine moral code of care had been obscured by the supposedly universal masculine mode of moral reasoning uncovered in previous psychological research. The latter code, she argued, had been transposed into Western legal systems in an idealised form as 'justice' through its association with the culturally prized values of objectivity and impartiality (Smart, 1989). Gilligan identified three key distinctions between the competing moral discourses of care and justice. First, the ethic of care is rooted in the moral frameworks of responsibility and relationships rather than rights and rules. Second, the care orientation is inseparable from concrete circumstances rather than being a formal and abstract system of thought. Third, care is primarily grounded in the daily activity of care rather than a set of universal principles (in Tronto, 1993, p 242).

Feminist theorists of the ethic of care have subsequently suggested that the origins of competing moral discourses lie in a gendered division of labour rather than innate psychological attributes. Tronto (1994), for example, traces the fracture line between justice and care to the model of the separate spheres upon which liberal democracy is based, arguing that the discourse of justice became the privileged voice of the public domain from the 18th century onwards. In the light of changing notions of social distance and the emergence of atomistic individualism, the classical liberal ethic of justice provided the proper morality not only for preventing abuses of power by protecting individual freedom, but also for regulating relations between the self-interested, autonomous self and relative strangers in the competitive public sphere of politics and civil society (see also Flanagan and Jackson, 1993). The ethic of care, by contrast, was relegated to the private sphere of family and friends as the proper morality for promoting individual well-being and for governing personal relations characterised by altruism, interconnectedness and dependence (Clement, 1998).

Furthermore, critics of Gilligan's thesis have identified care and justice as logically compatible rather than dichotomous moral orientations. Friedman (1993), for example, maintains that morally valid forms of caring presuppose prior conditions and understandings of justice. Within interpersonal relationships based on mutual intimacy, support and concern, she argues, the principles of distributive justice require that the privileges and responsibilities of care are shared appropriately among the participants, while the principles of corrective justice require that those who are harmed within abusive personal or family relationships receive redress and/or protection from further harm. Conversely, Baier (1993) points out that the moral disposition to be just (as opposed to a purely prudential commitment to justice) depends on a prior sense of attachment to, and care for, not only personal and family networks, but also some wider community. Otherwise, there is no commitment to search for a fairer, more equal distribution of resources, or any other sort of social justice.

Claims for distinct modes of moral reasoning have also been challenged. Identified as a contextual morality, the ethic of care is premised on the assumption that individuals can only determine the proper course of action by reference to the specific circumstances and needs of particular individuals whereas the ethic of justice – or the principle that everyone should be treated the same – is assumed to be universally applicable to the resolution of moral dilemmas. Inasmuch as the general principles of the justice ethic often conflict, however, Clement (1998) argues that settling moral dilemmas always requires some examination of their context in order to ascertain which principles should be applied and in what manner. Even legal judgements, as Broughton (1993) points out, frequently involve the necessity of taking particular, concrete situations into account when applying general notions of rights in specific cases. Certainly this interplay between rule-based and discretionary decision making is a taken for granted problematic of welfare administration.

Towards a political (and just) ethic of care

Establishing the logical compatibility of the two ethical frameworks is important, for the ethic of care, as several writers have argued, cannot be used as a guide to social action without reference to justice principles of some kind. Justice, as Goodwin (1987, p 279) observes, is both a legal term concerning the distribution of pains and penalties to the guilty and a political goal concerning the distribution of goods and 'bads'. Insofar as the care perspective may obscure the violence and harm associated with human interrelationships and community, then, interventions underpinned by the principles of corrective justice are required (Friedman, 1993, p 267). Yet a fundamentally conservative orientation towards the preservation of existing social arrangements means that, by itself, the care ethic lacks any satisfactory means of distinguishing between mutually satisfying or harmful relationships (Broughton, 1993). Indeed, the association of care giving with a proprietary sense of being in charge may give rise to the damaging power dynamic of 'paternalism–maternalism' identified by Tronto (1994). Certainly, the British disability movement has rejected the very concept of care as an appropriate institutional response to impairment, arguing that not only has it served to create and reinforce disabled people's dependency but that it is implicated in the abuse to which they are routinely exposed (Morris, 1993).

As a political goal, justice has regard both to the processes of human interaction and to their outcomes (Drake, 2001, p 76). Classical liberal formulations of justice are primarily concerned with second-order principles of justice, which, as Goodwin (1987, p 302) explains, are designed to determine the strategies and methods of distribution rather than particular outcomes. The procedural principle of ensuring that equal cases are treated alike is useful in countering the particularism of the ethic of care, originating as it does in the ties of affection and kinship. To the extent that the care ethic carries the danger of 'parochiality' – or the legitimation of special pleading on behalf of family, friends, group, even nation (Tronto, 1993, 1994) – a special significance may also be held to attach to the justice principle of impartiality in a society such as Britain where the notion of citizenship has been built upon the principle of excluding certain groups both within and beyond national boundaries (Williams, 1989; Dwyer, 2002). Yet a more substantive theory of distributive justice is required to counter both the relativism of the care ethic, which offers little assistance to policy makers faced with settling competing claims over the division of scarce material and other resources to meet care needs (Larabee, 1993), and its particularism, which serves to divert attention away from the wider (and unequal) social relations structuring caring relationships (Clement, 1998).

Fisher and Tronto's (1991) four-dimensional schema of a political ethic of care provides the means for analysing the justice of existing care arrangements in terms both of process and outcome. Each dimension of care within their schema is characterised by a core moral precept. 'Caring about', which is underpinned by the moral imperative of *attentiveness*, consists in recognising others' needs for care. 'Taking care of', underpinned by the imperative of *responsibility*, consists principally in assuming responsibility for meeting identified needs. 'Care giving', which is underpinned by the imperative of *competence*, consists in directly meeting others' needs for care to a competent standard. 'Care receiving', which is underpinned by the imperative of *responsiveness*, consists in providing care in ways that are responsive to the needs and interests of the care receiver. This schema has been taken up by several writers (Tronto, 1994; Clement, 1998; Sevenhuijsen, 2000; Williams, 2001) in order to examine the legitimacy of given sets of social arrangements for care in terms of the distribution of caring tasks, the allocation of resources and the quality of care provided.

Dependency, responsibility and rights

The development of critical tools for understanding care policy is particularly timely at this juncture given the increasing politicisation of care in the UK and Europe more generally (Williams, 2001; Daly, 2002). The National Carers Strategy, the Royal Commission on Long-term Care, the National Childcare Strategy and a number of interventions designed to help working parents, bear testimony to its importance to the New Labour policy agenda of the UK government. The following sections explore the salience of Fisher and Tronto's feminist (as opposed to feminine) schema for illuminating both the core concepts of dependency, responsibility and rights with which this book is principally concerned and the policy context within which they are currently situated.

Dependency

Within its classic liberal form at least, the ethic of justice is grounded in assumptions of equal personhood and common humanity, which are associated in turn with an individualistic conception of the autonomous self. By contrast, the ethic of care is characterised by a relational ontology in which the self exists solely through and with others (Sevenhuijsen, 2000, p 9). As this section will suggest, the 'third way' of British politics is analysable in terms of a care–autonomy dichotomy underpinned by the public–private divide and the differing conceptions of human nature within which the ethical frameworks of care and justice are rooted.

Inasmuch as individual autonomy is equated with paid work in the 'third way', the current government's raft of policies to support working parents and other carers has tended to privilege the work ethic, productivity and global competitiveness over an ethic of care (Sevenhuijsen, 2000; Williams, 2001; Henderson and Forbat, 2002; see also Chapter One of this book). As is the case across Europe more generally, care policy tends to be framed in terms of reconciliation between work and family life yet, in practice, to constitute a form of labour and employment policy (Daly, 2002). In the case of informal carers of older and disabled people, increased policy attention has been directed towards their support yet services have been located at the margins rather than within mainstream provision (Parker, 2002, p 1) and highly selective definitions of need continue to take their unpaid labour for granted. In terms of Fisher and Tronto's (1991) formulation of a political ethic of care, New Labour policy makers are discharging the duties of the powerful by caring about and taking care of, but delegating the activities of care giving and care receiving to the powerless. The schema, as Tronto (1994) argues, also makes visible the labour involved in care giving, both paid and unpaid, by promoting an understanding that human needs are not met simply by paying taxes and allocating resources to care provision. It also serves to debunk the myth of self-sufficiency by revealing that the powerful can use their resources to purchase care for self and family while ignoring the extent to which their power and privilege depends on the care they are given by others.

The grounding of the care–autonomy dichotomy in a distinction between those who can and those who cannot work not only obscures the contribution of care giving to the fulfilment of human need, but also links care receiving to negative concepts of powerlessness, incapacity and neediness. This denial of autonomous personhood to people receiving care is fundamentally associated with the mind–body dualism of liberal thought that constitutes bodies as separate from, and governed by, the self/mind. To the extent that, as Bacchi and Beasley (2002, p 331) point out, the pulls of emotion and bodily vulnerabilities constitute acceptable dependency only when contained within the private domain, active and autonomous citizens are expected to be in control of their bodies in the public domain and the state is justified in regulating political subjects who fail to exercise normal bodily control through policy interventions which determine what bodies can and cannot do, what shape they are to take, what resources they can expect in order to survive and where they can appear or assemble.

In the case of social care for adults, the policy of the UK government is directed towards 'promoting independence' through a range of strategies, such as rehabilitation, the use of technology, New Deal and direct payment schemes, which are designed to encourage greater functional as well as financial self-sufficiency. As Humphrey (2003) explains, social care is harnessed to wider government aims of absorbing as many citizens as possible into the majority of productive and tax-paying adults. She describes the underlying message of the Department of Health's Performance Assessment Framework, which sets out quantitative targets for local authority social services departments to achieve in terms of care and costs, as:

> they should take their 'raw material' – that is, the most impoverished or impaired people in the country – and transform them into 'robust products' such as independent citizens regardless of the limitations of their resource base. (Humphrey, 2003, pp 12-13)

The extent to which this privileging of independence has eclipsed the socio-liberal values underpinning the postwar welfare state, which readily encompassed the care of groups made dependent by the specific contingencies of life (Hill and Bramley, 1986, p 8), is evidenced by the following stricture:

> Social services must aim wherever possible to help people get better, to improve their health and social functioning rather than just 'keep them going'. (DoH, 1998, para 2.11)

Based on a notion of the essential interdependency of self and other, the care ethic is grounded in the twin assumptions that relationships between people are a good thing in and of themselves and that all individuals both give and receive care. In recent years, however, care givers have been constructed as the active participants in UK social care policy in ways that threaten the needs and interests of both care givers and care receivers. Thus, the National Strategy for Carers (DoH, 1999) is driven by an instrumental concern to assist the cared for by supporting informal carers in their role as care providers, while guidance on the 2000 Carers and Disabled Children Act continually associates intervention for carers to the notion of the 'sustainability' of caring arrangements (Parker and Clarke, 2002, p 354-56). Parker and Clarke (2002) point out that, under the 2000 Carers and Disabled Children Act, carers not only have a right to an assessment of their own needs as care givers, but can instigate the delivery of certain services to the cared for even if the older or disabled person refuses to be assessed.

Contemporary policy also perpetuates a long-standing tradition in social care of centring interventions round the fixed and dichotomous identities of 'carer' and 'cared for'. The construction of care as unidirectional (reinforced in the National Strategy for Carers by the recurrent use of terms such as 'dependent', 'service user', 'cared for') implies a passivity and lack of agency on the part of the care receiver which belie the active caring performed by both participants within the care relationship (Lloyd, 2000). In a context where, increasingly, social care is narrowly conceived as personal care, the strategy is also part of a longer run process of the professionalisation of informal care, particularly through training in basic nursing tasks, as a means of minimising service use and integrating unpaid care givers into formal provision. Yet, as Henderson and Forbat (2002) point out, professionalisation is at odds with the intimate and relational components of informal care from which the provision of personal care cannot easily be separated out.

In reality, while positioned on the virtuous side of the care–autonomy divide, paid workers in adult care are afforded little discretion over their conditions of work. According to Fisher and Tronto (1991), quality care results from an integration of the four dimensions of care outlined in their schema. Yet Tronto (1994) points out that the determination of need by the powerful is often distant from the actual care giving and receiving. Social care in the UK, where need has been defined highly selectively by a predominantly white male group of policy makers, employers and senior managers, is a case in point. The privileging of the value of cost efficiency in the contracting out of paid care to the private and voluntary sector has resulted in low employment benefits which undermine care workers' economic self-sufficiency (Ford et al, 1998). The value of competence, which is associated with care giving in Fisher and Tronto's (1991) schema, is set by employers and managers rather than by care givers or care receivers, part of a process of standardising and regulating work practices which has accelerated under New Labour with the setting up of the National Training Organisation for the Personal Social Services, the General Social Care Council and the National Commission for Care Standards. Women are attracted to paid care work not only because it can be fitted around domestic commitments, but also because they feel equipped for this type of work (Ungerson, 2000). Yet, while care workers tend to value the emotional and interpersonal dimensions of caring, their ability to provide care in line with their own notions of quality is limited by an emphasis on the physical tasks of personal care to be performed within dominant norms of productivity and efficiency.

Responsibility

According to Smith (2002, pp 48-9), New Labour's stakeholder society is informed by the notion of a quasi-contract based on the principle of reciprocity, which places the emphasis on mutual obligation and responsibility between state and individual. This principle is characteristic of liberal democracies where the drive to preserve individual autonomy gives rise to systems of justice based on notions of consent and contract, according to which equal persons mutually consent to certain obligations in return for reciprocal rights and freedoms. The ethic of care, by contrast, reaches beyond formal or legal obligations to apprehend responsibility as a moral imperative forged in networks of personal relationships which are shaped, in turn, by the social relations and practices of caring. Within individualistic conceptions of justice, as Clement (1998, p 13) explains, the grounding of social relatedness in reciprocal rights and obligations means that the self-interested individual enters into relationships with others only on the basis of consent rather than a sense of duty, whereas the roots of human connectedness in given rather than chosen kinship relations mean that the care ethic is largely based on the assumption that people recognise rather than choose their obligations to others.

Sevenhuijsen (2000) argues that both obligation and responsibility are ascribed rather than achieved within 'third way' thinking. Certainly, the responsibilities of informal carers in relation to community care have become increasingly formalised over the past two decades and have arguably acquired the status of citizenship obligations. As Lloyd (2000) points out, the vocabulary of the National Strategy for Carers, which includes 'value', 'worth', 'pride' and 'unsung heroes', exemplifies New Labour's emphasis on duty and responsibility as key elements of citizenship (see also Chapter Three of this volume). Such an approach may be seen as part of the wider 'third way' project described by Smith to establish a conditional reciprocal relationship between state and individual: government responsibilities and obligations to pay state welfare benefits or provide certain services only come into play when conditions are fulfilled relating to recipients' behaviour and/or status (Smith, 2002, p 48).

Moreover, if Daly (2002, p 260) is correct, citizenship obligations are being reinforced by the extent to which the increasing politicisation of care under the New Labour government represents a form of governance based on particular rather than collective relationships. Whereas the foregrounding of the informal carer within New Right welfare discourse may be read as part of a neoliberal ambition to roll back the state, in rhetorical terms at least, the 'third way' offers a response to the damaging impact that atomistic individualism is perceived to have had on social cohesion and a means of reframing the solution to social exclusion in terms of our responsibilities to family and community. At the macro-level, Daly (2003, pp 120-2) argues, the informal networks and communities of civil society are represented as a more desirable form of governance than either the bureaucratic state or private market, while at the micro-level of individual conduct, people are encouraged to become active in their own self-government by developing the capacities of responsible citizenship. In this fashion, Daly (2003, p 125) argues:

> We are increasingly governed in terms of our particular relations to communities of identity, families and so forth rather than our more general belongingness and our sets of relations to the larger society.

The ascription and enforcement of citizenship obligations to care can also be located within the wider system of power and group privileges outlined in Fisher and Tronto's (1991) schema. What this highlights is an unequal distribution of caring responsibilities that is embedded, in turn, within gender and other social relations. Tronto (1994) maintains that, from a position of 'privileged irresponsibility', the powerful use their group privileges to define needs in ways that maintain their position, while simultaneously passing caring work on to others, particularly working class and black women who are disproportionately likely to be among the least well-off and least powerful. According to Sevenhuijsen (2000, pp 23-4), 'third way' definitions of social exclusion similarly fail to acknowledge the difficulties experienced by the poorest women who undertake a considerable amount of caring work for the excluded poor and destitute, often under difficult conditions and with few resources at their command.

Rights

In classical liberal justice, civil and political rights derive from a particular interpretation of equality as sameness, as in the case of human rights for example, which are based on the notion of equal respect for the equal worth and dignity of each person. The equality of rights holders serves to preserve individual autonomy by equalising relationships among members of civil society while creating mutuality. From a care perspective, too, a commitment to the equal value of all humans is necessary to protect those who fall outside the compass of caring relationships. Yet abstracting claims for universal rights and equality from their cultural contexts carries the risk identified by Arendt (1966) of placing such an onerous moral burden on people that the response is tribalism, racism or hatred (in Tronto, 1994, pp 58-9). Unless a sense of connectedness to socially distant others is fostered by a politics of care then, as is starkly manifest in the populist stance that is being adopted by several Western governments towards refugees and asylum seekers, there is a danger that justice claims will be rejected by those who have duties to care about and care for.

The notion of the equal and autonomous rights holder dominating liberal systems of justice also perpetuates the unequal social relations underlying care. Not only does its individualism obscure the social disadvantages associated with racism, sexism, disablism, ageism and so forth, but the principle of equal treatment on the basis of equal worth only appears to overcome the problem of otherness by dealing with unjust discrimination. In reality, as Tronto (1994, p 70) argues, the equal and autonomous rights holder occupies the position of the generalised other, obscuring the real circumstances of the 'non-generalised other'. Moreover, insofar as the principle of equal treatment outlaws special pleading on behalf of 'others' (1994, p 70), it is an approach that is antithetical to the social rights necessary to deliver substantive equality. As Clement (1998, pp 103-5) points out, it follows from the formal equality principle that if people are not really different then they should normally become self-sufficient or rely on their families.

Aspects of the 'third way' approach to social justice are firmly rooted in a liberal model of formal rather than substantive equality. Egalitarian claims centre, firstly, on a commitment to securing a basic equality of opportunity for citizen workers after which goods are distributed primarily according to merit and, secondly, on the principle that different groups are treated as of equal value by guaranteeing equity of access to public services. So far as disabled people are concerned, the commitment to equality of opportunity has constructed paid work as not only a duty but a right (Williams, 1999). Yet to the extent that disability policy has tended to treat the individual rather than discriminatory barriers to paid employment as the focus for change, Powell (2000) argues that equal opportunities for disabled people have consisted principally in enabling 'them' (the different) to overcome barriers that prevent them from becoming like 'us' ('the normal'), while people who cannot fulfil their obligation to work are eligible for only a residual version of rights – if any at all (cited in Parker and Clarke, 2002, pp 352-3). In the case of social care, users' rights are confined largely to the right to coordinated and readily accessible services, including clear and comprehensive information, and to fair and consistent systems of charging and accessing support (see DoH, 1998).

The conditionality of rights in the 'third way' (outlined earlier in this chapter; see also Chapter One of this book), further narrows their scope. As discussed, this conditionality rests not just on the obligation to work but also on the politically constituted obligation (rather than the socially constituted responsibility) to care. As Parker and Clarke (2002, p 355) point out, 'rights' for informal carers are problematic both in principle and practice. First, in feminist terms, the responsibility to care exists prior to any possible articulation of rights. Second, services for informal carers 'reward' caregivers for discharging their moral duty rather than confer rights, even as their marginality reinforces the obligation to continue caring. In the case of care receivers, their rights to social care are balanced by the obligation to manage without help wherever possible and to pay for and make economical use of any services provided (Johnson, 1999).

Arguably, the political rights of caregivers and care receivers have also been eroded in recent years by the way in which dominant relations of care are reinforced in performance governance. The moral imperative of responsiveness outlined in Fisher and Tronto's schema, or taking the other's position into account as that other expresses it, hinges upon a democratisation of public services. Yet for all New Labour's rhetoric about decentralisation and consensual politics, performance management and budgetary controls ensure that power remains centralised. The Best Value inspectorate, set up under the auspices of the Audit Commission, is at the centre of what Humphrey (2003, p 5) describes as a massive expansion of regulatory apparatus under the current government. Best Value places a statutory duty on all public authorities to deliver services "to clear standards covering both cost and quality, by the most effective, economic and efficient means available" (DoH, 1998, para 1.5). Although the current government represents the increased emphasis on assessing outcomes as a move towards greater democracy in the public sector (Blackman and Palmer, 1999), top-down control through performance measurement and standardisation militates against local democracy and inclusive definitions of quality. Despite the promise that determinations of 'best value' will draw on a plurality of stakeholder approaches to and experiences of quality as a means of repositioning users and carers as local citizens rather than as atomised consumers (Rouse and Smith, 1999; Jacobs and Manzi, 2000), Best Value is ultimately an economic measure which links performance to value for money by targeting assistance only on those most at risk and minimising service use.

Care and social justice

So far in this chapter, the political ethic of care has been used primarily as a critical tool to highlight the force of the care–autonomy dichotomy in shaping New Labour care policy in the UK as an instance of liberal thought. In this part, more detailed consideration is given to the ways in which the ethical framework of care may be used to imagine different welfare futures and interpretations of social justice.

Integrating care and autonomy

A key task, as Williams (2001, p 481) argues, is to redefine the concept of autonomy to fit with the notion of interdependence. Care writers have pointed to those principles of justice and forms of selfhood that might be required to achieve 'relational autonomy', or a situation where people are able to pursue their own ends in the context of relationships in which others may do the same (Young, 2000, p 231). In her book *Care, autonomy and justice*, Grace Clement (1998, pp 42-3) has argued that this is both a theoretical and practical possibility. Clement rejects a classical liberal conception of justice, deriving as she sees it from a predominantly psychologistic account of autonomy grounded in the human capacity for rational thought. She points out that such a formulation has given rise not only to the concept of individual agency, but also to the political imperative in liberal democracies of protecting that freedom from an overbearing state. Relational autonomy, by contrast, depends upon positive not negative freedoms. Should autonomy be inseparable from an individual's sense of responsibility towards and relationships with others, both personal and social, then a substantive system of justice is required to bring about the social conditions necessary to exercise genuine agency. At the same time, achieving a selfhood based upon an idea of human uniqueness and discreteness requires sufficient separation between self and others to enable caregivers, for example, to avoid self-sacrifice and the denial of self-identity.

Reaching some accommodation between autonomy and interdependence provides a way of moving beyond a mere iteration of the centrality of relationships to human existence to offer some means of assessing their quality, and by extension the quality of social policy. Thus, policy that reinforces gendered stereotypes by taking women's care giving for granted at the expense of their own interests may be adjudged illegitimate. Insofar as contemporary care policy in the form of leave from employment tends to be either unpaid or remunerated at a low level, as Daly (2002, p 267) points out, it has a negative impact on gender equality in the UK because it encourages women rather than men to exit from the labour market. Furthermore, the lack of good quality, universal, affordable and flexible forms of day care in the context of a drive to fuller employment creates difficulties for working parents, particularly women (Williams, 2001). As Sevenhuijsen (2000) argues, social policies based on an integrated account of care and autonomy would seek to ensure that all citizens had the time and space to combine paid work and care.

Rethinking reciprocity

An integration of care and autonomy in policy making would also look beyond the reciprocal obligations of dutiful citizens for a guide to moral action in relation to care. As discussed earlier in this chapter, political obligations in a classical liberal system of justice tend to be constructed in such a way as to preserve individual autonomy, whereas Clement maintains that the ethic of care must show how the self can achieve individual freedom without violating moral obligations to others. What policy makers require, she argues (1998, p 13), are elaborated insights into the way in which caregivers handle the moral dilemmas that go with conflicting responsibilities for self, others and the relationships between them. As Finch (1989) has demonstrated empirically, it is not formal obligations that provide the guide when responsibilities to self and others conflict in care relationships, but rather situated questions about the 'proper thing to do'. After all, the result of any imposition of a universal obligation to provide care through policy interventions may be the abuse of the care receiver if the affective dimension of the relationship between care giver and receiver is absent.

Clement (1998) further suggests that it is vulnerability rather than reciprocal obligations that should serve as the moral imperative for those with the power to act on behalf of others. Yet, as Goodin (2002) points out, the shift from social insurance to workfare in Britain represents a move away from the principle of the powerful helping the vulnerable in anticipation of some future time when they too might be weak. Contemporary welfare discourse makes rights to welfare conditional upon their immediate reciprocation in the particular currency of paid work. From a care perspective, it is possible to imagine with Goodin that our responsibilities towards each other might be met by offering different kinds of support, such as care giving, at different points in time. As Smith (2002, p 52) points out, too, unemployed people and older and disabled people already contribute towards the life of the community through such means as voluntary work, community-based group activities, cultural and artistic participation. Moreover, such understandings appear to inform popular notions of the relationship between responsibility and rights to welfare. In Dwyer's (2002) research, for example, as in our own (see Chapter Four of this book), participants saw those who had contributed in some way to the wider welfare needs of the community as deserving of social security.

The foundational concept of human interdependence upon which the ethic of care is based, as Tronto (1994) makes clear, derives from the varying degrees of dependence and independence, autonomy and vulnerability experienced by the relational self throughout the life course. Yet, Williams (2001) rightly points out that claims for the universal nature of dependency and vulnerability serve to underplay disabled people's marginalisation and oppression and their historical constitution in the social relations of disability. The social model of disability challenges the link between impairment and dependency, relocating dependency in the social barriers constituting disability. Dominant definitions of independence as self-sufficiency are also rejected in favour of a version of autonomy that allows disabled people to achieve independence without the need to be self-sufficient in terms of daily living tasks (see Morris, 1993). Where autonomy is equated with self-determination, it can be accomplished by substituting personal assistance and direct payment schemes for disabling modes of care.

These distinctions have proved useful for making sense of care receivers' experiences of mainstream care services where overly narrow definitions of independence, which place the emphasis on people regaining or maintaining functional independence, have had a damaging impact on home care. While care receivers value their ability to perform tasks independently where possible, as Vernon and Qureshi (2000) found, people tend to equate independence less with self-sufficiency than with autonomy, or a sense of control over choices and decisions affecting their lives. Whereas simply 'keeping people going' is now tantamount to policy failure, empirical studies would suggest that receiving help to meet legitimate needs tends to promote rather than compromise people's sense of autonomy. Moreover, as Clark et al (1998) point out, the targeting of personal care on those most at risk of physical harm has been at the expense of low-level preventive services which are highly valued by many older people as well as arguably based on a far broader definition of social inclusion.

Embodying care

Yet the distinction between autonomy and self-sufficiency undermines claims for a universal vulnerability by suggesting that bodily dependencies are transcended if the social relations of disability are changed. Designed principally as a socio-political tool to challenge disabling power relations (Campbell and Oliver, 1996), the social model approach has had significant success in challenging dependency-creating policy and practice. However, inasmuch as it is founded on the liberal model of the rational and autonomous self, for whom political citizenship is based on control over the body, the social model is also in danger of reinforcing the very mind–body, public–private dualisms within which the social construction of disability is inscripted. Indeed, Scott-Hill (2002) argues that disability politics have spawned an undemocratic and exclusionary group identity of disabled people based on the 'truth' of the social model within which, it is assumed, all forms of experience can be accommodated. Certainly disabled feminist writers in particular have called for some recognition of the extent to which bodily vulnerabilities, such as pain, incontinence, illness, fear of dying, create restrictions which are personally experienced rather than socially created (Morris, 1991; Crow, 1992; French, 1993).

These debates are of more than academic interest as they have practical implications for care receivers and for care policy. Recognition that autonomy is both relational and embodied, both public and private, opens up areas of social policy hitherto hidden from analysis. In her account of the giving and receiving of intimate bodily care, Twigg (2000) highlights the myriad negotiations involved in care work, around touch and nakedness for example, and the power dynamics which underlie them. Given that personal care is largely delivered on a one-to-one basis within the privacy of the home, then the embodied nature of autonomy arguably matters very much to care receivers. Such issues have been thrown into sharp relief by the fragmentation of home care in the UK as a result of parcelling it out to a multiplicity of providers, who deliver intimate personal care in short shifts over an extended working day.

Visits by 'serial' care workers threaten the bodily integrity of care receivers by undermining the relational aspects of care provision, as well as compromising other valued qualities of home care, such as its flexibility and the security it offers to highly vulnerable people (Quilgars et al, 1997; Henwood, 1999; Ungerson, 2000).

Overcoming the politics–policy dichotomy

By developing the theory and practices of independent living in direct opposition to community care and to the concepts of dependency and need on which social welfare regimes have rested in the postwar period, disability activists and writers have tended to place the emphasis on independence rather than interdependence. Similarly, rather than substantive rights to care, the struggles of disabled people's organisations have tended to centre on civil rights, with legislative power presented as the principal source of protection against discrimination in the public domain. Anti-discrimination legislation is arguably rooted in dominant models of political citizenship that turn disabled people into full citizens through the right to equal treatment, particularly to be active in the public domain of employment and consumption. The accession in the UK of the incoming Labour government to demands from the disability movement for the setting up of the Disability Rights Commission may be taken as evidence that such an approach is entirely consistent with New Labour's workfare policies and its framing of citizenship in terms of equality of opportunity within and access to paid work.

Scott-Hill (2002) maintains that disability writers have set up a false dichotomy between 'policy' and 'politics', rejecting (welfare) policy because it is rooted in an individual model of disability while favouring politics on the basis that they derive from the social model. This is a dichotomy, she suggests, that not only risks positioning those people with impairments outside liberationary struggle as 'victims' of care policy, but, ironically, harnesses disability politics to the individualistic model of rights in which anti-discrimination measures are grounded. Certainly access to the paid economy is not a key preoccupation for older people, whereas substantive rights to care services of a particular quality are of critical importance. Moreover, Oldman (2003, p 53) points out that, even as ageism is tackled through citizenship initiatives such as Better Government for Older People and the National Service Framework for Older People, independent living policies provide the perfect justification for savage cutbacks persuading older people to stay at home reliant on family members.

As Scott-Hill (2002) argues, policy and politics are both collective voices that represent particular outcomes in the negotiation of difference. The pitfalls associated with reliance upon vulnerability as the point of departure for care policy might be avoided if the nature of reciprocal relations and the politics underlying care policy are reframed. Thus, Smith (2002, pp 50-7) claims that justice can be defended as reciprocity if we rethink the relations underlying both formal systems of justice, where reciprocal relations are based upon the obligations of the individual to return benefits given by others, and more substantive systems which exempt socially marginalised groups from the conditions of reciprocity on the basis of their vulnerability. Were reciprocal relations also seen in terms of the obligation of the powerful to receive benefits from others, then Smith suggests that, in the case of disabled people, this benefit might take the form of learning from the unique insights and levels of personal development gained through the experience of impairment. Nevertheless, Smith cautions that such learning can only occur if the reality of our interdependent social and human existence is acknowledged and if understandings of justice are broadened to include identity discrimination caused by a failure to acknowledge the diversity of experience of those defined as disadvantaged.

Overcoming these barriers requires that care policy is informed by a politics of recognition grounded in the assumption that justice should be seen not only in terms of unequal access to resources, but also in terms of the recognition of difference and "claims for the realisation of personhood, for cultural respect, autonomy and dignity" (Williams, 1999, p 673). Rather than attempting to refract a diversity of experiences through the social model, or any other universalising assumption of a common good or interest, such a politics would recognise differences among care givers and receivers on the basis of age, gender, ethnicity and so forth. It would also move away from individualistic notions of autonomy to encompass the principles and practices of relational autonomy discussed earlier. Relational politics would depend in turn on the practice of deliberative democracy, a central aim of which is to facilitate the participation of people in decision making affecting their lives through a democratic practice that takes proper account of inequality and diversity (see, for example, Drake, 2002). In the case of social care, as Barnes (2002) points out, such a practice would be responsive to differing communicative competences and challenge not only the substance of policy decisions but also the assumptions underpinning dominant forms of professional and managerial governance.

Conclusion

The first part of this chapter sought to establish the political ethic of care as a valuable feminist tool for examining contemporary care policy in the UK and its relationship to dependency, responsibility and rights. In theory, the overarching principle of 'third way' social policy is 'work for those who can, security for those who cannot'. In practice, a number of mutually reinforcing dualisms – care–autonomy, public–private, mind–body – not only divide care giver and care receiver from the self-sufficient citizen, but subjugate both the activities of care giving and care receiving and the relationships within which they are rooted to paid work. Indeed, the twin notions of care and dependency in which much social welfare was embedded in the postwar period have arguably been delegitimated in 'third way' politics. Certainly, they attract only residual and conditional rights. In the active preventive state, care giving is a citizenship obligation to be fitted around paid work or else integrated into service provision as a form of work in the case of adult social care. If care receivers cannot engage in paid work then at the very least they are expected to be active in their own rehabilitation or care management.

Adopting the perspective of a political ethic of care, therefore, has thrown into sharp relief a number of ethical and practical deficiencies characterising contemporary UK care policy. An overarching emphasis on the obligation to engage in paid work obscures the extent to which citizenship rights may be reciprocated in other ways, such as care giving or providing insights into the experience of managing age and impairment which most of us face at some point in our lives. An appreciation that we act in response to our responsibilities towards others within the context of given relationships rather than in response to ascribed obligations highlights the injustice of making caregivers' rights to support conditional upon individualistic obligations to continue caring. Only care policy based on the precepts of relational autonomy might enable citizens to manage the ethical dilemmas they face in balancing responsibilities to self and others and/or provide the practical means by which people are afforded the time and space to combine paid work with care giving or receiving.

Over the past decade, disability writers and activists have offered an influential critique of social care arrangements from the perspective of the care receiver. Writers have articulated the social relations of disability and their consequences in terms of social disadvantage as well as redefining autonomy as self-determination rather than self-sufficiency. Yet, in other respects, disability politics tend to reflect or reinforce the oppressive dualisms within which 'third way' care policy is forged. The struggle for the rights of the independent disabled person to formal equality in the public domain has relegated bodily vulnerability to the private domain. What is obscured in the process are the possibilities for imagining an embodied and relational autonomy that fosters an understanding of human connectedness and identifies ways of supporting people to both give and receive care in socially just ways. More particularly, care policy based on an appreciation of the interdependent nature of human relations would direct attention towards the ways in which meeting need at the everyday level embodies abstract ideas about need, power and relationships (Tronto, 1994).

This is not to mount a defence of the ethos of care or altruism towards the different person with special needs underpinning postwar welfare regimes. Such an approach, as Clement (1998, p 105) points out, merely serves to preserve the group privileges of the powerful while obscuring their own implication in the power relations that assign the problems to others. The political ethic of care is at one with disability politics in understanding difference as the property of social relationships rather than individuals, yet goes further by insisting that rights should be supported by universal and non-stigmatising forms of social provision. What is required, however, as Williams (1999) argues, is a 'differentiated universalism'. Such an approach signals a commitment to the inclusion and equal moral value of all citizens, and challenges structured differentiation, yet seeks additionally to incorporate people's own definitions of their own diversity.

This is a politics that is unlikely to flourish within the sterile apparatus of performance governance based as it is on individualised categories of need and unitary measures of quality. Identifying integrative means of promoting the shared interests of self and others demands a politics capable of generating solidarities based on a recognition of both universal and differentiated values, supported by a democratic practice which ensures a range of voices are heard.

References

Arendt, H. (1966) *The origins of totalitarianism*, New York, NY: Harcourt, Brace and World.

Bacchi, C.L. and Beasley, C. (2002) 'Citizen bodies: is embodied citizenship a contradiction in terms?', *Critical Social Policy*, vol 22, no 2, pp 324-52.

Baier, A. (1993) 'What do women want in a moral theory?', in M.J. Larabee (ed) *An ethic of care: Feminist and interdisciplinary perspectives*, New York, NY: Routledge.

Barnes, C. (2002) 'Introduction: disability, policy and politics', *Policy & Politics*, vol 30, no 3, pp 311-18.

Barnes, M. (2002) 'Bringing difference into deliberation? Disabled people, survivors and local governance', *Policy & Politics*, vol 30, no 3, pp 319-31.

Blackman, T. and Palmer, A. (1999) 'Continuity or modernisation? The emergence of New Labour's welfare state', in H. Dean and R. Woods (eds) *Social Policy Review 11*, Luton: University of Luton/Social Policy Association.

Broughton, J. (1993) 'Women's rationality and men's virtues: a critique of gender dualism in Gilligan's theory of moral development', in M.J. Larabee (ed) *An ethic of care: Feminist and interdisciplinary perspectives*, New York, NY: Routledge.

Campbell, J. and Oliver, M. (1996) *Disability politics: Understanding our past, changing our future*, London: Routledge.

Clark, H., Dyer, S. and Horwood, J. (1998) *'That bit of help': The high value of low level preventative services for older people*, Bristol/York: The Policy Press/Joseph Rowntree Foundation/*Community Care*.

Clement, G. (1998) *Care, autonomy and justice: Feminism and the ethic of care*, Boulder, CO: Westview Press.

Crow, L. (1996) 'Including all our lives: renewing the social model of disability', in C. Barnes and G. Mercer (eds) *Exploring the divide: Illness and disability*, Leeds: The Disability Press.

Daly, M. (2002) 'Care as a good for social policy', *Journal of Social Policy*, vol 31, no 2, pp 251-70.

Daly, M. (2003) 'Governance and social policy', *Journal of Social Policy*, vol 32, no 1, pp 113-28.

DoH (Department of Health) (1998) *Modernising social services: Promoting independence, improving protection and raising standards*, Cm 4169, London: The Stationery Office.

DoH (1999) *Caring about carers: A national strategy for carers*, London: The Stationery Office.

Drake, R. (2001) *The principles of social policy*, Basingstoke: Palgrave.

Drake, R. (2002) 'Disabled people, voluntary organisations and participation in policy making', *Policy & Politics*, vol 30, no 3, pp 373-85.

Dwyer, P. (2002) 'Making sense of social citizenship: some user views on welfare rights and responsibilities', *Critical Social Policy*, vol 22, no 2, pp 273-99.

Finch, J. (1989) *Family obligations and social change*, Cambridge: Polity Press.

Fisher, B. and Tronto, J. (1991) 'Toward a feminist theory of care', in E. Abel and M. Nelson (eds) *Circles of care: Work and identity in women's lives*, Albany, NY: State University of New York Press.

Flanagan, O. and Jackson, K. (1993) 'Justice, care and gender: the Kohlberg-Gilligan debate revisited', in M.J. Larabee (ed) *An ethic of care: Feminist and interdisciplinary perspectives*, New York, NY: Routledge.

Ford, J., Quilgars, D. and Rugg, J. (1998) *Creating jobs? The employment potential of domiciliary care*, Bristol/York: The Policy Press/Joseph Rowntree Foundation/Community Care.

French, S. (1993) 'Disability, impairment or something in-between?', in J. Swain, V. Finkelstein, S. French and M. Oliver (eds) *Disabling barriers – Enabling environments*, London: Sage Publications.

Friedman, M. (1993) 'Beyond caring: the de-moralisation of gender', in M.J. Larabee (ed) *An ethic of care: Feminist and interdisciplinary perspectives*, New York, NY: Routledge.

Gilligan, C. (1982) *In a different voice: Psychological theory and women's development*, Cambridge, MA: Harvard University Press.

Goodin, R.E. (2002) 'Structures of moral obligation', *Journal of Social Policy*, vol 31, no 4, pp 579-96.

Goodwin, B. (1987) *Using political ideas* (2nd edn), Chichester: John Wiley and Sons.

Henderson, J. and Forbat, L. (2002) 'Relationship-based social policy: personal and policy constructions of care', *Critical Social Policy*, vol 22, no 4, pp 669-87.

Henwood, M. (ed) (1999) *Our turn next: A fresh look at home support services for older people*, Leeds: National Institute for Health.

Hill, M. and Bramley, G. (1986) *Analysing social policy*, Oxford: Basil Blackwell.

Humphrey, J. (2003) 'New Labour and the regulatory reform of social care', *Critical Social Policy*, vol 23, no 1, pp 5-24.

Jacobs, K. and Manzi, T. (2000) 'Conflict and control in housing management', *Critical Social Policy*, vol 20, no 1, pp 85-103.

Johnson, N. (1999) 'The personal social services and community care', in M. Powell (ed) *New Labour, new welfare state? The 'third way' in British social policy*, Bristol: The Policy Press.

Kohlberg, L. (1981) *Essays on moral development. Vol 1: The philosophy of moral development*, San Francisco, CA: Harper and Row.

Larabee, M.J. (1993) 'Gender and moral development: a challenge for feminist theory', in M.J. Larabee (ed) *An ethic of care: Feminist and interdisciplinary perspectives*, New York, NY: Routledge.

Lloyd, L. (2000) 'Caring about carers: only half the picture?', *Critical Social Policy*, vol 20, no 1, pp 136-50.

Morris, J. (1991) *Pride against prejudice*, London: The Women's Press.

Morris, J. (1993) *Independent lives? Community care and disabled people*, Basingstoke: Macmillan.

Oldman, C. (2003) 'Deceiving, theorising and self-justification: a critique of independent living', *Critical Social Policy*, vol 23, no 1, pp 44-62.

Parker, G. (2002) 'Guest editorial. 10 years of the 'new' community care: good in parts?', *Health and Social Care in the Community*, vol 10, no 1, pp 1-5.

Parker, G. and Clarke, H. (2002) 'Making ends meet: do carers and disabled people have a common agenda?', *Policy & Politics*, vol 30, no 3, pp 347-59.

Powell, M. (2000) 'New Labour and the third way in the British welfare state: a new and distinctive approach?', *Critical Social Policy*, vol 20, no 1, pp 39-60.

Priestley, M. (2002) 'Whose voices? Representing the claims of older disabled people under New Labour', *Policy & Politics*, vol 30, no 3, pp 361-72.

Quilgars, D., Oldman, C. and Carlisle, J. (1997) *Supporting independence: Home support services for older people*, Oxford: Anchor Research.

Rouse, J. and Smith, G. (1999) 'Accountability', in M. Powell (ed) *New Labour, new welfare State? The 'third way' in British social policy*, Bristol: The Policy Press.

Scott-Hill, M. (2002) 'Policy, politics and the silencing of "voice"', *Policy & Politics*, vol 30, no 3, pp 397-409.

Sevenhuijsen, S. (2000) 'Caring in the third way: the relation between obligation, responsibility and care in Third Way discourse', *Critical Social Policy*, vol 20, no 1, pp 5-37.

Smart, C. (1989) *Feminism and the power of law*, London: Routledge.

Smith, S. (2002) 'Fraternal learning and interdependency: celebrating differences within reciprocal commitments', *Policy & Politics*, vol 30, no 1, pp 47-59.

Tronto, J. (1993) 'Beyond gender difference to a theory of care', in M.J. Larabee (ed) *An ethic of care: Feminist and interdisciplinary perspectives*, New York, NY: Routledge.

Tronto, J. (1994) *Moral boundaries. A political argument for an ethic of care*, New York, NY: Routledge.

Twigg, J. (2000) *Bathing: The body and community care*, London: Routledge.

Ungerson, C. (2000) 'Thinking about the production and consumption of long-term care in Britain: does gender matter?', *Journal of Social Policy*, vol 29, no 4, pp 623-44.

Vernon, A. and Qureshi, H. (2000) 'Community care and independence: self-sufficiency or empowerment?', *Critical Social Policy*, vol 20, no 2, pp 255-76.

Williams, F. (1989) *Social policy: A critical introduction*, Cambridge: Polity Press.

Williams, F. (1999) 'Good-enough principles for welfare', *Journal of Social Policy*, vol 28, no 4, pp 667-87.

Williams, F. (2001) 'In and beyond New Labour: towards a new political ethics of care', *Critical Social Policy*, vol 21, no 4, pp 467-93.

Young, I. (2000) *Inclusion and democracy*, Oxford: Oxford University Press.

THREE

Responsibility and welfare: in search of moral sensibility

Shane Doheny

In 1997, Britain's New Labour government promised "a modern welfare state based on rights and duties going together" (Blair, 1997, p 4). One of the striking features of New Labour's 'third way' discourse is that it moralises without making recourse to a moral sensibility. Theirs is a discourse that makes judgements about action without needing to provide ethical grounds for preferring one course of action to another. This moral reasoning fits easily with a social philosophy where responsibility has more to do with calculating the risks and benefits of providing for welfare than with any sense of solidarity for the stranger (Bauman, 1993; Fevre, 2000). New Labour takes up responsibility as part of a communitarian discourse offering both a critique of liberalism and, ostensibly, a vocabulary commensurate with ethical socialism (Driver and Martell, 1998). Responsibility is supposed to articulate the social web of relationships that bind communities together and to voice a critique of liberal individualism that holds out the possibility of social cooperation. However, without a moral sensibility articulating reasons for people to come together and cooperate – as opposed to reinforcing the ways that people do in fact come together – New Labour's discourse begins to look empty of any ethical socialist conceptions.

To help illustrate my argument, this chapter first reconstructs and analyses the discourses employed by New Labour in a series of press releases dating from the end of its first term of office. I reconstruct these discourses because of their special status as news stories written to be retold by the press and broadcasting media to (potentially) everybody (Jacobs, 1999). What we find in these discourses are four different constructions of the citizen, each requiring different kinds of information and services; but uncovering the sense of responsibility implied in these discourses means using a theoretical framework sensitive to social constructions of responsibility. For this reason, the second part of the chapter applies Dean's (2002) taxonomy of discourses of responsibility to map the repertoires New Labour takes up. We shall see that New Labour's press release writers draw principally on discourses of duty and obligation – and on occasions a discourse of obedience (see also Chapter One of this book). Their discourse largely excludes an ethical understanding of responsibility. What this suggests is that New Labour focuses on gathering people together into private contracts in civil society and the economy rather then into a public sphere.

Finally, in order to make sense of the issues involved in this construction of responsibility, this chapter discusses contemporary social philosophy of responsibility. I argue that the communitarian politics of responsibility favoured by New Labour (Driver and Martell, 1997; Heron, 2002) grants authority to the idea that being responsible will benefit the self, and so reduces the moral to a knowable social good. In this chapter, I show that there are other ways responsibility can be constructed that put ethical and moral solidarity at their core.

Constructing citizens through the news media

Within the government's publicity machine, the press release constitutes a channel through which information is circulated into the public sphere, where it becomes a text that people can use to gather information or as a way of understanding issues. Due to these characteristics, the press release is both an institutionalised channel through which information flows as news, and it is a text that people take up and read and perhaps retell to others. It can exert power, therefore, across time and space. For the government to successfully manage the frameworks for understanding the world that citizens use, it is important that press release writers successfully communicate information that conveys the government's preferred frames. This means the press releases have to be written to maximise media exposure and grab the attention of target audiences (Jacobs, 1998). As a text available in the public sphere, press releases consistently communicate information and New Labour's frameworks of understanding. In short, it is a highly managed form of communication.

The corpus of press releases that I discuss in this chapter consisted of 69 statements relating to a variety of cash benefits, government schemes to promote labour market participation, and the state regulation of private pensions that were issued within the six-month period between September 2000 and February 2001. The majority of the press releases were issued by the former Department of Social Security, while the former Department for Education and Employment issued six. All the press releases were accessible through government websites.

My analysis of these texts suggests they implicitly construct four kinds of reader/listener/viewer for news editors, corresponding to four kinds of citizen: the 'heroic citizen', the 'passive citizen', the 'good citizen' and the 'recalcitrant citizen'.

The heroic citizen

For the heroic citizen, the publicising role of the press releases was restricted to either providing information or informing about other sources of information. There was no need to construct elaborate discourses; rather, the press release writers could get straight to the point (Box 3.1).

Box 3.1: Press releases for Heroic Citizens

Claim your pension over the 'phone: new tele-claim service for pensioners
People who are about to retire can now claim their State Pension by telephone rather than by filling in a form Alistair Darling, Social Security Secretary, announced today.

Mr Darling said, "This new service will give people about to retire active assistance when they claim. It will provide a smooth, efficient and accessible service. This is part of my aim to modernise the services that the DSS offers" (DSS, 2000e).

Or:

Want information on Stakeholder Pensions? Ring a new helpline
People who want more information on stakeholder pensions can now ring a new helpline for impartial information, Social Security Minister Jeff Rooker announced today.

Launching the helpline Mr Rooker said: "Stakeholder pensions will, for the first time, offer millions of people a good value, secure and flexible second pension" (DSS, 2000c).

Both the press releases in Box 3.1 relate to the promotion of a new kind of specially regulated stakeholder pension scheme designed primarily for people with relatively low incomes. Each follows the same format. The titles bring two statements together, combining some kind of action with a solution. These are highly charged insertions into the public sphere designed to gain the attention of people who are actively trying to find rational solutions to problems. However, the particular issues raised in these attention-grabbing headlines are issues of choice and access to a businesslike organisation. The question of how to proceed to set up one's pension is answered with a telephone-based service, the need for information answered with a helpline. The presumption made is that a businesslike service and a route to information will satisfy a citizen whose attention is secured through issues of choice and access. The first two paragraphs in the body of these press releases elaborate further on these postulated sources of satisfaction (Box 3.1). However, what is notable in each case is the rational nature of the expectation. People who are retiring can expect "smooth" and "efficient", "active assistance" from the state. Those assessing their pensions options have a right to expect an option that is "good value, secure and flexible". In effect, this citizen expects options, incentives and a businesslike service. It is very much the classical liberal citizen dressed up in consumerist clothes.

The passive citizen

Whereas publicity for the heroic citizen was about providing information, publicity for the passive citizen was about reassuring and encouraging people actively to participate in providing for their own welfare. This interest in encouraging participation pushes information provision into the background. Instead, the press release publicises information in ways that reassure people about securing their own welfare themselves. The press release does this by generating space where the passive citizen can integrate with others into a larger society so that s/he feels safe and secure in approaching state systems for help, support and information. Accomplishing such a feat in a press release means using complex operations (Box 3.2).

Box 3.2: Press release for Passive Citizens

Getting on the dog and bone to find out about pensions
Shadow the sheepdog is pictured leading the line for people who want to collar a decent pension.

The canine TV advert star barked out advice to those who want to know whether stakeholder pensions are right for them.

With just six weeks to go before stakeholder pensions become available, Pensions Advisory Service (OPAS) stakeholder helpline staff are now answering calls from people looking for help and information.

Shadow's guest spot on the helpline came as new research reveals four out of five people find the technical jargon of pensions confusing and nine out of ten want simple advice.

The DSS' current pension education marketing campaign involving talking sheepdogs encourages people to consider their pension options as early as possible. A set of eight booklets is available covering the whole range of options including stakeholder, personal, occupational and state pensions and written in clear and simple English (DSS, 2001d).

The press release in Box 3.2 is concerned once again with stakeholder pensions, but describes the actions of the canine star of a television advertising campaign aimed at getting people to act to secure pensions. However, the people this campaign is aimed at are not receptive to information. Indeed, they find the "technical jargon of pensions confusing" (DSS, 2001d) and pensions themselves boring, making the press release writers work even harder:

> Too often people see pensions as a complex and boring subject that they do not want to think about.... The DSS had to produce a campaign very different from traditional public service information – something that would keep them watching when they hear the word 'pension'. (DSS, 2001a)

The sheepdog is recruited in response to this perceived apathy. In fact, one press release (DSS, 2001a), as we have seen, plays out the way that the sheepdog is supposed to "keep them [passive citizens] watching when they hear the word 'pension'". This is a citizen who is so easily turned off thinking about his/her welfare that it is at first necessary to convey messages to him/her by stealth. This press release does not publicise information; rather, it publicises an image of people being brought together by a sheepdog and directed towards the Pensions Advisory Service (OPAS) and an assortment of booklets. Therefore, this citizen is assumed to operate outside, or at the margins of, the public sphere. S/he needs to be drawn into the public sphere and made to feel safe and secure as part of the information gathering and options evaluating public.

In the case of the press release in Box 3.2, the initial emphasis is not on the available information but rather on "Shadow the sheepdog" integrating the passive citizen into the public sphere. The sheepdog, a dog defined according to its function in farming sheep, is used as a metaphor for the state. The sheepdog embodies many of the qualities of the state. It is a friend, a protector, the herder 'leading the line' and, although it has hunting instincts, these are subdued, allowing it to work in the best interest of sheepish citizens. Furthermore, naming the sheepdog Shadow familiarises it while the name describes the sheepdog state in the activity of shadowing. It is always there, shadowing the sheep or the passive citizen. Metaphorically, the state is familiar, reliable and always working to protect its citizens; but in this press release, the image of the state as sheepdog is shifted so that the sheepdog leads sheepish citizens towards taking on more of the burdens of responsibility for their own welfare themselves. Shadow "is pictured leading the line" for people who "collar [that is, both catch and burden themselves with a restrictive band] a decent pension". This sheepdog "barks out advice" and talks, but it is communicating not with people who want information, but with those who want to know the right answer. It barks at "those who want to know whether stakeholder pensions are right for them" and in talking it "encourages people to consider their pensions". The passive sheepish citizen is one who needs to be told what the right thing to do is, or needs to be encouraged into thinking about his/her welfare. Significantly, however much the press release writers seek to imagine the state as a sheepdog, the citizen is still expected to approach state agencies for information, or to pick up such information from the public sphere. This passive citizen who needs to be encouraged to think is supposed to "call" helplines for information, or else pick up booklets. The government extends the public sphere making it receptive to this passive citizen, but there is still no guarantee that this citizen will enter this sphere.

The good citizen

The heroic citizen was the rational adult of the liberal imagination and the passive citizen was marginally involved in matters of public welfare. Between the rational hero and the socially malleable passive citizen stands a good citizen who shares traits with both of the other two. Like the heroic citizen, the good citizen is independent and rational, actively looking for information. Like the passive citizen, the good citizen acts in ways that are defined socially. What differentiates the good citizen is also the very feature that elides him/her with these others. S/he wants to know how to be responsible like the heroic citizen, but not in the individualistically rational sense of the hero. Rather, his/her understanding of being responsible is negatively defined as not being a burden on others. This places him/her right between the hero, who is positively responsible by rationally choosing among his/her options, and the passive sheep that is influenced by the acts of others and loosely integrated into society as a public sphere. For example, the press release in Box 3.3 accompanies the one aimed at the passive citizen discussed earlier, but here it is aimed at the good citizen.

Box 3.3: Press release for Good Citizens

Pension awareness ad blitz begins

Man's best friend has taken the lead in a new Government campaign to get people to think about planning for their pension.

Using Oscar-winning techniques that brought 'Babe' to life the £6.5 million marketing campaign aims to make people aware of the need to plan for their retirement and consider all the pension options available to them.

Launching the campaign Alistair Darling, Social Security Secretary, said: "Obviously the basic state pension will remain the foundation of income in retirement". "But now people want to retire on the highest possible income and they can do that by saving through an occupational pension, personal pension or – from April – the stakeholder pension. Yet two out of five people in work today still have no provision except the state pension."

"This campaign is about getting people to consider all the options for retirement" (DSS, 2001a).

This press release (Box 3.3) is presented more as a discussion of the meaning and implications of advertising campaigns than as a piece of publicity about pensions initiatives. It draws the reader in by seemingly impartially observing how the cinematic techniques developed for the film *Babe* are being used in the context of pensions. This, of course, invites discussion of this development in opinion essays, suggesting pensions as at least a subtopic of discussion thereby gaining more publicity. But publicity for whom? Publicity, that is, for those influenced by public opinion as it is presented in the media. The press release goes on to offer its own interpretation of this development. The advertising campaign is first presented as a means of increasing awareness of the need to think about pensions and plan for retirement. The use of an advertising campaign is set inside a narrative about the continuities and changes in pensions systems. There is the continuity of a state retirement pension as a 'foundation', while there are changes in people's expectations in the consumer society. Significantly, the press release writers respond to this by providing a rule of thumb for the good citizen:

> The introduction of the Pension Credit from 2003 will reward those with modest savings and a small second pension with a cash top up. So the message from the government is whatever you can afford to put aside, it will always pay to save and the more you save and the earlier you start the better. (DSS, 2001a)

Those who want to know how to be responsible in the changing world are told "it will always pay to save".

Perhaps more than the heroic citizen, the good citizen needs clear signals about how to be a responsible person. It is not enough to simply tell this citizen to save; s/he also needs to have his/her saving clearly rewarded:

> 'For the first time ever the Pension Credit will make sure savings will be rewarded,' said Mr Darling. 'There is a fundamental fault in the system we inherited. Saving should be rewarded, not punished. The Credit will reward the thrift of millions of people who have worked hard to save for their retirement.' (DSS, 2000d)

The good citizen needs to have his/her responsible behaviour reinforced and positively conditioned by rewards and incentives. Yet, however much s/he is rational, the good citizen also shares some of the sheepish traits of the passive citizen. Hence, an initiative such as pensions statements is supposed to form good responsible citizens out of passive citizens:

> Jeff Rooker said: 'Once people see in black and white what they will have to live on I think they will realise the importance of saving for their old age and I hope it will prompt them to review the provision they have made for their retirement.... These statements will be one of the important factors in getting people to save by showing them how much pension they have built up and how much more they can get if they save.... Working people, who can afford it have a responsibility to save for their retirement. But the Government has a duty to help them'. (DSS, 2000b)

Good citizens, those who want to know how to be responsible (but responsible in the sense of not being a burden on others), can be made of passive citizens convinced of the need to take responsibility or people who are responsive to a changing world.

The recalcitrant citizen

As we have seen, the press release serves to circulate information into the public sphere where it becomes a text that continues to manage the information that people consume. Press releases differ according to how target audiences are expected to receive the information being supplied. Hence, the hero is expected to seek the basic point, looking for developments and sources of information; the good citizen wants to know how to avoid being a burden on others; and the passive citizen needs to be reassured while being drawn into the public sphere. However, a fourth kind of citizen is also manifest in the press releases, an unruly recalcitrant citizen who would play the odds to receive, or to increase their receipt of, welfare benefits. The role of the media in problematising the 'abuse' of benefits has been extensively remarked upon elsewhere (see, for example, Dean, 2001). What is interesting in this instance, however, is the way in which publicity issued in response to the recalcitrant citizen was aimed at restricting both his/her social space, and the administrative scope for his/her function. So, contrary to the other citizens who received some positive support, the recalcitrant citizen received threats and penalties.

One important feature of the language used in connection with the recalcitrant citizen was its hostility. For example, benefits agencies battle with "criminals who ... hijack the identities of innocent Irish citizens to make false claims in the UK" (DSS, 2000a). However, the recalcitrant citizen does not have to be a criminal at the margins of society; rather, it could be a person who earns "cash in hand while claiming, playing on the sympathy of friends to cadge free drinks" (DSS, 2001b). They are the kind that "blights the system and takes money away from the people who need it most" (DSS, 2001c). Using this kind of language, the recalcitrant citizen is built into a spectre that needs to be dealt with forthwith. The state battles the culture of the recalcitrant citizen by altering his/her systemic and cultural context. The systemic context is characterised by greater control over the gateways to fraudulent behaviour:

> The Government is playing its part in tackling fraud: tightening the gateways to benefit, improving the training of fraud investigators, modernising the technology to root out the cheats as well as seeking new powers to toughen the penalties against persistent offenders and to gather the information necessary to catch them. (DSS, 2001b)

The cultural context is altered through an advertising campaign aimed at altering the image of the fraudster:

> We produced a series of tough ads to demonstrate that targeting fraud is everyone's business; we have tested them thoroughly in the North West and now we are ready to take the campaign nationwide. (DSS, 2001b)

This is a battle that the state claims to be winning:

> The progress we are seeing must and will continue. Combating fraud is one of the reasons social security spending is under control and will remain under control. (DSS, 2000a)

But the recalcitrant citizen is not just a kind of person: s/he is a welfare client, a lone parent, pensioner or disabled person (DSS, 2001a). Yet as a client she is denied a voice or any form of ontology:

> People who work and claim benefits aren't loveable rogues, what they are doing is despicable. Benefit fraud costs every household in this country over £80 a year. People would be rightly angry if £80 was stolen from their wallets. (DSS, 2001b)

In transforming the welfare fraudster into a spectre of greater magnitude than bureaucratic waste, the benefits agency's relationship with its clients is discursively changed into one that is more conditional. Governing irresponsibility legitimates making rights conditional as a way of insulating a system against a hostile environment. Consequently, obedience is tied more and more closely to the administration's ability to control outgoings.

Interpreting discourses of responsibility

As this reconstruction of the discourses used by New Labour's press release writers shows, each kind of citizen is responsible in different ways, drawing the government towards them differently. However, the reconstruction cannot by itself make sense of this. One way of doing so is to draw upon a theoretically derived taxonomy of social discourses of responsibility provided by Dean (2002). This taxonomy distinguishes between individual duties, personal obedience, moral obligations and social responsibility as the conceptual locus for differences in social discourses of responsibility. The taxonomy is represented in Figure 3.1, in which the horizontal axis represents a continuum between solidaristic

Figure 3.1: Interpreting responsibility

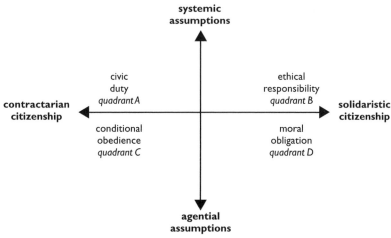

Source: Dean (2002, p 200)

and contractarian approaches to citizenship while the vertical axis is based on a distinction between thinking about responsibility using systemic and agential assumptions.

Where responsibility is construed along contractarian lines but using systemic ideas about the generalisability of being responsible, it takes the form of civic duty (quadrant A). A duty is first a private matter for the parties to a contract, each of whom expects the other to carry out his/her part of the bargain. This relationship, however, can also be generalised as the grounds for reasonably expecting contract bearers to carry out their actions. So, while civic duties are based on expectations, the reciprocal nature of these expectations means they can take a systematic form.

The contractarian view of responsibility can also take on a more particularistic form using agential assumptions (quadrant C). Considered along these lines, responsibility is manifest as conditional obedience. Within the contract, as we saw, responsibility is curtailed to the relations existing between parties to the contract. However, the participants have an interest in ensuring that every party acknowledges and acts upon his/her responsibilities. Looked on from this point of view, responsibility comes to be about eliciting obedience as much as promoting responsibility. The discourse focuses, not on context transcending arguments, but on the means to ensure individuals behave responsibly.

Responsibility can also be conceived in a more collectivist and solidaristic light; that is, the combination of solidaristic with systemic assumptions points in the direction of more ethical ways of thinking of responsibility. The solidaristic perspective starts by considering how people come together into relationships based on the force of their commitment to each other and their willingness to work on the meaning of this commitment. This perspective forms a discourse of ethical responsibility (quadrant B) as the issue turns on how coming together can be generalised, so that ideas of a solidaristic responsibility take on a more systemic form.

Where responsibility is considered from within a solidaristic perspective that emphasises how individual agency responds to social customs and cultural traditions, responsibility takes the form of moral obligations (quadrant D). From this point of view, the interest in protecting, sustaining or generating solidarity and a sense of community means shaping the individual's sense of agency so that the individual acts responsibly. Moral obligations are firstly based on appeals to good reasons, cultural tradition, collective loyalty, or to socially accepted norms. More importantly, however, obligations gain their force from expectations based on their membership of a community.

Using this taxonomy of discourses of responsibility, it is possible to analyse the links between the citizens projected in the press releases and to map the sort of discourse of responsibility used by New Labour.

Civic duty and the heroic citizen

New Labour's ideal is the heroic citizen, but s/he is not seen as a moral citizen. S/he is essentially a self-interested actor, actively seeking information, incentives, choices and a businesslike service so that s/he can decide on the best course of action for him/herself by him/herself. New Labour's press release writers use the repertoire of civic duty when dealing with this citizen. S/he is dealt with using both contractarian and systemic assumptions. On the one hand, s/he is understood as a rational adult who is seeking information, and on the other, the press releases publicise the information that this citizen is anticipated to be seeking. Effectively, the heroic citizen is doing his/her duty by looking for information on the best value service available to him/her, while the government responds by taking up a contract whereby it provides this information along with a range of businesslike services. This reciprocity draws the state and the heroic citizen into a relationship defined by a civic duty where each holds rights and duties in a contract that is rational and systemic.

Moral obligations and the passive citizen

If the hero citizen is left largely to him/herself to look after his/her own interests, the passive citizen is made to feel part of a bigger society. This citizen is difficult to communicate with, s/he gets bored easily and is mentally overtaxed by welfare issues. The press release writers deal with this citizen by setting out his/her moral obligations. S/he is gently informed as to what the right and responsible course of action is, and is assured that s/he can do the right thing. S/he should follow the common sense embodied by the sheepdog, accept that s/he is part of society and carry out the attendant obligations. The press release writers appear careful not to emphasise the morally conservative tendencies of this discourse. Rather, the press releases focus on integrating the passive citizen into the public sphere where s/he can make rational choices, framing moral obligation as the obligation to deal with one's own welfare oneself. Nevertheless, the passive citizen is shielded from the contractarian and alienating tendencies of this rationality by making him/her feel safe getting information from the state. State services are presented as approachable, working in the best interests of this citizen, like Shadow the sheepdog.

The good citizen and a thin discourse of ethical responsibility

As we have seen, the good citizen shares some of the traits of the heroic and passive citizens. S/he shares the heroic citizen's desire to be responsible, and s/he too engages in activities of evaluating choices. However, the systemic assumptions about the nature of responsibility that s/he uses draw him/her into thinking about wider trends in public opinion, and make him/her watchful of incentives and rewards. S/he wants to know s/he is doing the right thing about his/her own welfare, and that this is accepted as right by like-minded individuals and the state. In this way, s/he shares the passive citizen's need to be part of a collective. This use of systemic assumptions and solidaristic conceptions of citizenship appears to make room for an ethical conception of responsibility. But the ethical is limited to the good – as the duty to work and as consumer choice. Hence, a particularly 'thin' (that is, strictly formal) sense of ethical responsibility is entertained in the values of work and thriftiness, values that are prized in civil society and the economy.

Conditional obedience and the recalcitrant citizen

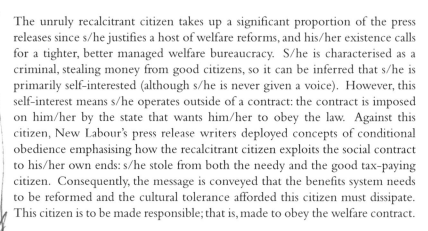

The unruly recalcitrant citizen takes up a significant proportion of the press releases since s/he justifies a host of welfare reforms, and his/her existence calls for a tighter, better managed welfare bureaucracy. S/he is characterised as a criminal, stealing money from good citizens, so it can be inferred that s/he is primarily self-interested (although s/he is never given a voice). However, this self-interest means s/he operates outside of a contract: the contract is imposed on him/her by the state that wants him/her to obey the law. Against this citizen, New Labour's press release writers deployed concepts of conditional obedience emphasising how the recalcitrant citizen exploits the social contract to his/her own ends: s/he stole from both the needy and the good tax-paying citizen. Consequently, the message is conveyed that the benefits system needs to be reformed and the cultural tolerance afforded this citizen must dissipate. This citizen is to be made responsible; that is, made to obey the welfare contract.

New Labour's repertoires of responsibility: a first characterisation

New Labour's press release writers, then, appear to take their conceptual resources from a number of quadrants in Dean's taxonomy of discourses of responsibility. Their discourse draws heavily on the repertoires of civic duty and moral obligation, making use of the language of conditional obedience to justify reform while using very formal – and thus almost meaningless – ideas of ethical responsibility. Consequently, New Labour brings together a liberal discourse that idealises the heroic citizen with a morally conservative discourse emphasising moral obligations to the collective. Insofar as it shows little regard for more ethical concepts of responsibility, this discourse also sidelines a democratic politics that puts collectively held reasons and values at its centre. This discourse firstly postulates membership as membership of civil society; however, in terms of the theory underlying this construction of responsibility, it draws on a discourse that is not concerned with morality.

The collective postulated in the press releases is consistently embodied as a public of information gathering and processing citizens. These are private people that are looking to make decisions about their welfare themselves, and so look for knowledge that has been made publicly available to them. It is a public of private people that come together to form private contracts in civil society rather than to discuss a common issue as a public. So, while New

Labour seeks to integrate the passive citizen into a public using a discourse of moral obligation, the public it has in mind is one where membership is defined through contracts in civil society. Membership of society is reduced to membership in civil society and the economy rather than membership of a public of citizens or a national community. Hence the exclusion of a properly ethical repertoire of responsibility in the coupling of civic duty with moral obligation forms a powerful focus on membership in civil society.

Theorising responsibility: between the interpersonal and the cultural

Alternatively, from a theoretical perspective, it is also possible to characterise New Labour's discourse of responsibility as more epistemic than moral. In this section of the chapter, I argue that this is consistent, for example, with the structure of Etzioni's (1993) communitarian approach to responsibility. Here, I compare this approach with those taken by Bauman (1993), Habermas (1995) and Apel (1990) to highlight how this is but one way of constructing the world.

The social theoretical and social philosophical approaches to responsibility are concerned with how people are drawn together into a relationship characterised by a sense of solidarity, an awareness of reciprocal interests, and/or recognition of each other. However, the models I choose to focus on here can be organised as theories focusing on interpersonal relations of responsibility and theories focusing on the social or cultural space between people. On the one hand, responsibility can be understood as a property of how two people interact. Here it is about how the self expresses its commitment or takes responsibility for the other. On the other hand, responsibility can be understood as a cultural property. In this case, responsibility is a cultural tool used to create or interpolate subjects who are responsible in the sense that they are responsive to the needs of others and society, and this tool is fashioned through socio-cultural discourse. We can peel this distinction apart so that it becomes instructive of the different theories of responsibility by separating theories that focus on moral problems from those that focus on ethical theories. Here I do not mean to create a strict separation between morality and ethics; rather, I want to highlight how, in theorising responsibility, the different contributors tend to bracket issues of the good life to focus on issues of the morality of responsibility and vice versa. Using these distinctions, we can generate a taxonomy with a horizontal axis separating interpersonal from cultural understandings of responsibility, and a vertical axis separating ethical from moral discourses. The different theoretical discourses of responsibility can be mapped into this taxonomy according to their dominant concern (Figure 3.2). It is important to emphasise that, in spite of some tantalising conceptual resonances, the taxonomy outlined in Figure 3.2 can not be empirically mapped on to that in Figure 3.1, since the two taxonomies have been constructed to fulfil quite different purposes.

Figure 3.2: Taxonomy of theoretical approaches to responsibility

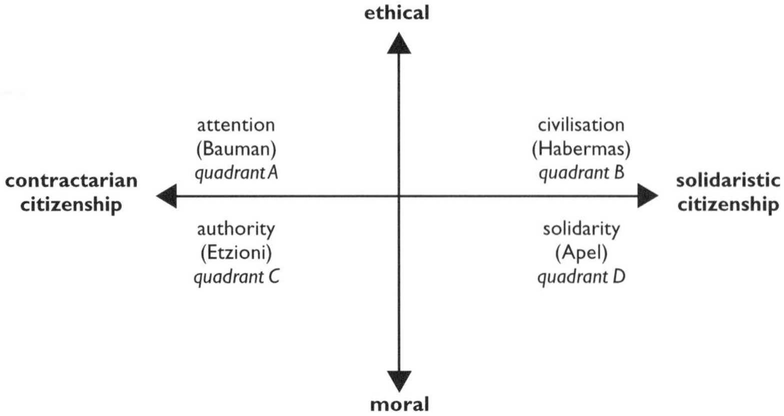

Source: Dean (2002, p 200)

To begin with, Etzioni's (1993) communitarian discourse is placed into quadrant C of Figure 3.2. Etzioni, as is well recognised, wants to reassert the moral space itself through appealing to community values. What he does is respond to contemporary hedonism and individualism by appealing directly to this individualism. The thrust of Etzioni's argument is that, if people are made critically aware of how they benefit from being responsible, they will become more conscious of their community and more willing to take on their responsibilities. Thus, it is necessary to work on the norms and values that promote a community consciousness and a sense of social responsibility. This sets responsibility up as a moral issue because no overarching ethic can be accepted in our individualistic and hedonistic society. Responsibility is also part of each of the interpersonal relationships that together make up society. The fragility of responsibility recurs in each encounter insofar as we expect people to behave responsibly but have no real reason to believe that they will. Etzioni's response is to argue for a heightened awareness of how everybody can benefit from being responsible. This is effectively the pattern of argument followed in New Labour's press releases. The recalcitrant citizen shows no awareness of his/her responsibilities and needs to be thwarted, while the passive citizen needs to take up the government's publicity and become aware of how s/he can benefit from being responsible. However, the trouble with this approach is that it places moral authority at its centre. It is the insight into how being responsible is beneficial to the self and the community that Etzioni believes is being eroded. It needs to be shored up by underpinning its authority under the law and in the framing of social policies. This turns responsibility into a social good that is beneficial to society. It begins to compete with other goods and responsibility loses its moral texture becoming a commonsensical insight.

Bauman (1993) contributes a more ethical construction of responsibility (quadrant A). For Bauman, following Levinas, the question of responsibility is not a question of knowing about the other. It is a question of the fundamental and originally ethical commitment to the other. It is about self-being for the other prior to having any knowledge about the other or expectation that the other might be for the self. The responsible self is for the other first. It gives to the other the power to call on the self to act, which means the self has to be attentive enough to recognise the call when it comes. This construction again uses an interpersonal understanding of responsibility because it is specifically concerned with the way the self shows itself as responsible by moving towards another. This, of course, also sets it out as concerned with ethical issues, because it is primarily involved (although by no means exclusively) in the ethical commitment to the other. This discourse is concerned with the meaning and fragility of taking responsibility, and the problems moral beings encounter in attending to the needs of the other. Unlike Etzioni's communitarian construction that appeals to contemporary individualism, Bauman, followed by Fevre (2000), deploys these concepts within a narrative about demoralisation. However, diagnosing demoralisation is made particularly easy by a range of concepts that emphasise moral responsibility as an ethical being for the other. As this space changes or shrinks, as it undoubtedly has, then it follows that people are less inclined to express solidarity with others. Bauman, like Etzioni, wants to reassert the moral space of the self, but he wants attending real others as a core value.

Habermas (1995, pp 162-70) sees moral responsibility as a reflexive cultural tool (see also Lara, 1998) that generates the individual's sense of self (quadrant B). Habermas describes responsibility within a narrative about socialisation, rather than about demoralisation or individualisation. He focuses on how moral and responsible subjects are generated in our plural multicultural societies rather than how moral spaces are being eroded. Habermas sees responsibility as an iterative task of self-understanding within a moral community. The responsible person has first to choose to understand his/her own history as identical with the kind of person s/he understands as him/herself. This activity is socially embedded so people weave stories about their own lives presenting them as valid constructions about themselves and how they take responsibility within and about their own lives. These stories are important because they contain an implicit 'vouch' that they will be this person in the future. To claim that I am who I am and have become, and to will that I be this person in the future, are entirely moral claims that can only be conveyed through a moral presentation of the self and the conscious continuity of an ethical life. These are directed to others because the individual wants his/her self-identity to be received as authentic and sincere. The public of others have a decisive role to play because they also mould the individual who becomes a responsible subject, "Because others attribute accountability to me, I gradually make myself into the one who I have become in living together with others" (Habermas, 1995, p 170).

Thus, being a responsible person is an activity of choosing, becoming, earnestly presenting and responding to the judgements of others. In taking up these concepts, Habermas comes to a different conclusion about the nature of responsibility today. For him, what has changed is the nature of the socialisation process. The important point is not simply that people are being individualised, but rather how people are individuated through a socialisation process that generates subjects capable of dealing with moral issues by themselves using abstract concepts. This is a theory of responsibility for the multicultural society. It constructs responsibility as both cultural and ethical because it is about how moral frameworks exert power over individuals who want to be accepted as responsible beings, and how they come to stand in the direction of civilisation.

A variant on this approach is provided by Karl Otto Apel (1980, 1996a), who theorises responsibility as a discursively achieved accomplishment (quadrant D). He starts his considerations from inside the 'unavoidable' presuppositions we make in formulating a serious argument. His argument goes like this. Every person who thinks about a problem does so in a real spatial and temporal location. In thinking, the person cannot be understood as an isolated subject, but as one who is considering a real issue that s/he has already adopted some responsibility for. But more, to think seriously is to think with a claim to validity, or to argue, and to think in the sense of arguing is to acknowledge certain ethical norms:

> Acknowledged is, so to say, the ethics of an ideal communication community, which consists of closely interwoven fundamental or formal procedural norms in the sense of *equality of rights* and *equal co-responsibility*, that is, of *solidarity*, of all possible discourse partners – in strong contrast to something like an amoral advocating of self-interest in a strategic discourse of negotiation (also in a contract à la Hobbes). (Apel, 1996a, p 6; emphases in original)

So, for Apel the subject already accepts responsibility for solving the problems that s/he thinks and argues about, and in arguing, accepts certain implicitly ethical moral norms. His point is that, in the light of these ethical norms, consensual agreements are in principle possible; but more, bonds of solidarity, of co-responsibility and equality of rights, are anticipated by thinking and arguing beings. These norms anticipated in the ideal communication community are approximated in discourse where they become something of a reality as participants actually engage with each other. Hence, for Apel, discourse is important as a 'moral strategy' for building a sense of co-responsibility for norms developed and in the light of their possible consequences and side effects. This again is a cultural approach, since responsibility is an achievement and a moral strategy, and it focuses on moral issues since ethical issues are solved as fundamentally recognised in the activity of arguing. This construction holds out the possibility of coming to consensual agreements about social problems through discourses that recognise rights and co-responsibilities. Beyond this, it means nurturing discourse on intractable social problems in the public sphere.

Conclusion

New Labour's 'third way' discourse of responsibility draws mainly on repertoires of civic duty and moral obligation, happily using the repertoire of conditional obedience while making very limited use of a discourse of ethical responsibility. The effect of this combination is to promote accessing publicly available information as private persons looking to make private contracts in civil society. Responsibility comes to be about the bonds of the social contract supported by the weak informal solidarity generated in civil society and economy, rather than bonds of solidarity generated as members of a society or of the public sphere. The problem with this, however, is not simply an issue of membership; more importantly, this approach to responsibility tends to reduce it to the status of one social good among many and empty of moral meaning. This is the price paid for taking up a communitarian vocabulary. In the chapters that follow, one sees the extent to which 'third way' constructions of responsibility are reflected both in popular discourse (Chapter Four) and in the discourse of welfare providers (Chapters Five and Six), but also how they may be challenged by welfare users' understandings of responsibility (Chapters Seven and Nine).

In this chapter, however, I have attempted to show that there are theoretical and normative alternatives that place different substantive moral concerns at their centre. For Bauman, this entails attending to the other; for Habermas, standing in the direction of civilisation; for Apel, the moral solidarity of co-responsibility. In particular, Habermas and Apel emphasise how responsibility could play a role at the core of a vibrant public sphere, thus restoring moral sensibility to questions of responsibility. Alternative ways to conceptualise responsibility will also be discussed in Chapter Ten.

References

Apel, K.O. (1980) *Towards a transformation of philosophy*, London: Routledge and Kegan Paul.

Apel, K.O. (1996a) '"Discourse ethics" before the challenge of "liberation philosophy"', *Philosophy and Social Criticism*, vol 22, no 2, pp 1-25.

Apel, K.O. (1996b) *Selected essays. Vol 2: Ethics and the theory of rationality*, New Jersey: Humanities Press.

Bauman, Z. (1993) *Postmodern ethics*, Oxford: Blackwell.

Blair, T. (1997) 'Introduction', in Labour Party General Election Manifesto, *New Labour: Because Britain deserves better*, London: Labour Party.

Dean, H. (2001) 'Defrauding the community? The abuse of welfare', in M. May, R. Page and E. Brunsdon (eds) *Understanding social problems: Issues in social policy*, Oxford: Blackwell.

Dean, H. (2002) *Welfare rights and social policy*, Harlow: Prentice Hall.

DSS (Department of Social Security) (2000a) 'UK and Ireland agree partnership to tackle transnational benefit fraud', DSS Press Release, 9 October.

DSS (2000b) 'Rooker says pension statements will get more people to save', DSS Press Release, 16 October.

DSS (2000c) 'Want information on stakeholder pensions? Ring a new helpline', DSS Press Release, 3 November.

DSS (2000d) 'Radical pension reform: the Government is doing more to reward saving for retirement', DSS Press Release, 9 November.

DSS (2000e) 'Claim your pension over the 'phone: new tele-claim service for pensioners', DSS Press Release, 27 November.

DSS (2001a) 'Pension awareness ad blitz begins', DSS Press Release, 11 January.

DSS (2001b) 'TV campaign against benefits cheats goes nationwide', DSS Press Release, 14 February.

DSS (2001c) 'Local authorities sign up for housing benefit support: £2.1m funding to train 900 new fraud investigators', DSS Press Release, 15 February.

DSS (2001d) 'Getting on the dog and bone to find out about pensions', DSS Press Release, 22 February.

Driver, S. and Martell, L. (1997) 'New Labour's communitarianisms', *Critical Social Policy*, vol 17, no 1, pp 27-46.

Driver, S. and Martell, L. (1998) *New Labour: Politics after Thatcherism*, Cambridge: Polity Press.

Etzioni, A. (1995) *The spirit of community: Rights, responsibilities and the communitarian agenda*, London: Fontana Press.

Fevre, R.W. (2000) *The demoralization of Western morality: Social theory and the dilemmas of modern living*, London: Continuum.

Habermas, J. (1995) *Postmetaphysical thinking philosophical essays*, Cambridge: Polity Press.

Heron, E. (2001) 'Etzioni's spirit of communitarianism: community values and welfare realities in Blair's Britain', in R. Sykes, C. Bochel and N. Ellison (eds) *Social Policy Review 13: Developments and debates: 2000-2001*, Bristol: The Policy Press/Social Policy Association.

Jacobs, G. (1999) 'Self-reference in press releases', *Journal of Pragmatics*, vol 31, pp 219-42.

Lara, M.P. (1998) *Moral textures Feminist narratives in the public sphere*, Cambridge: Polity Press.

Smart, B. (1999) *Facing modernity: Ambivalence, reflexivity and morality*, London: Sage Publications.

Part Two
Popular and welfare provider discourses

FOUR

Popular discourses of dependency, responsibility and rights

Hartley Dean and Ruth Rogers

This is the first of the three chapters that make up Part Two of this book, which recounts the principal findings from the ESRC-funded study described in the Introduction. It focuses on what might be defined as 'popular' discourses insofar that it is based on in-depth interviews that were conducted with a sample of 49 working-age adults drawn from Dover (seven), London (one), Sheffield (11) and Luton (30). The sample was evenly distributed between men (25) and women (24) and, although it was somewhat skewed towards older participants (30 were aged 40+, compared with only 19 under 40), it included representatives of the full working-age range. The youngest was 19 years of age and the oldest was 65 years of age at the time of the interview. Six members of the sample were from non-white minority ethnic groups (four Asian, one Caribbean and one Middle Eastern). Two thirds of the sample (33) were living with partners and nearly half (22) had dependent children. Eleven respondents regarded themselves as disabled and five reported that another member of their household was disabled. The sample was deliberately selected so as to be evenly distributed between four income bands, the poorest with incomes below £9,000 per annum (12), two intermediate income groups with incomes between £9,000 per annum and £18,000 per annum (12) and £18,001 per annum and £27,000 per annum (13), and the richest with incomes above £27,000 per annum (12). Nine participants were in professional or managerial occupations, 13 were in skilled occupations (manual or non-manual), ten were in part or unskilled occupations and 17 were unemployed or economically inactive.

The interviews sought to explore the participants' understandings of dependency, responsibility and rights and to locate these understandings in relation to their attitudes to the welfare state.

Dependency

When asked what they thought was meant by the word 'dependency', participants responded in a variety of ways. Almost half (23) responded immediately with images of those whom they regarded as dependent and identified stages within the life course – childhood, old age or periods of sickness – when people were necessarily dependent, frail or isolated. Others (17) recognised a difference between, on the one hand, physical or material dependence (on the state, for example) and, on the other, psychological or 'emotional' dependence: a state of helplessness or of familial attachment. In the course of the interviews, however, as the meanings of dependency were probed, participants would often express more considered views, so that most (27) acknowledged that dependency was unavoidable (Box 4.1): for example, since any one of us may experience times of need, including times when we are 'down on our luck', and need help (16); because there are some – such as those with mental health problems – who will always be dependent (six); or because everybody is dependent on someone or something (five).

Box 4.1: Popular images of dependency

- "I'd describe a dependent person as somebody that can't do a lot of things for themselves ... somebody that's in bad health that depends on someone else doing a lot of things for them."
- "An adult that's not able to look after themselves fully on their own and is dependent in whatever form or degree, maybe they just need somebody to come in and cook their meals but they can quite happily live on their own but they might not be able to live on their own at all."
- "I suppose on the broadest level, we are all dependent. We're all dependent on each other."

Others (13), and especially older participants and men, arrived at a clearly expressed view that dependency was not a good thing: it was something that most people should avoid. A distinction was made between the deserving (whose dependency was unavoidable) and the undeserving (whose dependency was not only avoidable, but may even have been encouraged by the nature of state welfare provision):

> When I was a child you had to be self-reliant, your family had to be self-reliant because you got nothing from anybody else.... You know, and so it was all self-reliance and I believe it taught you something. Nowadays they seem to, they ain't got that reliance on themselves, they've lost something. Because the state's virtually featherbedding them. So they're losing something out of their character.

> I've known people that have been on the dole for countless numbers of years, have no intention of getting a job, and to me that is not a good dependency.

The interviews then explored participants' views about their own dependency: did they themselves feel they were now, or had they ever felt they had been, dependent? Did they expect one day to be dependent? Half the sample (24), especially younger participants, participants from higher income bands and men, resisted the idea that they were or had ever been dependent, saying either that they were not or had never been dependent, or insisting that dependency arose only in exceptional circumstances, for example, during sickness. The other half (25) acknowledged that they were or had at some time been dependent on their families, on the community or friends, on the state and/or (more rarely mentioned) their employer:

> Oh yeah, you're dependent on that aren't you? I mean, we pay us dues and demands, but we're dependent. You know, hospitals – all that sort of thing.

> I'm still dependent on me family, and the weekly wage. I'm dependent on that.

Although some (five) concluded that it was impossible to foresee the future, when it came to regarding future dependency, most (27 of the 37 responding) acknowledged that they expected at some stage – whether during old age or ill health – to become dependent, although a few (five), none of whom were on low incomes, responded by claiming that they were financially prepared for the future:

> I hate to admit it, but I think I'm going to be worse as I get older because you have other problems with age.

> I hope not. I've made provisions, so I won't be [dependent].

These answers begged the question, 'Are there different kinds of dependency?' To which, of those who responded (34), most (24) replied that dependence on the resources of the state was quite different in nature from dependence on one's family, friends or employer (Box 4.2).

Box 4.2: Popular understandings of different kinds of dependency

- "Dependency on the state is a more financial thing, being dependent on a family member is more an emotional need, rather than a financial need."
- "I can't really imagine myself being dependent on an employer. I would hate to be dependent on friends.... If my husband were dependent on me it wouldn't worry me, it would worry him an awful lot, but not me. and the state, yes, I think it does have its commitment to people, whatever their dependency problems are. I think they have a big responsibility."
- "If you're dependent on your family, you're still working so you're earning your own income and what have you. If you're dependent on social [security], then you're *more* dependent because you're not doing nothing at all, just claiming benefits."

When asked, 'When is it acceptable to be dependent?', participants fell into two broad groups. The larger group (33) put conditions on the acceptability of dependency: people must clearly need help (18); their dependency must have been reasonably unavoidable (ten); they must themselves have reciprocally contributed in some way, for example, through work or taxes (five). The other group (14) were less inclined to impose conditions: they reflected on the unconditional nature of the dependency we experience as members of our families (six), or acknowledged that we are all dependent on each other (two) or else may occasionally be dependent (three), while others expressed pride in the universal nature of the British welfare state (three).

From a different perspective, participants were asked to define or to characterise an independent person. Although a few participants (seven) replied that there is no such thing, and even fewer (three) equated independence with a state of social or emotional self-sufficiency, most (37) equated independence, at least in part, with material sufficiency, referring either solely to financial independence (20), or identifying practical and physical aspects of independence alongside the emotional and psychological aspects:

> I don't think there really is any such thing as a truly independent person, regardless of what a person does or how much money they bring in, or whether they're paying other people or not they're always going to be dependent on somebody else, or something else, be it, just dependent on that one person who stays up until four o'clock in the morning working at the petrol station.

> Someone who's got a grip on life, they can do what they want basically. Got their life organised, money organised, preferably working … likes to do things on their own. Don't like handouts and can stand on their own two feet.

Imputing a final definition of dependency to our participants from a study of their responses, four broad positions seemed to emerge: the dominant view (for 21 participants, especially older and better-off participants and men) celebrates hard work and asserts that people should depend on themselves if at all possible; but almost as important (and dominant for 17 participants, especially younger participants, participants from lower-income bands and women) is a view that dependency is acceptable and inevitable for some members of society. Minority positions included a view (dominant for five participants) that dependency is a phenomenon associated with emotional, social and familial attachments, and a view (dominant for just three participants) that society is premised upon our interdependence (Box 4.3).

Box 4.3: Popular reflections on dependency

- "If you're young and able to work, I think it's acceptable that you go to work. I don't think it's acceptable that you live on the dole for the whole of your life. You know, in that sense of the welfare state: living on the dole."
- "I think everybody's dependent at any stage of their life.... You might be dependent on the state for the financial help at that time and then elderly – you're dependent on your family or care homes, and then mentally ill people or disability people again will be dependent on care workers."
- "Well, I think family is very important. I mean, I like to take my parents out, and I'd like to think they were always there for me. So probably, yes, I depend on them."
- "I don't think there's anything wrong with being dependent. I think the modern trend of wanting to be independent is actually a false thing and that we're actually made to be dependent. You should have relationships and be dependent on each other."

Popular discourse, therefore, exhibits a complex mixture of representations of dependency. However, it appeared that within the sample there was a general recognition – albeit sometimes highly reluctant – that there is at least *some element* of interdependency that arises in the course of the human life course. The transcripts were rigorously checked for disconfirming cases and of the 49 participants there were only five (three men and two women) who at *no* stage acknowledged the nature of human interdependency. In each case, this denial of dependency arose because the participants associated dependency with weakness, and *dependability* with strength. One very 'macho' 34-year-old man (a railway worker), while proudly acknowledging that he was putting food on the table and paying the bills for his young stepson ("until he's old enough to go on his own"), claimed that he himself would never be dependent because he had made 'provisions', and described himself as somebody:

> who goes out and earns his money and pays his way. Pays my own bills, without getting money off nobody or nothing from anybody. It's all on my own; what I work for.

In contrast, a 52-year-old woman (an 'earth mother' figure who was caring inter alia for a severely disabled neighbour) explained:

> I do a lot for everybody else, yet you can't find that you depend on them. I don't like depending on people. No matter how I feel, I like to think that I can depend on myself.... I've always been the type of person who's been a strong person, for everybody else to come to. So I don't like to think that I've got to depend on anybody.

Paradoxically, therefore, even those who denied their own interdependency demonstrated an acute awareness of the necessity that others should depend on them.

Although, on close examination most participants could and did recognise the realities of interdependency within their own lives, their readiness to do so was clearly tempered by a range of pejorative associations. A close examination of the interview transcripts revealed that all but five of the 49 participants at some stage in the interview called upon some version of what might be called the 'dependency culture thesis'; that is, the belief – or indeed the 'myth' (see Dean and Taylor-Gooby, 1992) – that long-term dependency on state welfare provision undermines independence; that it fuels a cycle of deprivation; and that it is associated with a culture of fraud or abuse of the system. Such associations continue to have a powerful purchase within popular discourse (see Golding and Middleton, 1982) and a corrosive influence on people's perceptions of state-provided welfare. Additionally, all but four participants at some stage in the interview problematised the dependency or irresponsibility of 'others'; that is to say, they criticised or denigrated other people or groups in society: the idle unemployed, feckless lone parents, drug addicts, benefit fraudsters, and so on. These 'others' were identified plainly as being beyond the sphere of the participants' own experiences and/or the intimate relationships within which they negotiated their own dependencies and responsibilities. Although this is hardly an unexpected finding, its significance in this context relates to the constraint such exclusionary prejudices can have upon people's understanding of dependency and interdependency.

It remains the case that, in spite of such constraints, as we have seen, popular discourse does nonetheless accommodate an albeit ambiguous awareness of interdependency.

Responsibility

When we turned, in the interviews, to the concept of responsibility, the broad question that participants were asked to address was, 'To what extent should people be responsible for their own welfare?' Some participants (15) responded to this immediately, usually in the affirmative, either indicating that people should in theory be responsible, but that it was difficult to generalise (eight); or else, agreeing that people should be able to save at least something for the future (four). Three participants indicated from the outset that they supported the principle of free health care and/or that they were opposed to private forms of welfare provision. When we explicitly asked what participants thought was meant by the word responsibility, most answers were focused either on the responsibilities one owes to oneself (or one's family) (23), or to others, as a good citizen (five), or a combination of these (13). Other participants referred to formal responsibilities to obey the law or pay taxes (three), or spoke in formalistic terms about being accountable for one's actions according to some personal code of conduct (five) (Box 4.4).

Box 4.4: Popular images of responsibility

- "I'm a responsible person. I brought a family up, with help [of my wife]. I've tried to help people and do what's right."
- "Well, I suppose to be responsible for maybe less fortunate members of society, and they do exist. You know, the old phrase – 'There but for the grace of God go I'."
- "Responsible is mature and knowing what they're doing and not abusing the law."
- "[Responsibility means] you can't blame anybody else if you've got yourself into a mess. You can't blame anybody else."

In the course of the interviews, however, as the meanings of responsibility were probed, participants would often express more considered views, so that two broad positions began to emerge. The dominant position (subscribed to by 28 participants, especially older participants, participants from lower-income bands and men) was fundamentally individualistic and associated responsibility with the use of initiative, with caring for one's own needs, and with independence. Alternatively, it was seen merely as an individual characteristic. There was another position (subscribed to by 17 participants) that was more holistic or existential, in that it associated responsibility with dependability or reliability (ten) or with 'owning one's own actions' (seven).

Other participants either struggled with contradictory notions of responsibility or saw responsibility and irresponsibility as no more than individual character traits. Depending on the degree of rapport established during the interviews, some participants (24) were asked whether they considered themselves to be responsible. Predictably, all but one declared that, by and large, they were. The participant who said she was not responsible was currently unemployed, and explained, "I can't say that 'Yes, I am responsible for meself', because I depend on social security".

Given the centrality within current political discourse of 'work' to notions of responsibility (narrowly construed as paid employment; see Part One and Chapter Seven of this book), participants were asked whether or not people have a responsibility to work, whether people can be responsible without working, and whether or when people might be allowed not to work. Most participants (41) agreed that people have a responsibility to work, but usually (in 23 instances) they qualified their agreement, emphasising, for example, that the benefits of work should outweigh the costs, and that people should have a choice of employment, implying a significant measure of scepticism towards government policy.

A clear majority of the participants (39) accepted that it was possible for people to be responsible without working, specifically when raising children, were 'genuinely' unemployed or unable to work, if they were responsibly engaged in voluntary work, or if they were financially independent. Very few insisted that people should be allowed not to work.

Asked whether people should take responsibility for such life course contingencies as redundancy or retirement, the opinions of the participants were divided. Some (22) agreed, but others gave only qualified agreement, insisting that this should only apply if people were able to do so financially (17), or else insisting that healthcare should be free (three), while some (four) disagreed, declaring that they preferred social to private insurance mechanisms (Box 4.5).

Box 4.5: Popular reflections on responsibility and welfare

- "I think that everybody realises that the state pension doesn't go very far and that if you are able to afford it, and if you start young enough paying into a private pension plan you should be able to afford it."
- "I mean, if you get really low wages ... you can't really save money and prepare yourself for the future if you just struggling to get to the end of the month. If you get maybe a £100,000 a year, maybe yeah, you can plan for the future. [Laughs] But I don't know any people get that sort of money."
- "I don't think they should be responsible for themselves if they've been sick, you know. I think good health, you know, and medical treatment, are things that are always looked upon as an entitlement."
- "That's the whole thing with the retirement thing: once you've reached that age then you earned your right to be old so they should look after you more."

Turning the issue of responsibility around, we asked participants what they thought was meant by irresponsibility. Initial responses were diverse, but most fell broadly into two categories: those addressing conduct adverse to society, such as criminal behaviour (mentioned by six participants) or forms of financial fecklessness that result in those who have squandered resources becoming a charge upon state funds (13), and those addressing the conduct of stereotypically defined 'others', such as the social fecklessness of those who are poor (who are perceived to be bad parents, wasteful and/or lazy) (14) or those who exhibit certain personality characteristics or lack of 'manners' (three). Participants from higher-income bands and women appeared to be slightly less likely than participants from lower-income bands and men to subscribe to stereotypical imagery. Some participants gave less specific answers (Box 4.6).

Box 4.6: Popular images of irresponsibility

- "An irresponsible person, I would say that type of person is somebody that relies on other people to provide for them when they're capable of providing for themselves, that does, has no regard for the law, thinks they can do what they want and disregard other people. That's the sort of person I would consider irresponsible."
- "A person who lives day-by-day, and spends their money. We know a lot of people like that and I don't think, I don't think that's right. I think you've got to, like, what

we do, we do save and what we've got, we've saved for it, um, so, I don't ... some people, I don't think they've thought about what's, what's going to happen. All they're doing is living by day-by-day and thinking ... and thinking well, we could get knocked over tomorrow. But then they're not thinking about the kids."
- "An irresponsible person, um, one without a job, as lazy as hell."
- "I suppose is somebody who has lack of respect, because obviously respect is something that enables you to, to live, as far as I'm concerned, to live a very useful life, but where you have lack of respect I think it breeds all sorts of emotions and attitudes."

However, as the meanings of irresponsibility were probed in the course of the interviews, some more considered definitions began to emerge. Although participants often became less certain about their understanding of irresponsibility, there were those who gravitated either towards a position that equated irresponsibility with a failure to contribute to society (18) or towards a position that equated irresponsibility with a selfish failure to consider the effects of their behaviour on others (16).

Participants were also asked what solutions there might be to deal with irresponsibility. Initial responses were polarised between punitive approaches – the irresponsible should be made to fend for themselves (four), be supported only for a limited time (seven), be supported for the sake of dependants (six), or only if they had not been wilfully irresponsible (four) – on the one hand, and paternalistic approaches on the other – the irresponsible should be educated (ten), or should enjoy the support of the welfare safety-net regardless of their behaviour (12). As interviews proceeded, some participants, and especially those who discussed the questions at greater length, appeared to modify their views, and in this instance, once again, they tended to become less certain. Small numbers of participants concluded that irresponsible people should have support withdrawn from them (four) or that they are, in any event, beyond help (three), while others concluded that there is no point in penalising irresponsible people, because they penalise themselves. All of the other participants who continued to engage with the question (21) concluded that irresponsible people might need to be supported, but they struggled to decide how far the state could fairly go (Box 4.7).

Box 4.7: Popular solutions to irresponsibility

- "They don't wanna be helping them. I don't know, just leave them.... Yeah, cut the benefits off if they don't wanna work."
- "I'd say to them, right, you've got a time limit of, let's say, six months.... We'll give you money for six months, that you haven't earned, that you don't deserve, but we'll give it you anyway for six month and after that you'll get nothing. You've got to make your own money or you don't get none at all."

- "Can't leave them to fend for themselves, 'cos we'd end up paying for that in the long run, it's a vicious circle. If they're not getting money from the dole, they'll go steal."
- "There should be certain measures that the state could do, to either make that person responsible for their actions or show them how to be responsible."
- "I think the bare minimum should be provided, but I don't think that in a reasonable society that one should let people be starving or whatever just because they can't be bothered to do anything."

As with dependency, so with responsibility: popular discourse exhibits a complex mixture of representations. Nonetheless, it appeared that the general tendency of the sample was to regard responsibility as an individual, rather than a collective, matter. Clearly, some participants did place responsibilities in a socially situated context, but they remained individual responsibilities. A close re-examination of the transcripts revealed that only two of the 49 participants in any way disconfirmed this: both were male and middle-aged. One declared himself to be a committed Christian, but also expressed left-wing views, misquoting the Marxist maxim 'From each according to his means, to each according to his needs', and asserting "We all have obligations towards each other as human beings". The other, who was in the highest income group, demonstrated an extensive knowledge of current and world affairs and an unusually reflexive approach to our questions. He deplored the unequal distribution of wealth in the UK and professed a sense of responsibility for those who are less fortunate, saying, "I dread to think of a society that doesn't look after its old, infirm and sick". It would be unfair to dismiss such radicalism as mere discursive gestures by privileged males, although they do demonstrate the extent to which notions of collective responsibility are somewhat marginalised within popular discourse.

It is consistent in several respects with this tendency to individualistic notions of responsibility that, without any prompting, no fewer than 38 participants called upon the social insurance principle as a way to square individual responsibility with collective provision. Although there were a few respondents who explicitly or implicitly spoke out against the principles of National Insurance, the idea that individual entitlements could be 'earned' by contributions (in cash or even in kind) made in the course of one's lifetime remains enduringly popular (see Dean, 1999). Similarly, and once again without any prompting, there were ten participants (nine of whom were women) who spontaneously identified the need for 'work–life balance' policies (although none used that expression), by which the caring responsibilities that working-age adults have to their dependants may be squared with their responsibility to participate in paid employment. Individualistic conceptions of responsibility in no way precluded awareness of social policy issues.

Rights

The broad question that we asked participants to address in relation to rights was, 'Should people's rights as human beings include the right to such things as state benefits, pensions and social care?' Most participants (41) agreed that they should, albeit that many (29) specified exceptions, suggesting that this should apply only to 'basic' rights to healthcare, education and pensions, or that rights should not be extended to people who had failed to contribute or were wilfully dependent on the state. Other respondents (eight) were initially hostile to the proposition that human rights should include social rights, some of them (four) contending that talk of human rights obscured the nature of our obligations and responsibilities to one another (Box 4.8).

Box 4.8: Popular linkages between welfare and rights

- "In this country I'd have to say yes, because tax, what we, as far as I can see that's what we stand for, that's what the system is all set up for and that's what we like to portray ourselves to the rest of the world, as, you know, we're a modern country, we look after people less fortunate and that."
- "Yes, I think it should. Unless we've proven over the years that they've deliberately refused to be ... [to] make contributions to the state pension et cetera, then yes, I think everybody has that right."
- "The world doesn't owe you a living and I think you have to take that on board ... but whether you have a right to those things, no, I don't believe you do."
- "I never really thought of rights as something granted by parliament. The nature of a right, I would have thought, is something that is intrinsic in human rights; in being human rather than coming from an external regulator."

The participants who had been completely opposed to the idea of social rights as human rights seemed to become less certain as the issues were explored; generally, however, views on this matter seemed to change very little in the course of the interviews. When it came to defining human rights, participants seemed to fall into two broad groups, by and large. The first (27), especially younger participants and women, might be said to subscribe, implicitly or explicitly, to a conception of inalienable rights, referring either to the substantive entitlements that human beings should have to dignity, food, clean water, sanitation and/or fair treatment (18), or else agreeing with the proposition that there are rights we would have simply by virtue of being human (nine). The other main group (19) adopted a more conditional view, believing either that demands for rights should be framed in relation to responsibilities and not taken to 'extremes' (ten) or that informal moral rights should not be conflated with legal rights (three); or else they simply disagreed with the proposition that there are rights we would have simply by virtue of being human (six).

The interviews then sought to link the issue of rights with the issues of dependency and responsibility. First, participants were asked when people might have the 'right' to be dependent. More than two thirds of the participants (31) expressed the view that people could be dependent, subject to the circumstances – such as, whether or not they were unable to provide for themselves and/or whether or not they were at fault. Other participants reflected upon the nature of human interdependency, concluding either that this was not a matter of 'rights' (five), or else that the only form of dependency that can be truly unconditional is dependence on our families (four) (Box 4.9).

Box 4.9: Popular linkages between dependency and rights

- "People with mental health problems, learning disabilities, they do, I suppose have a right to be looked after and cared for and their needs met and people that are ill would have a right to adequate healthcare."
- "I wouldn't say it's a right, but there are times when people will be dependent. The world in which we live, we are all interdependent. There are times and circumstances when someone will be dependent on another. I mean times of disaster and so on. I respond by giving help, because they are dependent on you for help."
- "Say you've got married, now your wife has a *right* to depend on you."

Second, participants were asked whether or not they felt responsible for people who were dependent. While half the respondents (25) recognised this as a personal responsibility – albeit in some instances (nine) a conditional responsibility – others appeared flummoxed by the question, sometimes admitting (in eight instances) that they had never thought about the issues in such terms:

> Yes, I think that's why we pay taxes. It goes to help those who are unfortunate, who are in need of help. We don't begrudge that at all.

> Well no. I don't feel responsible for them. You know, I mean, I don't mind money being used for those things, but I don't feel responsible, personally.

To unpack the question further, we asked participants whether they were 'comfortable' that taxpayers' money was spent on various social groups. The pattern of preferences demonstrated by their responses was wholly consistent with data from successive rounds of the British Social Attitude survey (see Taylor-Gooby, 1991, 1998; Lipsey, 1994; Brook et al, 1996; Hills and Lelkes, 1999). It confirmed that there is a hierarchy in the mind of the public concerning who is more and who is less deserving of public support (Table 4.1)

We asked whether participants themselves would be comfortable to receive such benefits or services, whether they felt that people have a 'right' to such provision, and whether such provision is the responsibility of those who pay for them. The responses demonstrate the extent to which participants did not

Table 4.1: Attitudes to social spending

Would you say you are comfortable that taxpayers' money is spent providing benefits/pensions/care for:	Yes	Yes (with exceptions)	No (with exceptions)	No	Total
Disabled people (social care)	48	1	–	–	49
Elderly people (social care)	48	1	–	–	49
Retired people (pensions)	43	6	–	–	49
Informal carers (benefits)	43	5	–	1	49
Disabled people (benefits)	39	10	–	–	49
Unemployed people (benefits)?	20	22	3	4	49

necessarily associate rights to welfare with their responsibilities as members of the community that provides welfare (Table 4.2). While a substantial majority accepted that we have rights to welfare (albeit subject sometimes to conditions), only a minority accepted that we have responsibilities to contribute to the welfare of others, and, indeed, a majority could not even engage with the question. While this finding is consistent with the idea that public opinion exhibits a mixture of pragmatic instrumentalism and guarded altruism (see Dean, 1999), it provides further confirmation that public perceptions of collective, as opposed to individual, responsibility, are substantially constrained. One young man, who encapsulated the diffidence expressed by some participants, said:

> You're paying taxes and that to support the *idea*. It's not so much supporting the people. It's just in case you happen to be in that situation. You've paid your money, you expect that treatment.... Yeah, like [insurance]. But it's not that you're paying your taxes to support other people.

Table 4.2: Attitudes to welfare entitlement

	Yes	Yes (with exceptions)	No (with exceptions)	No	No reply/ don't know	Total
Would you be comfortable to receive such benefits/services?	26	15	2	2	4	49
Do people have a 'right' to welfare provision?	23	21	1	2	2	49
Is welfare provision the *responsibility* of those who pay for it?	11	5	3	3	27	49

Finally, during this part of the interviews, participants were asked, 'Which is the bigger responsibility – working or caring?' We had anticipated that most participants would 'play safe' and say they were equally important, but the responses were more interesting. A majority (27), especially older participants, participants from higher-income bands and women, were prepared to say that caring was the more important and only a few (eight) chose working, with about a quarter of the sample (12) contending that working and caring are equivalent (Box 4.10). Popular discourse may be more accommodating towards an ethic of care – which does not necessarily recognise the language of rights (see Chapters One and Two of this book) – than is political discourse.

Box 4.10: Popular perceptions of working versus caring

- "Caring I'd say. I've cared for my Mum and that's the biggest responsibility. Yes."
- "I would say working, because, I mean, if they didn't work, we wouldn't have no taxpayers, so the carers wouldn't be able to care because they wouldn't get the money from the taxpayers."
- "I don't think you can distinguish between the two. Caring is important and it's also a job, so you're working."

Popular discourse on the subject of rights would appear to be especially complex and ambiguous. The general view of the sample appeared to be that, although there may well be certain inalienable human rights (and there is little consensus as to how these might be defined), it is not possible to include universal social or welfare rights among these: provision for welfare, if it is a right at all, can never be a wholly unconditional right. A careful re-examination of the transcripts revealed that only five out of 49 participants disconfirmed this. Of these, one was the middle-aged Christian man (mentioned earlier in this chapter) whose ideas of collective social responsibility extended to the view that rights flow unconditionally from needs. Another was a 34-year-old woman who, by chance, was a social worker and, like others in the social workers' sample (see Chapter Five of this book), said, "I don't believe we have a right to anything really". For her, "We have expectations of how we should be treated and hopefully they are met". Between these two extremes were three respondents: one a partly disabled man, and two women, one of whom was a lone parent on benefits and the other had recently experienced a dramatic reduction in financial fortunes after her husband had been made redundant. Their view of rights appeared to flow from the fact that – unlike the participants who had equated dependency with weakness (see earlier in this chapter) – they were themselves reasonably comfortable with and/or expressly tolerant of others' dependency:

> I don't think you should be ashamed of accepting that fact [for example, if you are physically or mentally impaired] and accepting the help that comes.

> Yes we must be responsible for dependent people. [In reference to asylum
> seekers/refugees] I'm probably a lone voice in this area [Dover], because I
> happen to feel very, very sorry for them and, I mean, people like that come
> into this country and they are, I suppose, they're dependent on us for
> everything because they've left everything that they ever had behind.

This participant was indeed a 'lone voice' within the sample. It was striking
that no fewer than 19 other participants also spontaneously brought up the
subject of immigration and asylum, not as this participant had, but in order to
justify *limits* to the applicability of a rights-based approach. In some instances,
this stemmed from explicit racism or xenophobia. In others, it was clear that
the high profile of immigration and asylum as a political issue seems to have
framed the way that people think about human rights issues. There is a chain
of association between human rights and the allegedly unsustainable challenges
posed by 'illegal' immigrants and 'bogus' asylum seekers.

Given the ambivalence exhibited within the sample as a whole towards social
rights as human rights, a re-examination of the transcripts was undertaken to
see to what extent the rights of extremely dependent people might be discounted
within popular discourse. In the event, only two participants, having defined
dependency in terms of helplessness, went on to suggest that dependent people
lack the autonomy necessary in order properly to enjoy or exercise rights.
There were in fact no fewer than 14 participants who explicitly contradicted
such a view and asserted that, for example, severely disabled people should
have rights.

As we have seen, however, a general acceptance of human interdependency
is not by and large translated into an acceptance of unconditional social rights.
The reason for this, arguably, is the individualistic nature of popular conceptions
of responsibility.

The welfare state

The final part of the interviews explored participants' attitudes to state welfare.
First, participants were shown a flashcard which displayed four statements that
have been used in standard questions asked by the annual British Social Attitudes
survey. Whereas respondents to the BSA survey are asked to say whether they
agree or disagree with each statement, our participants, on the other hand,
were asked with which they *most* agreed, and why. As would be expected from
the general pattern of recent BSA findings (see Taylor-Gooby, 1991, 1998;
Lipsey, 1994; Brook et al, 1996; Hills and Lelkes, 1999), a clear majority was in
favour of additional welfare spending (Table 4.3).

Those who were unprepared to pay more towards welfare provision
characteristically said either that they paid enough tax and could not afford to
pay any more (five), or that the present system is satisfactory and does not need
any more money (three). Over a quarter of the sample (14) indicated that,
although they might be prepared to pay more, they would want to be assured

Table 4.3: Attitudes to taxes

Statement	Preferred by participants in our study	Agreed with by respondents in 1998 BSA survey[a]
We should pay *less* in taxes and spend *less* on services like health, education, social benefits and services	3 (6%)	3%
We should keep taxes and spending on these services at the same level as now	11 (22%)	32%
We should pay *more* in taxes and spend *more* on services like health, education, social benefits and services	32 (65%)	63%
Don't know	3 (6%)	2%
Total	49 (99%)	100% n=3,146

Note: [a] See Hills and Lelkes (1999)

(depending on their particular priorities or prejudices) that money was spent on the right things and was not 'wasted'. Those who were unequivocally in favour of paying for improved services believed that current systems are underfunded (nine), while over a quarter of the sample (14) argued that Britain is a wealthy country and needs high-quality services (Box 4.11).

Box 4.11: Popular beliefs about taxes versus benefits

- "I wouldn't like them to pay more because ... I wouldn't like to be taxed any more than I already am. A lot of people get taxed too much anyway, don't they?"
- "I think it works quite well at the moment, well they're working for me anyway."
- "We should pay more in taxes, I think, if we could guarantee it goes, rather than on defence spending or, you know.... Some things being more important, yeah. I don't think it's important, necessarily, to buy sort of weapons or even, call me an old cynic but, you know, like sort of, you know, the nudist Rastafarian lesbian league or something, you know ... but proper, what I call proper services like health, education, and social services, you know, then yes. I think more money should be spent on those."
- "Because I think that it's totally underfunded. I mean there's a lot of people that need these services, they just cannot get them because there isn't enough funding going into them."
- "Well, they never seem to have enough money to pay for all these different things and I think if you paid a little bit more in tax you wouldn't notice it."

This ostensibly strong support for the welfare state was not necessarily reflected in optimism about its future. Asked what they thought was likely to become of the welfare state, only 11 participants considered the welfare state to be satisfactory as it is and/or that it is likely to remain unchanged. A majority of participants (37) anticipated that it was going to change. Of these, most believed that it would have to change in view of the demands being placed upon it (22), or else recognised that it would become more privatised and/or less universal in nature (five). The inevitability of impending change was attributed to external forces or trends, rather than the government. In contrast, a fifth of the sample (ten) expressed their unhappiness with current services and fears for the future of the welfare state, often specifically blaming the government (Box 4.12).

Box 4.12: Popular reflections on the future of welfare

- "I think, Labour government is trying to turn it around and if things carry on as they are, I think it'll be alright, you know, I think things will probably carry on for the better really."
- "I think people are going to have to take more responsibility for themselves because you have an antique population and old people ... are living a lot longer and the state in the end just doesn't have enough money to support people. I mean people's expectations are high, probably a lot higher than they used to be and in order to cover those, you need more money and there's just, they're at a limit to the amount the state can do."
- "Maybe education might start leaning more towards privatisation and stuff like that, private schools and definitely start to move away from the state schools."
- "I think we're in a mess at moment. I *hope* things can get better, but I'm not sure they *will*. But I just hope, the idiots running, running the welfare state – I think we've got a chance of ... but at the moment, no chance at all."

When asked how they would feel if the welfare state were to be cut back or disappear, over two thirds of the sample (34) expressed negative feelings, some (31) contending that society somehow has a responsibility to care for its members (a sentiment often contradicted by other statements that participants might have made), others (five) that they would feel cheated by the government. A few participants (three) did not accept that the welfare state would ever disappear, but a fifth of the sample (ten) seemed untroubled at the prospect. Of these, a half (five) believed that, for some people, welfare provision should be cut back, claiming that some individuals are too dependent on the welfare state. Another half (five) were very 'matter of fact' about the prospect, believing they would not be directly affected as they would be more than capable of supporting themselves. Of the latter group, some even welcomed the idea, provided that they had their National Insurance contributions either reduced or removed altogether (Box 4.13).

Box 4.13: Popular reflections on the end of the welfare state

- "I think that would be a real step back into the dark ages, if you like. I think the country really would fall to bits then, you're going to have lots of groups of people,

---

the homeless, not being able to support themselves, hungry. Yeah, I can see that being just terrible really."

- "Well, for myself, I would be astronomically hurt, I would feel aggrieved because I have paid a lot of money out for a long time. You know my money has been taken and it's also like, this sounds awful, but you work hard, your salary is taxed, National Insurance et cetera, and if you get a pension they tax that again. So you sort of think 'I'm paying out twice so I'm entitled to some return on that'."

- "I don't think so, not in these circumstances what we're hearing in the news. People need employment and with the latest issues, I don't think that they will try to cut back but to improve it and put more into it."

- "I think things like single parent mothers, they say 'Oh, nobody chooses to be a single parent'.... Yes, they do. You know, you can choose to use contraceptives. [Laughs] I dunno, personal viewpoint I suppose. But I think that area of it perhaps should be cut back more."

- "If they cut the welfare state completely then they'd have to cut taxes, therefore I'd be able to make provision for myself ... I'm paying a hell of a lot of tax, which would go a long way to paying for myself."

As ever, popular discourse is complex and diverse. Nonetheless, the general view of the majority within the sample might be taken as being broadly consistent with what Hills and Lelkes (1999) characterise as the New Labour government's 'selective universalism' and 'patchwork redistribution'. That is to say, participants wanted improved public services, but they tended to be particular about who should benefit from additional spending: there is, as we have seen, an abiding hostility – that is itself fuelled by political and media rhetoric – towards welfare provision for certain groups. Nonetheless, our interviews also revealed a pessimism and concern about the future that does not *necessarily* signal an endorsement of New Labour's 'third way' policies (see Taylor-Gooby, 1994). Clues to understanding popular interpretations of the politics of welfare lie, we suggest, in the patterns of discourse relating to dependency and responsibility and the implication these have for popular conceptions of rights.

Conclusion

Were we to characterise crudely the prevailing 'third way' political orthodoxy that has already been outlined in Part One of this book, it might be supposed that it is inimical to a human rights approach to welfare because it entails:

- a one-sided approach to dependency;
- an individualistic interpretation of responsibility;
- a strictly conditional approach to rights.

We have seen that popular discourse does not constitute dependency entirely in accordance with 'third way' doctrine. There was a majority in our sample that favoured a view that dependency is unavoidable rather than avoidable. Admittedly, certain kinds of dependency and certain causes of dependency could be regarded quite markedly as more acceptable than others, and there were those who endorsed the 'third way's' celebration of independence through 'work' (that is, labour market activity). Nonetheless, there was wide acknowledgement that there can be times in the ordinary life course when dependency cannot necessarily be avoided. Instances in which there was no acknowledgement of human interdependency as a constitutive feature of the human life course were exceptional and, in their own way, paradoxical: participants would deny their own dependency in order to assert their dependability for others.

We have also observed that popular discourse tends to constitute responsibility as a personal or individual (rather than a social or collective) matter, and this is very much in keeping with 'third way' doctrine. The majority in our sample interpreted responsibility in an explicitly individualistic manner. There was a minority who looked upon their individual responsibilities in more holistic or existential ways and acknowledged, therefore, that responsibility must be socially situated. However, notions of shared responsibility or of responsibilities that are *constituted* through the individual's social context were really quite rare.

Finally, we have observed that popular discourse on the subject of rights remains ambivalent. There was a majority that favoured a view that there are at least certain rights that are (or should be) inalienable rather than conditional in nature, a view that is not necessarily in step with the implication of 'third way' orthodoxy that citizens' responsibilities precede their rights. Nonetheless, although there was a prevalent sense that there are at least certain basic rights that should apply unconditionally, certain kinds of rights – which tended explicitly to include social or welfare rights – were regarded as less universally applicable than others. Instances in which this did not apply were exceptional and confined largely to participants who were unusually tolerant of others' dependency.

This may, to an extent, cast some light on the ambiguity of people's attitudes to welfare reform. A majority of our sample believed the welfare state would or indeed had to change, but most were prepared to pay to defend it, and some were plainly apprehensive about the future of welfare provision. Participants appeared mistrustful, if not of New Labour itself, then of government in general. The evidence outlined suggests that popular discourse can accommodate an understanding of both dependency and rights that is wider than that promoted from within the 'third way', but is fettered in particular by an individualistic interpretation of responsibility. Whether or not this is an interpretation born out of some secular process of 'individualisation', as Beck and Beck-Gernsheim (2001) might argue, it is an interpretation that tends to construct individual agency in a manner that problematises human interdependency and marginalises rights-based claims to welfare (see Chapter Seven of this book). Certainly, it is an interpretation that nourishes fears about the sustainability of the welfare state.

Arguably, therefore, the most significant moral or ideological obstacle to a human rights approach to welfare is the purchase within popular discourse of 'third way' individualism, and what might be portrayed as an ethically deficient interpretation of responsibility (see Chapter Three of this book). This tends to confirm that any debate about our understanding of welfare rights as human rights must start with a debate about the nature of our collective responsibilities as interdependent beings. It is an issue to which this book returns in Chapter Ten.

References

Beck, U. and Beck-Gernsheim, E. (2001) *Individualization*, London: Sage Publications.

Brook, L., Hall, J. and Preston, I. (1996) 'Public spending and taxation', in R. Jowell et al (eds) *British social attitudes: The 13th report*, Aldershot: Dartmouth.

Dean, H. and Taylor-Gooby, P. (1992) *Dependency culture: The explosion of a myth*, Hemel Hempstead: Harvester Wheatsheaf.

Dean, H. with Melrose, M. (1999) *Poverty, riches and social citizenship*, Basingstoke: Macmillan.

Golding, P. and Middleton, S. (1988) *Images of welfare: Press and public attitudes to poverty*, Oxford: Martin Robertson.

Hills, J. and Lelkes, O. (1999) 'Social security, selective universalism and patchwork redistribution', in R. Jowell et al (eds) *British social attitudes: The 16th report – Who shares New Labour values?*, Aldershot: Ashgate.

Lipsey, D. (1994) 'Do we really want more public spending?', in R. Jowell et al (eds) *British social attitudes: The 11th report*, Aldershot: Dartmouth.

Taylor-Gooby, P. (1988) 'Citizenship and welfare', in R. Jowell et al (eds) *British social attitudes: The 1987 report*, Aldershot: Gower.

Taylor-Gooby, P. (1991) 'Social welfare: The unkindest cuts', in R. Jowell et al (eds) *British social attitudes: The 1990 report*, Aldershot: Gower.

Taylor-Gooby, P. (1994) 'Welfare outside the state?', in R. Jowell et al (eds) *British social attitudes: The 11th report*, Aldershot: Dartmouth.

FIVE

Fostering a human rights discourse in the provision of social care for adults

Kathryn Ellis and Ruth Rogers

In this chapter, we examine the findings of interviews conducted with 14 social workers/social care staff working in three local authorities in the South East of England. In terms of the composition of the sample, three were men and 11 were women. All were white. Three were aged under 40 and the others 40+. Five were graduates and the others were all qualified to Diploma level (one had a nursing qualification, the other 13 a social work qualification). Between them, they had a range of experience with a variety of user groups, but their present roles were mainly focused on services for older people and people with mental health problems. Given their numerical superiority (13/14), participants are hereafter referred to as 'the social workers'.

The chapter is divided into two main sections. The first presents the findings as they relate to the three core themes of dependency, responsibility and rights explored during interviews. The second offers an analysis of those findings that takes account of the policy and practice contexts within which social workers currently operate. In particular, we evaluate the promised cultural transformation of public authorities in the wake of the implementation of the 1998 Human Rights Act (HRA) and its potential impact on social care practice with vulnerable adults. As in Chapter Six of this book, we acknowledge that a considerable degree of caution must be observed in relation to the suggested interpretations that are offered in the following discussion, given the small sample size.

The interview findings

Dependency

The social workers were proportionately more likely than the core sample to see dependency in terms of practical factors (10/14, compared to 17/49). Eligibility criteria governing social care for adults are generally based on levels of dependency and the attendant risk of physical harm were services not provided. It is unsurprising, therefore, that in their initial definitions a majority associated dependency with physical or cognitive incapacity and a consequential inability to function without assistance:

Dependent is basically that they can't function in their body in day-to-day living.

... people who need services from us ... they would be dependent on us in some way because they can't construct their lives, either in a physical way, or an emotional way or a psychological way.

Perhaps because of their proximity to human vulnerability, the social workers differed from the core sample in their unanimous view that dependency was unavoidable. In response to our question about the nature of independence, too, all of the participants were of the view either that no one could be entirely independent and/or that interdependency was the nature of human existence:

I think we're all dependent on others at times, I mean, if you're ill, you're dependent on other people for things you can't do yourself, erm, I suppose we're all dependent on certain sort of systems and things that are around, that you don't always realise.

Well there's a kind of interdependency, you can't do everything on a human level so, yes, we're all interdependent on each other.

This group of participants was also proportionately more likely than members of the core sample (12/14, compared to 25/49) to acknowledge their own past and present dependency, or to anticipate their future dependency. Yet that dependency was viewed in qualitatively different terms to dependency on welfare benefits and services. The majority (12/14) described their own dependency in terms of an emotional reliance on support from family and personal networks and/or dependency on employers. While dependency was an inevitable consequence of using services – "by the very nature that they're our clients, they are dependent", in the words of one – social workers' own autonomy was not threatened by dependency because their relationships were viewed as reciprocal (Box 5.1).

Box 5.1: Social workers' reflections on professional interdependency

- "They're [employer] just as dependent on me as I am on them – it's a bit of give and take."
- "I think there's a value that you can be dependent on an employer, which is seen as returning something, seen as earning that, whereas if you are dependent on the welfare state, it's seen as one directional with regards to the person who's receiving."
- "You can *choose* to be dependent on a friend or a colleague, I can *choose* whether I want to ask for help. I can get by if I don't get it but if you're dependent on the state for benefits, you are completely dependent, and I think it's one of the worst things you can be."

Social workers may have regarded dependency as an inevitable aspect of human existence, but they had differing expectations of welfare dependency. In their definitions of independence, the social workers were proportionately less likely than members of the core sample to mention issues relating to material sufficiency (4/14, compared with 38/49). Independence was more likely to be associated with free will. To the extent that half of the participants believed that those reliant on welfare benefits and services could achieve greater self-sufficiency by demonstrating mental resolve, dependency was at least partially under voluntary control:

> It's almost a state of mind actually, because you can have people that, for example, are financially dependent on the state and yet you still define them as independent because they've still got sort of dynamism and urge about them, even though they may be, you know, completely physically and financially dependent, they still may be independently minded.

Unsurprisingly, then, social workers were nearly as likely as the core sample to attach conditions to when it might be acceptable to be dependent on state welfare (7/11 responding to the question, compared with 33/47). Legitimate dependency arose out of age, illness or impairment, or other factors for which the individual could not be held to account, such as caring for a relative. Over a third of participants (5/14) echoed the current policy emphasis on investing in human capital through health and education as a means of preventing future dependency and encouraging self-reliance:

> I think a clear dependency is when you are, when, there is a physical or a mental health issue that, prevents you, for example, prevents you from working maybe, and also prevents you from functioning and being able to make, choices and decisions.

> I think there should always be opportunities, I think there should always be education, there should always be healthcare, and those are the things that mediate against poverty ... there should always be opportunities to 'get out'.

Close examination of the interview transcripts shed further light on the tendency of some of the social workers to distance themselves from people dependent on state provision. Half of the participants (7/14) were shown to believe in the existence of a 'dependency culture' (see Chapter Four of this book). Not only did the very existence of welfare benefits and services serve to undermine autonomous thought and action, but dependent others, including disabled people, were prone to abuse resources when they ought to have been working (Box 5.2).

> ## Box 5.2: Social workers' perceptions of 'dependency culture'
>
> - "Another line in where I see dependency in my line of work is people who through illness have become dependent and then remain that way. Even though they could start to move away and become more independent, they come to see social services or whatever as being providers, erm, that can become quite entrenched in some ways."
> - "I don't want my tax to go to somebody in their twenties to sit on their arse and watch Richard and Judy in the middle of the day when they could go out and do something for X amount a month."
> - "There are people who don't want to work and there are people who say they're disabled who literally just fall on the line when really they could get a job."

Yet the views of half the participants were more solidaristic. Detailed analysis revealed a consistent reluctance on their part to problematise others' dependency, while two explicitly objected to the pejorative nature of the term:

> I suppose in the wider sense of the term they are different yeah, but if you break it down there's not really that much difference is there? It's just the way people view it, because people don't see claiming benefits as being a good thing and the whole Blair thing about ... we'll look after the very few dependent people that there are, just the bottom layer, and that, that in itself makes it seem derogatory.

> ... dependency is on many levels, isn't it? And that's why I don't like that word really, it has negative connotations, whereas we all have needs, and I think needs is probably a better word, we all have emotional needs, physical needs, and I think needs is a better word than dependency. It's a negative word, immediately, you label somebody.

This group was either sympathetic to the difficulties faced by people dependent on state benefits and services or mindful that there may be factors leading to dependency which were beyond the individual's control.

Responsibility

Although social workers' definitions of responsibility were generally less individualistic than those of the core sample, the majority of participants held simultaneously to individualistic and other regarding definitions. Thus, responsibility was variously defined as an individual character trait (two); as taking responsibility for one's self or one's own family (six); and as accountability for one's own actions (four) (Box 5.3).

Box 5.3: Social workers' definitions of responsibility

- "A responsible adult would I suppose be seen as someone who is reliable and dependable and if they have said that they'll do something will do it and won't let people down."
- "I think being responsible is perhaps being aware of what your own needs are and then being able to find the best way of meeting them."
- "You have to own our own actions. Sometimes we don't always know *why* we do things but at the end of the day we have done it and it's no good saying, 'Well so and so down the road said to do it and it was a good idea – we had no money and we needed it'."

And yet, only two of the participants saw responsibility solely in individualistic terms. The majority (12/14) also defined responsibility variously as not causing harm to other people (five) and taking responsibility for others' practical or emotional needs (seven); while some definitions (five) had a wider purview, referring to responsibilities owed as citizens or as otherwise socially responsible actors. Two of the latter participants commented that the individualistic nature of contemporary culture served to discourage a sense of responsibility for others (Box 5.4).

Box 5.4: Social workers' accounts of socially situated responsibilities

- "I think it's about the consequences for other people, isn't it, that your actions will have. If you like, the least unhelpful consequence for everybody else ... because whatever you do, the chances are that somebody somewhere isn't going to like it very much, but if you can steer a course whereby most people are OK with it, then perhaps that's responsible."
- "Erm, I mean classically I think it's a person who is able to conduct themselves in a way that takes due regard to other people's practical and emotional aspects. Just a basic, just a fundamental thing, I would guess that responsibility towards one another and responsible to anything around the environment or...."
- "I actually think a lot of the younger generation, this is just my own view, but I actually think people tend to think only of themselves and not to be responsible for others or society so much, you know."

Five participants, three of whom proffered socially situated definitions of responsibility, pointed out that people could only act responsibly if they had the capacity to do so:

> I think a responsible person is somebody who, we are talking about someone with mental capacity, someone who would, say, understand you know, what

they're doing and can have some insight. Because I don't see that you can take responsibility if you haven't got mental capacity.

We have to be responsible for ourselves as far as we can, but that it is not always easy for people who can't do a day-to-day living and look after themselves.

While just over half of this group of participants (8/14) equated responsibility with paid work, the social workers were as likely as the core sample to qualify or challenge the idea promoted by the present government that paid work is a universal responsibility of citizenship. Unsurprisingly, ill health or impairment were most frequently cited (11/14) as legitimate reasons for drawing benefits rather than being in open employment. Half of the participants also pointed to demand-side factors, such as low pay, the poor quality and insecurity of some employment, as well as its uneven geographical distribution, as reasons for not branding a wider population of unemployed people as irresponsible (Box 5.5).

Box 5.5: Social workers' reflections on responsibility and labour market participation

- "There's jobs out there and people should go and do them. I do think you should have personal responsibility."
- "Yeah, I mean, there are some people who, I guess for various reasons, are not actually able to be, erm, [be] employed. [Pause]. Sort of health reasons, all sorts, or other problems that prevent them having access to, erm, employment."
- "I'm sure that there are a number of areas where people can't work either because of commitments or because there is not work available in some areas. That doesn't make them *irresponsible*."

The social workers were also just as likely as the core sample to point out that people could be responsible without working – by caring for others (seven) or by serving the community in some way (five):

… there's people that do voluntary work, community work and things like that so there's, there's lots of ways you can be [responsible]. I don't think work is the be all and end all.

The social workers were proportionately much more likely than members of the core sample (10/14, compared to 17/49) to agree with the proposition that people should take responsibility for protecting themselves against the risk of redundancy or providing for their own retirement. Their responses were evenly divided between those that suggested a commitment to the principle of taking personal responsibility wherever possible and those that indicated a pragmatic adjustment to the current direction of welfare systems:

> I think that as human beings we should be responsible for ourselves. I don't personally believe that we should expect that we reach old age and that there's going to be a nice state provided pension there.

> I think you have to be realistic as to what the future's gonna hold and how much money's going to be around, you know, like this, like with pensions coming up, you know and 'Oh, there isn't gonna be one' and, you know, state pension and all the rest of it, erm, well, maybe we have to move on from post-war initiatives, it's like, you know, we're not that anymore.

A majority (10/14) of participants, however, significantly qualified their support for the notion that people should protect themselves and their families against life-course contingencies. Whether by reason of ill health or impairment, or by virtue of occupying a marginal position in the labour market, vulnerable people could not be expected to provide for their own future. Three of these participants also felt strongly that the current generation of older people had acted responsibly by contributing towards their own retirement, only for governments to renege on their side of the bargain by allowing the value of pensions to be significantly eroded:

> … you'd have to be living a certain life to be doing that. So you'd be in full-time employment for instance or, you know, quite structured and quite planned with what you're doing in life and I think some people haven't got that so, you know, getting critical life, sickness insurance, life insurance and, pensions and private schemes and all that is *not* going to be high on their agenda.

> I work with older people and the pension is a pittance, how people live on it I don't know … they feel that they've paid in, so why isn't it happening. and I feel that happens with a lot of things, is that people feel that they've already paid into a scheme and the government then decide to say, they're not going to run a national scheme anymore, everybody must set up their own.

While apparently less individualistic than the core sample about the nature of people's responsibilities, the overall pattern of social workers' replies when defining irresponsibility and suggesting solutions for dealing with irresponsible or antisocial behaviour was quite similar to that of the core sample. The majority (12/14) saw irresponsibility in terms of a failure to provide for their own or their family's welfare when it was within their powers to do so and/or as a lack of regard for the harmful impact of their actions on others at interpersonal and social levels, including welfare abuse (Box 5.6).

Box 5.6: Social workers' images of irresponsibility

- "Someone who prefers to spend all their money and not save, considering that they are fairly well off, and consider that it's the state's problem basically. I think that that is irresponsibility at its extreme."
- "Well, people may act and don't think about the effect of the impact of their behaviour on whatever level, on other people or society as a whole."
- "Somebody that takes their benefits and smokes and drinks when their children are going without, that sort of thing."

Three participants felt that 'irresponsible' people should be forced to engage in productive activity rather than depend on benefits or else be left to their own devices, provided they were not harming other people. The majority (11/14), however, were reluctant to propose punitive action against vulnerable people who had not provided for themselves or who otherwise acted 'irresponsibly':

> Eh, I'm not too hot on a nanny state I have to say. I think this government gets over involved whereas the last one didn't get involved enough, I think there's got to be a midway.... I think if it affects their children then you have to get involved. Erm ... or if they're a nuisance to other people you have to get involved, but otherwise, I'd be inclined to let them get on with it.

> I think society has to, I mean you *can't*, what's the alternative? You know, you're back to Victorian days with kids and people living in circumstances that are *totally* unacceptable.

Rights

Two social workers considered rights to be a mere social or legal construction. The majority (12/14), however, subscribed to the proposition that people had rights simply by virtue of being human. Over half of this latter group linked their views about the origins of rights to notions of a fundamental human interdependency (Box 5.7).

Box 5.7: Social workers' reflections on 'rights'

- "Erm, I think human rights legislation is man-made, or, I mean, 'person made'."
- "Things change all the time, boundaries change and as technology and society develops, I think that changes as well ... it can't be ... set in, enshrined in stone. Basics, basic human rights can be, because they'll always be basic."
- "I think that we all have a responsibility to each other, before the Human Rights Act was even brought out. To have certain care towards each other and certain responsibility towards each other."

The social workers' initial responses to the question of whether people's rights as human beings should include social rights were rather more cautious towards a rights-based approach than those elicited from the core sample. Compared with a substantial majority of the core sample, just over half the social workers agreed (or agreed with qualifications) with the proposition (8/14, compared with 41/49). Ultimately, two remained opposed to the idea of 'rights' to welfare, while four remained ambivalent or undecided (Box 5.8).

Box 5.8: Social workers' linkages between welfare and rights

- "I think people ... have their rights to benefit, have their rights to pension, to decent housing, decent education, et cetera, I see that as a right."
- "I don't think there's any God given human right to do anything. People say, 'Oh, I've got a right to live how I want and raise my children how I want and breed'. I actually think that's a crying shame because you don't have a right to, you just can, and you don't necessarily do it very well at all."
- "They do have basic rights, but then so do animals.... What concerns me is how far that is taken, because it's almost a sense that people have rights and that's taken to such a degree that it impacts on other people."

Accordingly, the social workers were proportionately more likely than members of the core sample (although less likely than the benefits administrators) to ascribe to a conditional definition of rights (7/14, compared with 19/49 and 6/9, respectively). Close examination of the transcripts confirms that acceptance of the inalienability of human rights by a majority of participants (11/14) did not translate into support for universal social rights on their part.

The qualifications expressed by social workers derived from a belief that rights depended on the fulfilment of responsibilities. Detailed analysis suggests that generalised statements about the existence of responsibilities beyond self and others do not necessarily translate into some notion of collective responsibility for others' welfare. Only four out of the 14 participants expressed views about the collective nature of responsibility which were not elsewhere contradicted or challenged by the view that responsibility should be seen primarily in such terms as dependability, being accountable for one's actions or taking responsibility for one's own life. There was also a marked resistance among social workers to the notion of *legally* enforceable rights in contradistinction to the 'natural' rights generated by kinship and human interdependency. Even those participants who most strongly supported the proposition that human rights should include social rights were uncertain about the term 'right' and/or located the roots of their support within the informal domain (Box 5.9).

Box 5.9: Social workers' scepticism about rights

- "I think that every human being should ... have what we would call the basic needs adhered to. But I think that at the end of the day we can't always rely on other people to do those things for us. We can't sit back and wait. We have to get out and do something for ourselves."
- "If it's someone in their family whom they have looked after ... they have the right to be looked after in turn [if] they're just generally expecting other people, strangers who they don't know to support them, I don't know."
- "I think rights, the rights of the individual should be extended as far as, as far as possible to protect the individual, they should, you know, they should be allowed, I think as citizens, that should be, er, extended as far as possible. It doesn't follow that it has to be statute."
- "I think it becomes more legal ... the more sophisticated we become the more unsophisticated we become ... in bringing sophistication and culture and philosophy it becomes more unsophisticated I would say, because we're having those basic human rights imposed on us. Whereas ... those basic things to me as a human being are enshrined in my kind of human sense."

In response to our questions as to whether they were comfortable that taxpayers' money is spent on providing benefits and services for various groups, the social workers – unlike the core sample or the benefits administrators – were unanimous in their support, including, for example, the principle of benefits for unemployed people. Yet again, however, the social workers were more likely than the other groups of participants to specify qualifications or exceptions to the general principle. Just over half (8/14) raised concerns about welfare abuse or the potential for welfare dependency to undermine personal responsibility:

> ... people should demonstrate that they've been trying and if all else fails I think it is reasonable to do some sort of community service for the [unemployment] benefit if they are able-bodied.

Their qualifications extended to disabled people and informal carers (although three participants thought that entitlement to carers' benefits should be extended to older people). Detailed analysis of the transcripts reveals that the highly paternalistic discourse towards disabled people as rights-holders found among the core sample was absent among social workers. If disabled people were sufficiently autonomous to exercise their rights then, by extension, they should be regarded as capable of behaving responsibly unless proven otherwise:

> I think it has to be monitored very closely that one because in my experience in my job, I know the sort of people that were claiming benefits but weren't really caring for them at all.

> As a principle yes I believe in it [disability benefits]. Again I think, I think there has to be criteria though.

Notwithstanding the resistance of some of the social workers towards legally constituted rights, the majority (11/14) supported the proposition that people had rights to at least certain kinds of welfare. The minority objecting (3/14) baulked at the term 'right', favouring the notion of state beneficence towards weaker members of society. When considering the question of whether welfare provision is the responsibility of those who pay for it through their taxes, social workers were perhaps more likely to agree than members of the core sample (5/7 of those giving unequivocal responses, compared with 11/22 of those in the core sample):

> I don't see them as rights. I see them as part of, you know, the society that we live in, that we've reached a stage of sophistication where we say that that's perhaps the right thing to do, to support perhaps the weaker members of society.

> I think we're all responsible for each other. So if there are dependent people in the country, I pay my tax, which goes towards benefits for them.

Two social workers were highly resistant to the notion of their own welfare dependency, one of them saying, "My nightmare is that I'd have to receive benefits I'd hate it". However, the group overall was marginally less likely to say they would feel comfortable about receiving benefits or services themselves (7/9 of those asked, compared with 26/45 in the core sample). In part, this may be taken as evidence of the distancing from 'other' (dependent) people discussed previously. For example, one of these participants, who was partially reliant on her income from benefits, was anxious to point out that "I'm not your traditional dependent type". Insofar as detailed analysis also revealed that half the participants favoured the contributory principle as a means of squaring the rights–responsibilities circle, both for themselves and dependent others, their discomfiture is also indicative of a desire to link rights to reciprocal responsibilities (the other seven participants expressed no particular commitment to social insurance, favouring a more or less generous system where entitlement was based on need):

> Retirement pension, yes, seeing as I've had to pay into it I would. If I hadn't had to pay into it I might feel a bit more uncomfortable as I would think that it was a bit like charitable benefits.

> ... my view is that it [retirement pension] should be twofold. If you've paid a National Insurance contribution, that demonstrates, in the main, that you've worked and contributed, you've paid into the scheme of the day or the scheme of the government. Therefore, I think that should be at a level. But

I also think there's got to be something to safeguard poverty and all that goes with it.

Perhaps unsurprisingly in a predominantly female group of participants, the social workers were proportionately more likely than members of the core sample to recognise that caring is a form of work (8/11 answering the question, compared with 12/49). Seven participants viewed informal care and paid work as equally responsible activities, four saw caring as a more significant responsibility than paid employment. What is less clear-cut, however, is whether social workers' view of caring as a responsible activity necessarily translated into the view that it generated *rights*. While three participants pointed out that carers saved the state money, two believed the all important principle of self-sufficiency was compromised if people withdrew from the labour market to provide care:

> … caring for somebody, whether you're caring for a child or you've chosen to stay at home and not go out to work or whether you're caring for a disabled member of your family, you're still doing a very valuable job that someone else would have to do if you went out to work.... You may be in a position that you can't afford not to go out to work because there would be no money coming in if you stayed at home and cared for someone. So it is a very, I don't think that one should be rated as more important than the other.

> Well, from a humanitarian view, caring is, has got to sit, sit higher than anything at the end of the day. But if care is looked at in terms of the holistic, holistic view and caring for somebody's needs, I suggest that, that comes to the top of the agenda. Yeah, that's how, yeah, if I was to look at the importance of the two on, in humanitarian terms, but again, I would suggest other people would suggest that, you know, without work, you don't have an income and then we go along the route of, you know, [provision] for yourself and others and whatever.

Finally, in response to our questions about the welfare state, the social workers were proportionately more inclined than members of the core sample to favour increases in taxes and social spending (12/14, compared with 32/49). Their expectations concerning the future of the welfare state demonstrated a greater critical awareness of the effects of cost-cutting and managerial control (4/14) and the likelihood of privatisation (6/14) than the core sample (none and just 5/49, respectively):

> Everything is so weighted now with paperwork, with proving that you are [and] they've been gathering statistics too long. We are all doing it every day but it does actually make, it costs money and it is not that useful to the day-to-day work.

The only thing that, that concerns me is you know, this, this sort of fad for public–private partnership, which I think is almost to the extent that, we're going to do it whether it's working or not.

Human rights and social care: the policy and practice context

Prior to full implementation of the HRA in October 2000, the government announced its intention of moving beyond mere compliance with the European Convention on Human Rights (ECHR) towards the creation of "a new human rights culture" which "requires all of us in public service to respect human rights in everything we do" (Home Office, 1999a, p 2). In this second part of this chapter, we locate our findings within the wider policy and practice contexts of social care as a means of examining in greater detail the potential for developing a human rights culture on the front-line of social work practice.

In line with the Lord Chancellor's (1998) statement that the introduction of the ECHR into domestic law would "promote a culture where positive rights and liberties become the focus and concern of legislators, administrators and judges alike" (p 1), some commentators have argued that, in certain circumstances, radical change in the development of social care could be brought about by the requirement for local authorities to take positive action in furtherance of people's human rights (Schwehr, 2001, p 76; Watson, 2002, p 35). Articles 2 and 3 of the ECHR, for example, place positive obligations on public authorities to intervene in order to protect the right to life of adults known to be at risk and to ensure that vulnerable adults are not subjected to inhuman or degrading treatment respectively. Other commentators have pointed out that Article 8, which prevents any interference in an individual's right to private and family life, places a positive duty on social services departments to take action to protect vulnerable people from physical, psychological and sexual abuse (Thompson, 2000; Sale, 2001; Williams, 2001; Clements, 2002).

The HRA may challenge the tight rationing regimes governing social care in other ways. While current prioritisation criteria protect an individual's right to life, local authorities may not be able to justify interference with other ECHR rights on the grounds of lack of resources, or their allocation according to agency criteria (Williams, 2001; Clements, 2002). For example if, as Daw (2000, pp 54–5) asserts, the general principle of interpretation is that the ECHR should guarantee "not rights that are theoretical or illusory but rights that are practical and effective", then Article 5, which protects an individual's right to liberty and security, may be invoked if a person's freedom to leave an institution cannot be realised because the local authority fails to provide the means to support an independent lifestyle. To the extent that there must be proportionate reasons for inaction under the HRA, then the right to respect for home, family life and privacy under Article 8 could also be invoked to secure the resources to enable people to stay together as a family unit and receive services at home (Schwehr, 2001; Watson, 2002).

Promoting positive obligations in a discretionary service such as social care, however, arguably requires front-line practitioners to advocate on behalf of a group of service users who are, by definition, among the most disadvantaged. Social workers were last urged to embrace cultural change during the implementation of the 1990 National Health Service and Community Care Act, at that time as a means of negotiating the shift towards a new mixed economy of care based on 'markets and managers' (Taylor-Gooby and Lawson, 1993). Promoting a human rights culture would appear to accord more readily with the core principles governing the 'caring professions' than consumerism should, as Hugman (1998, p 62) claims, these principles derive from the human personhood of anyone in need of professional help, and the responsibility of the caring professional to that humanity. Moreover, the common emphasis within human rights conventions and professional codes of conduct on respecting the life and dignity of the individual, and protecting the vulnerable from harm, would tend to favour a positive interpretation of rights.

Yet day-to-day practice in social care is arguably shaped less by professional codes of conduct than by the organisational context of practice. Given the wide-ranging scope of the ECHR, which has the potential to develop still further in the UK courts (Daw, 2000, p 49), the government has advocated a 'good practice' approach to the 'mainstreaming' of human rights by local authorities, assisted by national frameworks and standards (Sale, 2001). Gibbs (2001) is optimistic about the implications for social work of newly established institutions such as the Social Care Institute for Excellence, the General Social Care Council and the National Care Standards Commission, describing them as "indicators of our determination to root social work values in principled institutions which will support them". Others are more sceptical about the top-down 'quality agenda' (Burton, 2000). Insofar as the primary intention behind such institutions is perceived as centralising control over both workforce and service delivery, they tend to suggest a continued mistrust of professionalism on the part of the present government. Over the past decade, what Hugman (1998) terms the 'technicalisation' of the social work task through care management and the wider performance management regime within which it is located has curtailed professional discretion (Foster and Wilding, 2000). Furthermore, the distinctive nature of social work has been eroded by linking access to social care to service criteria based on managerial definitions of risk, transforming much front-line practice from a process of human interaction to a linear sequence of calculations about the negative consequences of not intervening to prevent harm (Davis et al, 1997).

A recent report from the British Institute of Human Rights (Watson, 2002) suggests that, not only has there been no serious attempt by the government or public authorities to use the HRA to create a human rights culture, but that there is a lack of understanding among front-line staff in the social care sector in particular about either the rights it contains or their responsibilities to uphold them. A survey of visitors to the *Community Care* website further revealed that nearly three quarters had reportedly received no training on how the HRA affects their work (*Community Care*, 9 January 2003). Our own investigation, moreover, suggests that it is not simply a lack of awareness that impedes progress towards a human rights culture but a deep-seated resistance to rights talk on the part of social workers, borne partly out of a principled commitment to self-determination but also out of occupational exigencies.

Promoting independence

As Preston-Shoot (2002, p 192) points out, "self-determination is invariably regarded as a core social work value". Thus, when describing their practice, participants in our study appeared to regard dependency as unavoidable but not necessarily immutable. At least half saw independence as a matter of personal aspiration on service users' part, with six voicing the view that users were prone to over-dependency on staff or services when they ought to be demonstrating greater self-reliance. As illustrated in the first section of this chapter, participants regarded welfare dependency as qualitatively different to the normal (inter)dependencies of human relationships. Provided there was no risk of harm to self or others, a majority of social workers (9/14) considered that users should take as much responsibility as possible for their own welfare:

> I do have clients who are referred to us who are capable of getting by, but know the system and *could* be independent but, again, it is how they see themselves.

> If you're looking at how people are responsible for themselves. Thinking about 'If I run out of money and my benefit didn't last until the end of the week then I'll ring up social services or whatever and I'll get something there'. It's just complete ... they know what they need to do but choose not to.

Policy and operational objectives for social care articulate with a professional commitment to self-determination. The government's White Paper, *Modernising social services* (DoH, 1998), identifies a key aim for adult services as "promoting independence" to be achieved by gearing provision towards "the support needed by someone to make most use of their own capacity and potential" (DoH, 1998, para 2.5). Both financial and functional independence are targeted through measures such as improved rehabilitation, systematic review of the level of assistance provided, extension of the direct payments scheme and improving access to paid employment. Independence, as Vernon and Qureshi (2000) point out, is defined largely in terms of increasing self-reliance.

An emphasis on independence in social care accords well with the classic liberal model of human rights on which the ECHR is based. Citizens are endowed with predominantly negative (and relatively costless) rights, such as freedom from torture and the right to 'dignity' of treatment, or rights that cannot be in short supply, such as equal consideration under the law. The right to access social care relates more closely to the negative right of freedom from interference than a positive right to the means to live a dignified and autonomous life. Moreover, the entitlement of citizens who are unable to demonstrate the capacity to become more self-reliant is uncertain:

> social services must aim wherever possible to help people get better, to improve their health and social functioning rather than just 'keep them going'. (DoH, 1998, para 2.11)

While a majority of social workers in this study (9/11 responding to the question) acknowledged a sense of responsibility for dependent people, both as professionals and as local authority employees, these responsibilities were seen by over half of the participants (8/14) in terms of promoting independence or empowering service users. With its roots in the Victorian doctrine of self-help, as Gibbs (2001) points out, a professional commitment to fostering self-determination finds its contemporary equivalent in a widespread commitment to 'enabling' and 'empowering' service users. Participants in this study who expressed a commitment to 'promoting independence' in their practice appeared to be motivated both by the desire to foster self-determination and to target resources appropriately:

> ... sometimes I have to say well, you don't meet the criteria anymore. I always like us to agree if we can, because I think that's much better, because then they've actually seen that they've grown and they can cope. Because you don't want them to be dependent on you, because that's the whole idea, the idea is that you go in there and you help them but sometimes you have to say, 'Look, you *can* do this and you can do that and at the moment you're not meeting the criteria'.

Balancing rights and responsibilities

According to Hunt (1999, pp 89-90), the foundation of civic order is the recognition of mutual rights, duties and responsibilities. In this vein, Home Office guidance on the HRA states that:

> It is a key part of the Government's programme to encourage a modern civil society where the rights and responsibilities of our citizens are clearly recognised and properly balanced. (Home Office, 1999b, p 2)

There is a similar attempt to balance rights and responsibilities in *Modernising social services* (DoH, 1998). People's rights in relation to social care are specified as coordinated and readily accessible services – including clear and comprehensive information – and fair and consistent systems of charging and accessing support (DoH, 1998). Yet, as Johnson (1999) points out, rights are matched by reciprocal obligations to manage without assistance wherever possible, and to pay for and make economical use of any services provided. In cash-strapped local authorities, only people who are at serious risk of harm without assistance are prioritised for social care, particularly since the 'Gloucestershire ruling' (R v Gloucestershire County Council and the Secretary of State *ex parte* Barry, 20 March 1997) effectively confirmed the right of local authorities to tailor provision to the resources available.

Analysis of our findings suggests that the pattern of a proportion of the social workers' responses was broadly in tune with a 'third way' welfare agenda in a manner that was both principled and pragmatic. While human rights were regarded as fundamental, linked as they were to an ontological view of human interdependency, this translated into no more than a reluctant acceptance of rights to welfare among participants. Unconditional rights were not only seen to undermine personal responsibility and pave the way to welfare abuse, but were regarded as untenable in an increasingly residualised welfare state. Five of the participants, moreover, saw users' responsibility in terms of cooperating in social work interventions:

> I think they need to take part of responsibility in a way because if you've got a client who doesn't engage properly, or doesn't engage with the service, there's only so much you can do. They need to take some responsibility in seeking out support, as much as you can give it, like people don't answer the door and you know, you're constantly going back, there's only so much you can do.

As Dwyer (1998, p 494) argues, where individual responsibility becomes the central focus of citizenship and the role of the state is reduced, welfare rights become increasingly conditional, and state funded provision is made dependent upon the individual conforming to particular obligations or patterns of behaviour.

Rights and front-line practice

Hugman (1998, pp 62-4) traces the codes of conduct adopted by the 'caring professions' to the two contrasting ethical traditions of Kantianism and utilitarianism (although the term utilitarianism is here accorded its original philosophical meaning as opposed to the meaning later acquired through association with Benthamism). Whereas the former is based on the concept of the individual as an autonomous moral agent, which gives rise in turn to a professional commitment to empowering the individual, the latter implies a social construction of the good towards which people might be directed in their actions. It is this compassionate form of utilitarianism that has found expression in anti-racist and anti-oppressive social work, which Dominelli

(1998) has linked to challenges to structural power differentials, the valuing of 'difference' and promotion of social justice as well as to power sharing and an emphasis on process in professional interventions. As some social work commentators have pointed out, it is on this tradition that any advocacy role in respect of promoting positive rights to social care would depend. Thus, George (1999, pp 21-2) argues that, if social work as a profession espouses a commitment to social justice, then it has an implicit role in promoting human rights, while Cemlyn and Briskman (2002, p 65) suggest that a human rights framework needs to be placed at the centre of social work practice in order to value 'difference' and counteract oppression, and assist social workers in examining their own assumptions.

The pattern of social work responses outlined in the first part of this chapter indicates that about half were based on socially situated views about dependency and responsibility. If individuals could not be held to account for their dependency then, by extension, their social rights should be upheld. In respect of their own practice, six social workers referred to their professional responsibility to advocate, or support, users' rights of access to benefits and services. Two of these participants, who belonged to the same authority, made specific reference to their sense of responsibility for advocating on service users' behalf when employers' decisions threatened to contravene human rights legislation:

> ... in terms of working with people ... I make them very aware of the rights that they have which is the clash that I have with my employers in that if they decide that they want social work practice to go one way, and we know that's not in the person's best interest, so, you know, it counteracts the Human Rights Act, I will jump up and down, and say, 'I'm sorry, you can't do that, this person has human rights'.

Four participants in this study, however, expressed overt hostility towards rights talk within the context of social work practice. Rights were seen not only to be used to advance 'unrealistic' claims for state support while avoiding responsibility for self-reliance, but to undermine the relationship at the centre of traditional social work practice with its associated skills of negotiating with clients to reach a compromise solution:

> ... if you don't get it right, it looks from the outside that they've [disabled people] got all rights but no responsibilities.

> It seems to me that we're getting into a situation where there is no compromise, there is no negotiation. It's either/or, you know, you infringe my human rights, I'll take you to court. I mean, you know, it's something that gets quoted a lot at us. This Human Rights Act ... that's about getting into a situation where litigation is all people think about. Because people are thinking of rights as being purely legal instead of moral, I think.

Social care providers echo participants' resistance towards legally enforceable rights more generally. A review of *Community Care* at the time of implementation evidences a predominantly defensive response to the HRA which is variously described as a "weapon of litigation" which threatens to engender a "compensation culture" and "swamp" social services with dubious legal challenges. The fear is that the 'compensation culture' will further erode professional judgement and stifle flexible and imaginative practice as social work managers and professionals are obliged slavishly to follow procedures to avoid the risk of being sued (*Community Care*, 6 September 2001; Whelan, 2000, p 14). Professional criticisms of the HRA enmesh with those directed at performance measurement to the extent that, as Schwehr (2001) points out, explicit risk management procedures are required if public authorities are successfully to establish justifications for interfering with people's human rights or demonstrate that their decisions meet the new test for judicial intervention – 'proportionality'.

Conclusion

Analysis of the interview findings suggests that the social workers held contradictory views about the nature of dependency, responsibility and rights. While their qualified acceptance of people's social rights can be linked to the individualistic terms in which participants defined dependency and responsibility, the extent to which people were expected to avoid dependency by taking personal responsibility for their welfare was limited by a counter tendency among social workers to see dependency and responsibility in wider societal terms. These competing views are intelligible when account is taken of the ethical codes of conduct underlying social work, which simultaneously commit practitioners to fostering self-reliance and promoting social justice.

While there was support among participants for a more expansive welfare state to which those in need should have access by right – solidaristic views which were further bolstered by an ontological view of interdependency from which human rights was largely seen to derive – their commitment to human and social rights within the context of front-line practice was more circumscribed. First, a rights-based approach appeared to threaten professional authority. Second, a belief in the virtue of personal responsibility articulated with the gearing of policy and operational objectives in social care towards the promotion of self-reliance. Third, as Watson (2002, p 8) notes, social care practitioners perceive the HRA to lie predominantly within the domain of the legal profession with the result that any change is perceived to rely on the courts rather than on good practice. Indeed, when reflecting on their front-line practice, social workers in this study perceived human rights less in terms of confirming a shared humanity than as a legal battering ram which threatened to breach tightly constructed eligibility criteria.

Implementation of the HRA carries the potential for placing positive obligations on local authorities to expand the currently limited nature and scope of social care. Not only has the government's stated objective of promoting a positive human rights culture in the public services proved largely rhetorical, however, but our interviews with social workers suggest that contemporary policy and practice regimes are inimical to the professional advocacy role which might assist in bringing such change about.

References

Burton, J. (2000) 'A heart and soul in jeopardy', *Community Care*, 14 September, p 15.

Cemlyn, S. and Briskman, L. (2002) 'Social (dys)welfare within a hostile state', *Social Work Education*, vol 21, no 1, pp 49-69.

Clements, L. (2002) 'Community care law and the Human Rights Act 1998', in B. Bytheway, V. Bacigalupo, J. Bornat, J. Johnson and S. Spurr (eds) *Understanding care, welfare and community*, London: Routledge/Open University.

Davis, A., Ellis, K. and Rummery, K. (1997) *Access to assessment: Perspectives of practitioners, disabled people and carers*, Bristol/York: The Policy Press/Joseph Rowntree Foundation.

Daw, R. (2000) *Human rights and disability: The impact of the Human Rights Act on Disabled People*, London: The Royal Institute for Deaf People/Disability Rights Commission.

DoH (Department of Health) (1998) *Modernising social services: Promoting independence, improving protection and raising standards*, Cm 4169, London: The Stationery Office.

Dominelli, L. (1998) 'Anti-oppressive practice in context', in R. Adams, L. Dominelli and M. Payne (eds) *Social work themes, issues and critical debates*, Basingstoke: Macmillan.

Dwyer, P. (1998) 'Conditional citizens? Welfare rights and responsibilities in the late 1990s', *Critical Social Policy*, vol 18, no 4, pp 493-517.

Foster, P. and Wilding, P. (2000) 'Whither welfare professionalism?', *Journal of Social Policy and Administration*, vol 34, no 2, pp 143-59.

George, J. (1999) 'Conceptual muddle, practical dilemma', *International Social Work*, vol 42, no 1, pp 15-26.

Gibbs, M. (2001) 'Debate: are our values safe?', *Community Care*, 27 September, p 25

Home Office (1999a) *Putting rights into public service: An introduction for public authorities*, London: Home Office Communications Directorate.

Home Office (1999b) *Private sector public service: Human rights for all*, London: Home Office Communications Directorate.

Hugman, R. (1998) *Social welfare and social value: The role of the caring professions*, Basingstoke: Macmillan.

Hunt, M. (1999) 'The Human Rights Act and legal culture: the judiciary and the legal profession', *Journal of Law and Society*, vol 26, no 1, pp 86-102.

Johnson, N. (1999) 'The personal social services and community care', in M. Powell (ed) *New Labour, new welfare state? The 'third way' in British social policy*, Bristol: The Policy Press.

Lord Chancellor (1998) 'Creating a nation of real citizens: partnership between the people and the state', Speech to the Citizenship Foundation, London, 27 January.

Preston-Shoot, M. (2002) 'Evaluating self-determination', in B. Bytheway, V. Bacigalupo, J. Bornat, J. Johnson and S. Spurr (eds) *Understanding care, welfare and community*, London: Routledge.

Sale, A. (2001) 'Caught in the Act?' *Community Care*, 10-16 May, pp 20-1.

Schwehr, B. (2001) 'Human rights and social services', in L-A. Cull and L. Roche (eds) *The law and social work*, Basingstoke: Palgrave.

Taylor-Gooby, P. and Lawson, R. (eds) (1993) *Markets and managers*, Buckingham: Open University Press.

Thompson, A. (2000) 'Trials and tribulations', *Community Care*, 14-20 September, p 25.

Vernon, A. and Qureshi, H. (2000) 'Community care and independence: self-sufficiency or empowerment?', *Critical Social Policy*, vol 20, no 2, pp 255-76.

Wainwright, H. (2001) 'A piece of paper and a team of lawyers isn't enough', *The Guardian*, 31 May.

Watson, J. (2002) *Something for everyone: The impact of the Human Rights Act and the need for a Human Rights Commission*, London: The British Institute of Human Rights.

Whelan, R. (2000) 'New rights, many wrongs', *Community Care*, 11-17 May, p 15.

Williams, J. (2001) '1998 Human Rights Act: social work's new benchmark', *British Journal of Social Work*, vol 31, pp 831-44.

SIX

Administering rights for dependent subjects

Hartley Dean and Ruth Rogers

In Chapter Four of this book, we described the findings from a set of in-depth interviews that we conducted with a 'core' sample of working-age adults in the UK. The same basic interviews were also conducted with a small sample of benefits administrators working for the Department for Work and Pensions (DWP) in local offices in a district in England. It should be said that negotiating access to the sample through the DWP had been difficult, not least because the fieldwork was conducted at a time of major reorganisation (late 2001–early 2002, as the Benefits Agency and Employment Service organisations were being brought together under the auspices of the newly constituted DWP). In the end, nine benefits administrators were interviewed, of whom two were men and seven were women. One was under 40 years of age and eight were aged 40+; seven were working in senior supervisory or managerial roles, and two fulfilled mid-range decision making or advisory roles; eight were white and one was from a minority ethnic group; two were graduates, two had sub-degree post-16 qualifications, and five had been educated to GCSE/'O' level standard (but all had received civil service training and at least three had had 20 or more years' experience). Members of the sample were responsible for the administration of a range of benefits, including income support, a range of disability related benefits and retirement pension.

This was a diverse and interesting sample and, in spite of the very small sample size, the quality of the data elicited justifies a detailed discussion of the findings (subject of course to a warning that these should be interpreted with caution). In this chapter, we first draw out some of the apparent similarities and differences between the discourse of benefits administrators and that of the core sample. Second, we shall look at certain distinctive features of the benefits administrators' discourse, including the way the administrators appeared to look upon claimants as dependent subjects and claimants' rights in terms of administrative responsibilities, and the evident ambiguity of their discourse as 'messengers' of the 'third way' policy regime.

Comparing benefits administrators with the 'core' sample

The interviews elicited a broadly similar range of responses to those of the core sample, albeit with certain differences that will have reflected an awareness stemming from the nature of the benefits administrators' occupation. Given the limited size of the sample, it is not possible to draw wholly conclusive inferences concerning differences between the benefits administrators and members of the core sample and caution should be observed in relation to the discussion that follows.

Dependency

As might be expected, given the context, the benefits administrators were proportionately more likely than members of the core sample to frame initial definitions or images of dependency in terms of financial dependency on the state (3/9, compared with 2/49), but they also appeared to be slightly more likely to regard such dependency as inevitable (5/9, compared with 17/49). This apparently heightened, but less than uniform, awareness seemed to extend to a greater readiness on the part of benefits administrators to acknowledge that they themselves had at some stage been, were now, or might in the future become, dependent on others. In part, however, this may also have reflected the fact that the benefits administrators' sample was also proportionately older and contained more women than the core sample. The ways in which benefits administrators framed their definitions or images of 'independence' were broadly similar to those of the core sample, although one benefits administrator sought to define independence in terms of the ability to make choices.

Asked whether they regarded benefits claimants as dependent, four of the benefits administrators said "yes", one "no" and three said "it depends". Here again, questions of choice emerged, with differing views as to whether on the one hand claimants have choices or whether on the other they are exercising illicit choices:

> I wouldn't say all of the customers [the officially preferred term for claimants] are dependent. I think that there, there are groups of customers that might know nothing else but being dependent on social security. That doesn't mean to say that ... it's a choice, it's a conscious choice on their part, it may be that there's always been a culture of that in their particular family, on social security, for whatever reason.

> That's not a straightforward question I suppose. They should be [dependent on the benefits we administer], to my mind that's the point of the welfare state, but whether or not some of them actually are is another matter.

We return later in this chapter to discuss the ways in which the benefits administrators perceived or 'constituted' claimants, but one benefits administrator in particular expressed very palpable resentment based on his perceptions of certain claimants:

> There are an awful lot of people in there [the benefits office] who are taking the money. They may also be doing whatever, on the side [that is, working without declaring their earnings].... People on benefit here, they come onto the benefit, they're a lone parent with a couple of kids and then another baby is born, so we pay for it, and then another one, and we pay for that. Whereas in America what you had when you started is how it stays, the state doesn't fund ... somebody else should be paying for those, well, I suppose somebody else should be paying for the existing two [laughs].

The benefits administrators were proportionately more likely to recognise all forms of dependency as being the same (4/9, compared to 5/49 in the core sample), which tends on the one hand to confirm that some benefits administrators may come to recognise dependency as an inherent fact of life. On the other hand, as with the core sample, nearly half the benefits administrators (four) saw dependency on the state as being clearly different from other forms of dependency, and at least one of the explanations offered reflected a very particular understanding of the one-sided nature of the relationship between social security claimants and the state, compared, for example, with the nature of familial relationships:

> I think that dependency with a partner is really one arriving out of a mutual understanding and it's a partnership that's entered into. A dependency on the state is really, as the system works at the moment, less of a partnership. It's a situation people find themselves in. It's not something that they'd entered into.

Although benefits administrators were proportionately slightly less likely than the core sample to attach conditions to the acceptability of anybody being dependent (5/9, compared with 33/49), a majority (five), nonetheless, did attach conditions and, as we shall soon see, this was translated into understandings of rights that were often strongly conditional in nature.

In broad terms, however, the discourse of the benefits administrators to whom we spoke was consistent with popular discourse insofar that, perhaps reluctantly on occasions, it embodied a general recognition that there is an element of interdependency that arises as part of the human life course (see Chapter Four of this book). Only one of the benefits administrators appeared to disconfirm this proposition, a middle-aged woman who dismissed the idea that dependency was anything other than a 'state of mind'. She reacted to the suggestion that she might herself be emotionally dependent, on a partner, for example, by saying, "Sorry, you're speaking to the wrong sort of woman about that – how pathetic [laughs]!". However, what distinguished the benefits administrators was not the way their own experiences of (inter)dependency had been fashioned, but the significance the concept of dependency had for them in constituting the claimants whose claims they processed. This is an issue to which we return in the second part of this chapter.

Responsibility

Benefits administrators were proportionately rather more likely than the core sample to accept the proposition that people should in theory be responsible for their own welfare (3/9, compared with 8/49), although this was still not a majority view. As with the core sample, however, a majority (five) of benefits administrators defined responsibility in strictly individualistic terms, and those who did subscribe to rather more socially contextualised notions of responsibility articulated them primarily, nonetheless, as responsibilities that are individually, not collectively, borne. None of the benefits administrators disconfirmed this proposition, suggesting quite possibly that benefits administrators may be even more individualistic in their approach to responsibility than other members of the working-age population (see Chapter Four of this book). It was striking that, whereas in initial responses to our question about the meaning of responsibility, a few of the participants in the core sample had defined it in terms of citizenship and wider responsibilities to other people; none of the benefits administrators did so.

Benefits administrators were asked expressly what responsibilities claimants had: two were not prepared to generalise; one said that claimants' responsibility was not to defraud the system; and six suggested that claimants' responsibility lay in cooperating with them as benefits administrators. (The significance of this last type of response is more fully explored later in this chapter.)

In spite of the emphasis placed by policy makers on the responsibility of benefits claimants to work, this was not *initially* mentioned by any of the benefits administrators. Nonetheless, when pressed to talk about people's responsibility to work and the circumstances in which people may be responsible without working, the pattern of the benefits administrators' replies was very similar to that of the core sample. Some expressed themselves in terms that are consistent with current government policy:

> Once you're on benefit then you get comfy with the life and particularly with people who have got large families. Why go to work for an extra 20 quid? I don't think that they realise just how much you would gain just from being at work. You get a reason for life, well not a reason for life but you get out of the habit of going round and round.

> I've had this conversation many years ago with a customer ... he was going 'Oh, so you think it's OK for me to go and sweep the streets, when I've got this qualification and that'. And obviously I can't turn around and say, 'Yes, I do think it is'. But at the end of the day if you can earn your own living

and support your family, OK it is a low-paid job and hopefully it's an incentive to get yourself a better paid job, or something you're more suited to.

Others, however, expressed a degree of dissent from government policy, and we shall be returning to this issue later in the chapter.

Where the pattern of the benefits administrators' replies noticeably differed from those of the core sample was in their responses to the question about whether people should take responsibility for particular life-course contingencies, like redundancy or retirement. As might be expected in view of the nature of their jobs, benefits administrators were much more likely to say that National Insurance arrangements should be sufficient and/or to express opposition to private insurance schemes (5/9, compared with 4/49 in the core sample):

> I suppose I come from the culture of the welfare state. So for me, if they've made contributions through their working life then that's where their responsibility ends. I mean, they've done it via paid employment they've been in, or if they have children and have stayed at home, that was their job then. I think that's where it ends. I don't agree with having private health or private insurance or private pension.

> And a lot of people will argue that we paid X number of pounds every week into National Insurance which is for the National Health Service as well as paying for benefits. A lot of people would argue that we're paying all this money why should we have to pay again for a service that we're already paying for.

Although the tendency cannot be said, in view of the small numbers involved, to be marked, in their responses to our questions about irresponsibility, benefits administrators seemed rather more inclined than members of the core sample to stereotype irresponsible people in terms of their social fecklessness or personality traits (6/9, compared with 17/49); rather more likely to associate irresponsibility with individual selfishness than a failure to make a social contribution (6/9, compared with 16/49); and perhaps slightly more inclined to think in terms of punitive rather than paternalistic solutions to the problem of irresponsible behaviour (6/9, compared with 21/49). While tending to support a collectively funded/state administered benefits system, benefits administrators seemed to incline towards an individualistic approach to the regulation of personal conduct. A particular preoccupation, shared by the present government but not so strongly by members of the core sample, was with benefit fraud and alleged abuse of the system:

> [Irresponsible people are] people who try and work and sign on at the same time, try and cheat the system because it undermines it for everyone.

> We get social security families. We get mother and father not working and
> then the children. They think that 'Well, they don't work and they get
> money', and you do get this sort of thing. These people are irresponsible
> because they're not prepared to make the effort and, a lot of people, they
> know how to work round the system.

On the other hand, the minority of benefits administrators who subscribed to
paternalistic forms of intervention harboured quite definite views as to the
nature of the government's responsibilities:

> If they've got children there is not a lot you can do but pay them some sort
> of income support because at the end of the day, you can't see the children
> going without because of the parents' irresponsibility.

> No, you can't leave someone alone cos they can't get out of it. In some areas
> of the country they have debt counsellors; we used to do it. Our department
> used to be very socially responsible, we used to have a special caseworker [a
> relatively short lived initiative in the late 1970s/early 1980s] that would go
> out to the person on income support and sort it out for them. That was
> their job. But it doesn't happen any more.

Rights

In response to our general question as to whether people's rights as human
beings should include social rights, the pattern of the benefits administrators'
replies was, once again, broadly similar to that of the core sample, with a majority
(six) in support, albeit usually subject to certain exceptions (five). However,
the benefits administrators' definitions of rights revealed a pattern that suggested
they were definitely more inclined than the core sample to the view that rights
are conditional rather than inalienable (7/9, compared with 19/49):

> I have a problem with the word 'rights'. It just sounds too much like people
> banging on, saying 'This is my right'.... I would say it's a responsibility of –
> I hate the phrase – of a caring society to look after people in the community
> that can't care for themselves.

> No, I don't think we have 'rights'. These things have to be earned.

When asked when people might have a right to be dependent, benefits
administrators gave a range of responses quite similar to those of the core
sample, but when asked whether they themselves felt responsible to those who
are dependent, most of them (seven) understandably interpreted this (at least in
part) in terms of their responsibilities as benefits administrators:

> I feel very strongly about this. I always make sure that if someone makes a claim and for some reason there's a delay, I mean it could be for all sorts of reasons, I make sure as it is dealt with as efficiently as possible. Most people out there [in the benefits office] are very, very caring towards the public. In fact we, literally, about 10 minutes before you arrived we were only talking about certain things, about certain aspects of the job. And one of the people said, 'Well, actually, we are actually, we are actually here to pay people', and that is actually what we're here for. So, yes, I take it very, very strongly that I make sure that people get what they're entitled to.

> I think, yes absolutely, we have a responsibility, erm, and I think we should be very much held accountable, it shouldn't be just a matter of 'Yeah, that's for that department to sort out'. I think there should be, I think the sort of things that have been brought in the last few years where there are penalties if the government departments don't do what they're supposed to do, I think that I'd go along with that because we should be accountable.

Responding to our question as to whether they were comfortable that taxpayers' money is spent on providing benefits and services for various social groups, the benefits administrators were more strongly supportive than the core sample. They were unanimous in their support for provision for elderly and disabled people, although one administrator expressed reservations about benefits for informal carers, arguing that caring for family members should be provided in addition to earning one's living:

> Well, some people live off it, don't they? That's the trouble. You know, if you do too much ... I've never claimed anything as a carer and I've always worked. Whereas some people would say 'Oh I couldn't possibly' and they would take, take, take.... Why should I keep throwing money into this fund that I might not get anything out of? But then there are people who have not worked and have claimed benefits and have done less than me, in my spare time.

The benefits administrators' support for provision for unemployed people was more qualified but still stronger than that of the core sample (with 6/9, compared to 20/49, expressing unqualified support). The benefits administrators were proportionately rather more likely than members of the core sample to say that people have a right to welfare provision (5/9, compared to 23/49), but slightly less likely to say unequivocally that they would be comfortable receiving benefits and services themselves (4/9, compared with 26/49). Reflecting, possibly, the extent to which several of the benefits administrators had experience in administering benefits for disabled people, they were proportionately rather more likely than the core sample to say in response to our question about work and care that caring *is* working (4/9, compared to 12/49). Additionally, at least three of the benefits administrators had had personal experience in the course of their lives of providing informal care for relatives. Nonetheless, the world-weary scepticism of certain benefits administrators was exemplified by the one who said:

> Given that choice, I'd have to say working, under normal circumstances. A lot of people do hide behind the caring thing.

In broad terms, however, the discourse of the benefits administrators to whom we spoke was consistent with popular discourse insofar that although there may be certain inalienable human rights – such as the right that claimants have to be treated 'with respect' – substantive rights to welfare can never be wholly unconditional (see Chapter Four of this book). Only two of the benefits administrators appeared to disconfirm this proposition, and for very different reasons. One, a woman in her 30s, who we shall call Constance, stood out from her colleagues in believing that rights should not be withdrawn even when people behave badly, but she acknowledged that she was subject to a considerable amount of peer pressure to change such views. At the opposite end of the spectrum there was an older woman who believed in rules rather than rights and insisted that people exclude themselves from *any* rights if they do not obey the rules of the system. She was giving expression to an extreme form of a 'rights as procedure' discourse that we discuss in the second part of this chapter.

The welfare state

Finally, in response to our questions about the welfare state, while some benefits administrators (three) suggested that taxes and social spending should be kept at current levels, a majority (six) said they were prepared to pay more in return for better services: a pattern similar to that observed in the core sample. However, the benefits administrators' replies concerning the future of the welfare state were rather different from those of the core sample. None of the benefits administrators suggested that the current system was satisfactory, yet none anticipated that the benefits system itself would be privatised. Two of the benefits administrators spoke specifically about the excesses of bureaucracy and 'red tape' within welfare systems and complained about complex cost cutting policy initiatives that they did not believe to be working. Nonetheless, the benefits administrators were proportionately more likely than members of the core sample to believe the system is in crisis and has to change (5/9, compared with 22/49) (Box 6.1).

Box 6.1: Benefits administrators' reflections on the future of the welfare state

- "What I fear is that you see things that are so top-heavy. There are as many managers as nurses in the Health Service and there is something wrong there. Stop doing bits of paper. There are so many glossies [expensively produced policy documents] come through here. If they stopped all the glossies and worked out how much. We had a launch thing. They worked out that it must have cost £10,000 to have glossies, and whatever. We could have had another member of staff. Please give us another member of staff!"

- "It all seems to be going full circle. Different names, same process, principles the same ... they will do their very best to keep the costs down ... [but] I can't see radical changes ... you can't, fundamentally there are too many problems within the system, it's too complicated. If you could simplify it there'd be no problem. The most radical thing would be, right we'll scrap everything, we'll just means-test anyone who needs support. But that's about as radical as it could get."

- "I think it's going to have to change radically, because I don't think there is, if you listen to all the pundits, in terms of there's not enough people working in this, that and the other. I think there's fundamental problems.... But I think it's going to change."

Benefits administrators' understandings of the welfare state, of course, are specifically situated and informed and we return in this chapter to discuss the tensions to which their discourse gave expression.

Client dependency and responsible administration

In summary, therefore, it is suggested that benefits administrators' discourse tends to share with popular discourse some recognition of the nature of human interdependency, an individualistic construction of responsibility, and a largely conditional conception of rights. However, dependency can have a particular meaning for benefits administrators insofar that social security claimants may be constituted through the nature of their dependency. For benefits administrators, claimants' responsibilities may be constructed in terms of obedience to the rules of the benefits system and claimants' rights in terms of the obligations that such rules impose upon them as the administrators of the system. At the same time, recent policy developments (see Chapter One of this book) have been attempting to reconstruct benefits administrators as interpreters or messengers of a new policy discourse that does not always sit easily with either the popular discourse in which benefits administrators share or the particular discourse through which the benefits administrators' role has conventionally been established. Insofar that, according to Hill (1997, p 146), "the implementation process *is* the policy-making process", the implications are significant.

Constructing the client

The benefits administrator is a classic example of what Lipsky (1976, 1980) has defined as the 'street-level bureaucrat'. It is officials dealing with the public at 'street-level' who must give effect to policy changes and who must confront the practical implications that may flow from policy defects, inadequate resources and/or public opposition. As policy is translated into practice, the quotidian survival strategies of street-level bureaucrats may result in pragmatic and often subtle adaptations. This might characteristically entail informal methods of rationing demand, stretching resources or eliciting client compliance. As street-level bureaucrats, benefits administrators are engaged in a process that Prottas (1979) has characterised as 'people processing'. Through the attitudes they exhibit to claimants, the information they impart and the discretion that they exercise benefits administrators can control the substantive effects of policy as it is experienced. However, they can also transform or 'reconstitute' the claimant in particular ways. Prottas and Lipsky have suggested that the process characteristically reconstitutes the claimant as a 'client', but under the influence of new public managerialism, as we shall soon see, claimants are increasingly constituted as 'customers' (Clarke and Newman, 1997; Dean, 2002).

The process of constituting the claimant occurs at several levels. At one level, it entails a 'partitioning' process (Dean, 1991) by which claimants are sorted into the various legislative categories upon which their entitlement to benefit may depend. At another, it entails a process which, almost in spite of itself, reinstates the distinctions once enforced under the Poor Laws between 'deserving' and 'undeserving' cases: between complaisant and difficult clients. The result is that day-to-day practical priorities may tend in the end to "impugn, by implication, the motives of most claimants" (Howe, 1985, p 65). A similar observation has been drawn by Wright (2001, 2003) in recent research based on observations and interviews in a Jobcentre office, including interviews with 48 Employment Service administrators. Wright makes the distinction between the administrative and moral categorisations by which benefits administrators identify claimants, and in relation to the latter, between 'good clients' and 'bad clients'. A good client was one "whose case was administratively straightforward, whose circumstances were 'deserving', whose behaviour was compliant and whose attitude was keen and respectful" (Wright, 2003, p 243). Bad clients, on the other hand, fell into a variety of overlapping categories, including "wasters" (who would not get jobs), "unemployables" (who could not), "nutters" (who could be frightening), "numpties" (a local colloquial term for clients that were inadequate but harmless) and those who were "at it" (that is, believed to be claiming fraudulently while engaged in undeclared employment) (Wright, 2003, p 248).

Such findings square precisely with our own. The benefits administrators to whom we spoke were concerned by and large to emphasise that most claimants were indeed 'genuine' and, by implication, deserving, but their preoccupation was often with an alleged minority of 'scroungers', 'unemployables', the 'obnoxious' (which included violent claimants with mental health problems), 'inadequates', and those engaged in alleged fraud. However, what our study would seem to indicate is a chain of association within the discourse of benefits administrators between welfare dependency and 'otherness'. Every one of the benefits administrators in our sample at some stage called upon some version of the 'dependency culture thesis' to account for claimants' conduct and all but one at some stage criticised or denigrated the dependency or irresponsibility of certain 'others' in society (see Chapter Four of this book). As with members of the core sample, 'others' were plainly identified as people – and especially claimants – whose habits, upbringing or lifestyles lay beyond the sphere of the benefits administrators' personal experiences and the intimate relationships within which they negotiated their own dependencies and responsibilities.

Some benefits administrators distinguished themselves from claimants in terms of upbringing or in terms of the standards of conduct that they expected (Box 6.2).

Box 6.2: Constructing the claimant as different

- "other people are not brought up that way [the way they should be] ... they see it as part and parcel of leaving school is knowing how to claim benefit."
- "[a responsible person] is one that makes an effort to have a reasonable education ... to get a job and ... to stick with that job. I would like to think that that is the way that I have brought my sons up to be. I mean they've always worked. They've never relied on the state. I consider a responsible person as someone who looks after themselves and their family, who doesn't expect the state to provide, which a lot of people do."
- "I seem to have one view about acceptability for other people and one view about myself."

Others sought to illustrate the ways in which certain claimants are beyond the pale of civilised conduct, to which they lack any sense of shame or have somehow, as it were, fallen from grace (Box 6.3).

Box 6.3: Constructing the claimant as 'other'

- "most days there are people out there [outside the office] sitting on the wall with their cans of lager and they're effing and blinding and they've got children running around."
- "people have got no shame that someone else can pick up the tab."
- "we've all got the same rights, certainly to start with, but ... you get the scenario where people go for years and years – something goes wrong maybe in their personal life – maybe go onto drugs or alcohol and they've lost it [ie their rights] then.... I mean they started out with the same rights as somebody who is maybe unfortunate

---

> enough to be *born* to parents who were drug addicts – and [then] *became* drug
> addicts themselves.... I think we've all got rights to start with and circumstances
> change those."

The one exception was Constance, who did not seek at any point in the
interview to portray any particular groups of claimants as undeserving. However,
she was conscious that she was out of step with her colleagues and illustrated
this most clearly when asked whether she would be comfortable about claiming
benefits herself or whether she would be prepared to take a menial low-paid
job in preference to claiming benefit:

> I have to say that sometimes, because of the negative atmosphere in which
> we work and people constantly harping on about getting things they don't
> deserve and what have you, it's probably made me more reluctant than I
> would have been before I started to work here to actually claim benefit....
> I could be persuaded by the idea now – having worked in the benefits
> system I wouldn't want to be in a position of being overly dependent on the
> state. But that's because I'm perhaps swayed by attitudes within the
> department.

Her case seems to illustrate the conflict that Lipsky (1980) suggests is experienced
by public servants who may start work in the expectation that they will be able
to do something socially worthwhile, but who then either become disenchanted
and leave or else come under pressure to adapt to the culture of street-level
bureaucracy. In spite of the cynicism expressed by some of the benefits
administrators we spoke to, it should be stressed that street-level bureaucracy
does not necessarily entail cynicism, but is, rather, a culture in which citizens
are constituted in terms of their dependency on the systems that street-level
bureaucrats administer; systems in which there is pressure to sanction or to
exclude those citizens that are adjudged to have forfeited their entitlement
under those systems.

Rights as procedure

Benefits administrators are engaged with an administrative process, and it is
primarily through that process that they conceptualise the rights and
responsibilities of claimants and their own responsibilities as administrators.
Benefits administrators would sometimes call upon established principles –
such as the contribution or needs principles – to justify the functioning of the
benefits system, but in this respect they were not so very different from members
of the core sample. What really did mark them out was their awareness of the
rules of the benefits system and the extent to which they subscribed to a
'blackletter' interpretation of rights and responsibilities (Box 6.4).

Box 6.4: 'Black letter' accounts of claimants' rights

- "There are rules and regulations for every benefit."
- "Provided they [claimants] fall into certain categories and they satisfy certain conditions, then they have a right to claim."
- "Unless they [claimants] satisfy certain criteria then they don't get any money.... Most people do get them [benefits] if they apply and satisfy the criteria."
- "If they [claimants] make a claim and they satisfy their contributions or the conditions of the benefit, then yes they do have a right to receive it."

As we have seen, however, the context in which that process is administered has been changing. There are two aspects to this. First, as was discussed in Chapter One of this book, there has been an attempt at the political level to re-conceptualise the relationship between rights and responsibilities (we consider the extent to which benefits administrators have become messengers for that project shortly). Second, there have been major attempts to change the nature of public services. This began in the 1980s with the development of new public managerialism (Lawson and Taylor-Gooby, 1993; Clarke and Newman, 1997), which entailed the introduction or adaptation of organisational structures and processes that had hitherto been the preserve of private enterprise. In the case of benefits administration, it involved the creation of new governmental agencies operating at 'arm's length' from departmental control, subject on the one hand to their own business plans, and on the other to ministerially prescribed performance targets. Such attempts have been redoubled under the New Labour government under the rubric of 'modernisation' (Blackman and Palmer, 1999; Cabinet Office, 1999). In the case of benefits administration, the drive is to develop an "Active Modern Service" (DSS, 1998, p 71), which is to be more efficient and 'customer-focused'.

We might have expected a managerialist approach to benefits administration to change the parameters of street-level bureaucracy and to prioritise policy objectives over administrative process. It may be, however, that it has reinforced the processual nature of benefits administration. Central to the shift towards new managerialism and service modernisation has been a reconceptualisation of the rights of citizenship. This began in the 1990s with the promulgation of the *Citizen's Charter* (Prime Minister's Office, 1991). The charter reconstituted the citizen as a consumer of public services, with the kind of rights that customers enjoy in the marketplace, including the right to complain or to choose an alternative provider (Dean, 2002). The users and providers of public services were cast as opponents of each other's interests. The 'business' of public service provision was uncoupled from the 'politics' of welfare. Applied to the 'business' of benefits administration in which claimants as 'customers' lack any real power, the managerialist approach can actually amplify the potentially adversarial but strictly technical nature of the benefits administration process.

The New Labour government's modernisation agenda has embraced and extended *Citizen's Charter* principles and provides for the development of 'customer charters' for each of the various agencies responsible for benefits administration. At the time of writing, a new Customer Charter for the Jobcentre Plus agency is awaited, but in the meantime the principles of the former Benefits Agency's *Customer Charter* (DSS, 1999) continue to apply (Box 6.5) and can also been seen, for example, in Customer Charters issued on behalf of the new Pension Service and Disability and Carers Service agencies (DWP, 2002a, 2002b).

Box 6.5: Customer Charter principles

Our responsibilities
We will help you by:

- **dealing with your claim as quickly as possible and keeping you informed about progress and decisions** – we will also make it clear what information you need to provide us with;
- **being polite and easy to talk to** – our staff are specially trained to meet your needs. They will treat you with respect and will do their best to understand your personal circumstances;
- **giving you accurate benefit advice and information including help with applying for child support when needed;**
- **being fair** – your race, ethnic origin, age, gender, sexual orientation, religious beliefs or any disability you have will not affect how we treat you;
- **following the rules of the Social Security and Data Protection Acts, and the principles of Open Government** – this includes giving you information you ask for, if the law allows. But it is a criminal offence for us to give your personal information to anyone else unless the law allows or we have your permission. We will treat what you say to us confidentially;
- **asking your views and using them to give you the service you want** – this includes talking to organisations which represent our customers.

Your responsibilities
To help us we need you to:

- **give complete and accurate information** when you contact us, and give all the evidence we need to decide your claim correctly. By law, we need certain information before we can pay your benefit;
- **tell us about changes in your circumstances as soon as possible;**
- **give the correct National Insurance (NI) number** when you contact us about your benefit or make a claim. We may also need your partner's NI number;
- **provide some means of identification** – for example, wage slips, your passport, driving licence or chequebook.

Source: DSS (1999, pp 6-7)

It is clear that certain of these principles, which have presumably been impressed upon benefits administrators through their training, play a key role in validating their administrative practices. The *Customer Charter*, with its ostensibly reciprocal sets of responsibilities, provides a language that can be adopted, adapted and even elaborated in defence of the benefits administrators' people processing. The discourse of the benefits administrators we spoke to constituted the process in which they were engaged in terms of compliance issues on the one hand, and 'customer service' issues on the other. The principles of the *Customer Charter* were immediately called upon by a majority of the benefits administrators in order to define the responsibilities of claimants. And for some, the language of the *Customer Charter* was inflated so that the claimants' responsibility to furnish information becomes a more general requirement. Taken to its extreme, this responsibility was escalated to assume the status of an act of confession or submission by which claimants might redeem themselves from the stigma of their welfare dependency. This is illustrated in Box 6.6 (in which emphasis has been added to certain phrases to illustrate the escalation effect referred to).

Box 6.6: Benefits administrators' perceptions of claimants' responsibilities

- "The responsibilities of our customers are mainly to give us the *right details*."
- "It is their responsibility if you like to ensure that *we have the information* in order to pay them their benefits."
- "They've equally got responsibilities to tell us should something change."
- "[A claimant's responsibility is] to *be truthful*; give accurate information. Really, I suppose that is it. If you are wanting help then I think the help should be there, but you've also got a responsibility *not to bend the rules* and not to withhold information ... *to play the game*."
- "Their responsibility is to be *as open as possible*."
- "...and as long as they are looking for jobs then the payment [of Jobseeker's Allowance] goes out. So no, I don't think it's a dependency as long as they *do what they are required to do*."

However, it was Constance who acknowledged the extent to which benefits administrators must surely realise the unequal relations of power that are constituted by the process through which they engage with claimants:

> [Claimants] often feel that they're in a position where they don't hold anything like the information that we hold, and therefore can't be held responsible as sometimes we hold them to be.

At the same time, customer service discourse is appropriated in a way that enables benefits administrators to distance themselves from 'customers', since the administrator's responsibility is limited, on the one hand, to the proper conduct of a strictly technical process, and, on the other, to erecting no more than a facade of respect or politeness (Box 6.7).

> ### Box 6.7: Benefits administrators' reflections on 'customer service'
>
> - "I have to ensure the work has been processed in a way that's going to meet our targets set by the Secretary of State, and I have to make sure we deal with things promptly and in a courteous and polite manner."
> - "If they've got rights it's my responsibility to make sure they get everything that they're entitled to, that it's right and it's on time."
> - "We all have the right to be treated with respect."
> - "Everyone's got the right to be treated with respect.... Sometimes it can be extremely difficult."

Once again, it would not be fair to paint a negative image of benefits administrators nor to imply they were entirely hardened and uncaring. The point that Lipsky (1980) had sought to underline is that street-level bureaucrats adapt to survive: they have to be pragmatic. This was touchingly illustrated by one benefits administrator who defended the distinction on which she relied – that is, between the moral rights in which she personally believed and the blackletter rights with which people must in practice be satisfied – in the following terms:

> Definitely there are [other rights]. To be loved. You can't have that written in your – by government can you? To be cared for. Again, I mean in a *loving* way, not just by the state.... I don't think the government can dot every 'i' and cross every 't', so no, I think there are a lot that we can look at as a right throughout our lives.... We should have rights to shelter, but even that, you know, in this country, we don't. Otherwise we wouldn't have homeless people would we?... We've sold most of those [local authority houses] haven't we? So, erm – ideal worlds are wonderful, but they're not practical.

In the course of their working lives, benefits administrators have to deal with a process and its rules, and to do so under circumstances that make it difficult to conceptualise these in terms of citizenship and its rights.

Ambivalent messengers

Although the benefits administrators we spoke to had all volunteered to be interviewed, some of them (initially at least) were quite reticent in the course of their interviews and appeared to be torn between an allegiance to the departmental 'party line' and their personal reservations and opinions. Certain of the administrators insisted that some of their remarks were off-the-record (and we have respected this wish).

On the basis of on-the-record remarks, however, it is possible to say that benefits administrators tended, on the whole, to be at least partly sceptical of the neoliberal elements of New Labour's 'third way' agenda, but to be divided between those whose loyalty would lie with a redistributive social democratic state and those who would support the more communitarian and/or socially conservative elements of the 'third way' agenda. We have already touched above on the benefits administrators' attitudes to the welfare state and some of their frustrations and fears for the future and observed that these were not so very different from those of our core sample. However, one of the features consistently to emerge from a thorough rereading of the transcripts was a certain tension – even on the part of the benefits administrators who broadly supported the 'third way' agenda – between their knowledge and understanding of the benefits system and the expectation that they should be 'on message' so far as the New Labour project is concerned. Thus, one benefits administrator, who fully supported New Labour's welfare-to-work policies, still sought to distance himself from the political rhetoric of certain politicians:

> *They* [the public] think *we* think like that. We don't. We buy the same newspapers, we watch the same TV programmes and what have you. Our influences are exactly the same – slightly different, working from the inside out – but we all know too that that could so easily be me sitting there [in the benefits office waiting room].

On the welfare-to-work issue, a majority of the benefits administrators to whom we spoke – once they had been persuaded to step out of their role as departmental ambassadors – were prepared to dissent from government policy. They felt upon reflection that government policies intended to channel disabled people, lone parents, and people with complex problems into employment were simply going too far (Box 6.8).

Box 6.8: Benefits administrators' scepticism about 'welfare-to-work'

- "I think we're doing a good thing encouraging [disabled people] to work. But you've got to accept that not everybody can and I think we're in danger of not being specific enough looking at individual cases ... they're pushing it through without stopping to think."
- "Not every single parent should work. This government considers they should. They are not all capable of it. Some people are stretched to their limit caring for a child and doing a good job in the end."
- "It's taking the people that haven't got the abilities or the inclination and it is putting them more into the poverty trap."

> - "I think there are limits ... there are people that employers wouldn't want to employ at the end of the day. And there are people whose situations health-wise or other mean they can't work."
> - "I don't think that being prescriptive about it is necessarily the best thing for society as a whole. I think it is down to the individual, and I don't think people ought to be forced into poorly paid jobs ... I suppose from my point of view I would say that if I was unemployed I would take on any job, but as I say, that's based on my own sort of values and beliefs, I wouldn't say that that's right for everybody."
> - "You can lead a horse to water but you can't make it drink, and I think the government would like us to make 'em drink."
> - "I don't like the idea that there's a sort of unsaid subtext – you know, of 'let's get them scroungers back to work' ... it's too all sweeping."

On wider issues, however, the picture that emerged was less clear-cut. Insofar that there was scepticism about the policies the benefits administrators were required to implement, this tended to stem from one or a combination of two sources. The first related to the benefits administrators' commitment to a form of public service ethos. The other related to the evidence of the longer-serving administrators' experience.

One benefits administrator spoke of her work as "the job that I love". Another explained the commitment of benefits administrators in these terms:

> There's always these people spouting off – these ministers and Heads ... about targets and stuff, but when it comes down to it, it's the people in here [the benefits office] working through their dinner breaks ... and we are on a pittance compared to outside bodies for what we are required to do.... People put so much effort in.... They rely totally on that, just like they rely on the nurses, they rely on the firemen, they rely on the police, they rely on everybody to do their job well and to have pride in their job.

Others complained that new managerial practices were undermining this public service ethos not only because of poor pay, inadequate IT systems and increasing workloads, but because of "amateurs doing professional jobs", and inexperienced staff being pressed into roles for which they are not properly prepared. Our findings tend to confirm that intensification of workloads can threaten the morale of benefits administrators and their commitment to reform (see Foster and Hoggett, 1999).

Several of the administrators with extensive experience would pessimistically recount the similarities between policies that were being tried now and those that had been attempted in the past, or else they would explain just how complex the benefit system is, how intractable are the problems that it faces, and how difficult it is in the short term to effect anything other than relatively superficial changes (Box 6.9).

Box 6.9: Benefits administrators' pessimism about welfare reform

- "I'm not sure that [the system] will change *radically*, because most of the things that they're introducing now are actually things that have been done before and worked quite well. But they were seen as cost-cutting exercises then and now they're being brought back in as the answer. For some of us who have been here a bit longer would say – you know people are saying 'well this is a good idea' – and we say 'yeah, well it was when we did it before'.... Silly things that they *say* are radical, like wearing name badges all the time ... I don't need to wear this all the time: that's not radical, it's stupid."
- "We try and get people off the books and to get back to work. They appeal and nine times out of ten they go back on benefit."
- "The new Jobseeker's [Allowance] ... will help towards employment those who are able ... and for a tiny minority that are too idle to get a job ... it won't make a scrap of difference. They'll still not get a job."

The ideological substance of 'third way' social security policies does not appear to have in any way politicised the benefits administrators who are charged with implementing such policies since, as street-level bureaucrats, they must continue to pursue the practical preoccupations and pragmatic priorities dictated by the need to survive in their jobs.

Conclusion

The street-level bureaucrat is in one sense a citizen like any other, albeit that s/he has a particular part to play in the implementation of policy. In the case of benefits administrators our evidence suggests that their particular discourse tends:

- to harbour a distinction between the kinds of dependency that characterise their own lives and the particular form of dependency that constitutes the benefit claimant. While the dependency of some or most claimants is acceptable, it remains problematic because of the 'otherness' of a minority of claimants whose dependency cannot be excused or cannot be understood;
- to be especially individualistic in its understanding of responsibility, since responsibility is for the benefits administrator's purposes primarily defined by rules and through compliance with rules, rather than by a concept of citizenship;
- to prioritise a 'blackletter' conception of rights, which tends to regard the rights of benefits claimants more as a constraint on the conduct of administrators than as the purpose of the process to be administered;

- pragmatically to resist key ideological premises of the 'third way', which if it is not construed as inimical to the public service ethos and/or the traditions of the welfare state, is seen as in some respects impractical or unrealistic.

At one level, this does not augur well for the development of a human rights approach to welfare. The nature of the street-level bureaucrat's discursive strategy is not one that can easily translate a street-level awareness of dependency into an ethical commitment to substantive rights. Additionally, it does appear that benefits administrators may have taken to heart the narrowly procedural rights and responsibilities discourse of their *Customer Charter*. At another level, however, it is clear that benefits administrators are not by any means ideologically committed, for example, to the idea that responsibilities in relation to substantive labour market activity must necessarily precede rights to substantive welfare assistance. What benefits administrators can contribute is pragmatism and experience, and this must have a part to play if we are in time to re-conceptualise the relationship between dependency, responsibility and rights.

References

Blackman, T. and Palmer, A. (1999) 'Continuity or modernisation? The emergence of New Labour's welfare state', in H. Dean and R. Woods (eds) *Social Policy Review 11*, Luton: Social Policy Association.

Cabinet Office (1999) *Modernising government*, Cm 4310, London: The Stationery Office.

Clarke, J. and Newman, J. (1997) *The managerial state*, London: Sage Publications.

Dean, H. (1991) *Social security and social control*, London: Routledge.

Dean, H. (2002) *Welfare rights and social policy*, Harlow: Prentice Hall.

DSS (Department of Social Security) (1998) *New ambitions for our country: A new contract for welfare*, Cm 3805, London: The Stationery Office.

DSS (1999) *The Benefits Agency Customer Charter*, Leeds: Benefits Agency.

DWP (Department for Work and Pensions) (2002a) *The Pension Service Customer Charter*, Leeds: The Pension Service.

DWP (2002b) *The Disability and Carers Service Customer Charter*, Blackpool: Disability and Carers Service.

Foster, D. and Hoggett, P. (1999) 'Change in the Benefits Agency: empowering the exhausted worker?', *Work, Employment and Society*, vol 13, no 1, pp 19-39.

Hill, M. (ed) (1997) *The policy process in the modern state* (3rd edn), Hemel Hempstead: Prentice Hall/Harvester Wheatsheaf.

Howe, L. (1985) 'The "deserving" and the "undeserving": practice in an urban local social security office', *Journal of Social Policy*, vol 14, no 1, pp 49-72.

Lawson, R. and Taylor-Gooby, P. (eds) (1993) *Markets and managers: New issues in the delivery of welfare*, Buckingham: Open University Press.

Lipsky, M. (1976) 'Towards a theory of street-level bureaucracy', in W. Hawley and M. Lipsky (eds) *Theoretical perspectives on urban politics*, Englewood Cliffs, NJ: Prentice Hall.

Lipsky, M. (1980) *Street-level bureaucracy: Dilemmas of the individual in public services*, New York, NY: Russell Sage Foundation.

Prime Minister's Office (1991) *The Citizen's Charter: Raising the standard*, Cm 1599, London: HMSO.

Prottas, J. (1979) *People processing: The street-level bureaucrat in public service bureaucracies*, Massachusetts: Lexington.

Wright, S. (2001) 'Activating the unemployed: the street-level implementation of UK policy', in J. Clasen (ed) *What future for social security? Debates and reforms in national and cross-national perspective*, The Hague: Kluwer Law International.

Wright, S. (2003) 'The street-level implementation of unemployment policy', in J. Millar (ed) *Understanding social security: Issues for social policy and practice*, Bristol: The Policy Press.

Part Three
Service user experiences

SEVEN

Agency, 'dependency' and welfare: beyond issues of claim and contribution?

Peter Dwyer

This chapter is concerned with the concepts of agency and dependency in relation to contemporary welfare reform. In order to explore such issues, it is divided into two main parts. The first begins by critically discussing 'third way' theory and its implications for future welfare provision. Notions of agency and dependency are central to such theorising and it is argued that the ways in which these ideas are used and constructed is flawed. The negative implications of a welfare philosophy that over-prioritises the 'active welfare subject' (Williams, 1999) while simultaneously understating the importance of continuing (and, in some cases, worsening) social divisions are also briefly discussed. The second part of the chapter draws on two recently completed qualitative studies (see Dwyer, 2000a, 2000b, 2001, 2002; Ackers and Dwyer, 2002) with different groups of welfare service users, and moves on to consider the ways in which users themselves seek to legitimise their own (and certain others') claims to public welfare, while at the same time justifying the exclusion of other individuals or groups from collective support.

In line with dominant 'third way' theorising, many users discriminate between what they see as 'welfare dependants' and 'active citizens' when making decisions about who deserves the right to public welfare. It is argued that this approach is deeply flawed for three reasons. The first reason is that the dichotomy between passive dependant and active citizen is false (Williams, 1999). Every one of us is welfare dependent in some way at some time (Titmuss, 1958; see also Chapters One and Two of this book), but some are more visible than others (Sinfield, 1978; Mann, 1992). The second reason is that this approach prioritises certain types of 'responsible' agency above others (see Chapter Three of this book). Thirdly, it fails adequately to acknowledge that a person's ability to act in an approved manner is highly dependent on the social and economic resources that they have at her/his disposal (Mann, 2001; Taylor-Gooby, 2001). Finally, in conclusion it is asserted that a society of 'positive welfare' (Giddens, 1998) will only become a reality when (or/if) two important elements are adequately acknowledged: first, the continuing significance of structural factors in enabling or constraining the ability of individuals to become active agents; and second, the importance of prioritising our collective *interdependence* when theorising welfare and enacting social policies in the future.

New times, new welfare?

Societies in Western Europe are undergoing a number of economic, political and social changes that have, potentially, profound implications for welfare states and the social rights of citizens (Taylor-Gooby, 1993, 2000; Giddens, 1994, 1998; Walters, 1997; Williams, 1999; Ellison, 2000; Mann, 2001; Wetherly, 2001). In recent years (most notably, but not exclusively, in the UK), there has been much talk of a new 'third way' politics, as advocated by Giddens (1994, 1998), and subsequently embraced with some enthusiasm by New Labour in Britain (Blair, 1995, 1998). A brief examination of the ideas and values that underpin the 'third way' for welfare will build upon Dean's outline (see Chapter One of this book) and provide a suitable starting point when considering the emergent 'new' welfare settlement. A central theme within such theorising is the assertion that welfare states and individuals will best meet the challenges they face only if future welfare policies primarily concentrate on ensuring individual agency.

'Third way' welfare

In *Beyond Left and Right*, Giddens (1994) asserts that the solidarity promised in the postwar welfare settlement (PWWS) has been eroded by two interlinked factors: first, the (perceived) inability of the state effectively to meet the welfare needs of its citizens; and second, the 'egoistic refusal' of the middle classes to continue playing their part in the welfare game. The increasing affluence of some sectors of society, accompanied by a reduction in the quality and quantity of state services, and the simultaneous expansion of alternative private provision, have encouraged middle class opt out from public welfare. After all, why would someone agree to contribute if they have little interest or need to claim?

The fact that state welfare promotes and sustains a welfare-dependent 'underclass' is, however, Giddens' greatest concern. Within his work there is stress upon the importance of both individual and group agency as a counterbalance to the dependency that he associates with *some* state-led programmes of welfare. Arguing that we must ditch the outdated, state-led, top-down approach to welfare, he believes that this will facilitate greater levels of individual autonomy and encourage a new 'positive welfare' in which individuals recognise their personal responsibilities both to themselves and wider society. However, this stress on political participation, of citizenship in its most active sense, coupled as it is with a rejection of a fundamental role for the state in the provision of welfare is not without its problems.

Although aware of the problem of solidarity within his theorising, Giddens (1994) maintains that the possibility of social renewal rests upon individual agents recognising the importance of obligations to others that are binding and authoritative. A centrally important question, however, remains unanswered: in a world of disparate views and needs, and the inevitable disagreement that ensues, which voices will endure and come to dominate? His approach appears to rest on the highly contentious view "that for the first time in history we can speak of the emergence of universal values" (Giddens, 1994, p 20). The twin problems of differential power and conflicting values remain unresolved and seriously weaken his analysis.

More recently, Giddens (1998) has revisited these themes. Once again, he outlines a new role for the 'social investment state' that will meet its future commitments to social justice and equality via the redistribution of 'possibilities' (primarily the opportunity to work and the right to education), rather than wealth. A government's role in relation to welfare is to encourage an "entrepreneurial culture" that rewards "responsible risk takers". Giddens (1998, pp 65-6) is also unequivocal in making a reciprocal relationship between rights and responsibilities central to his approach:

> One might suggest as a prime motto for the new politics, *no rights without responsibilities*.... As an ethical principle 'no rights without responsibilities' must apply not only to welfare recipients, but to everyone ... because otherwise the precept can be held to apply only to the poor and needy as tends to be the case with the political right.

Although this declaration that the new rights–responsibilities rule must be evenly and universally applied is commendable, it fails to reflect reality. In relation to the social element of citizenship, it is almost exclusively the rights of the poor and needy that are being reduced while simultaneously the attendant responsibilities required to access those rights are being increased (Dwyer, 1998, 2000a, 2002).

A further, and perhaps more worrying, aspect of Giddens' theorising is the general lack of vision when considering 'welfare' and the 'problem' of dependency. Titmuss (1958) reminded us long ago that we are all welfare dependants to a certain extent. Giddens' analysis would perhaps have greater authority if he also considered the fiscal and occupational benefits available to the better off rather than (taking his cue from the New Right), concentrating solely on the more visible 'social welfare' element discussed by Titmuss (Mann, 1998). This narrow focus when discussing dependency has, as later discussions illustrate, profound implications for any subsequent theorising of agency and dependency among differentially sited welfare service users.

From 'welfare society' to 'active society'

While Giddens optimistically endorses welfare that prioritises *responsible* individual agency as a panacea for dependency, others are more sceptical about the current direction of welfare reform. Walters (1997) argues that the 'welfare society' of the past that promised, theoretically at least, a common citizenship status that guaranteed a universal minimum of welfare rights has today been superseded by the 'active society' in which increasingly individuals can only access social rights if they are willing to become workers in the paid labour market (PLM). Walters is not asserting a naive view that all was well in the past. He is aware of the 'false universalism' (Williams, 1992) of the PWWS and the fact that a person's participation and position in the highly stratified PLM has long been of central importance in defining the quality and extent of an individual's access to public provisions. His key point is that a fundamental shift has occurred. Although imperfect, the state defined people in the 'welfare society' of the past according to various categories with certain 'inactive' groups exempted from PLM participation, either because they were making what were recognised as socially valid contributions elsewhere (for example, women engaged in informal/familial care work) or because they had previously contributed (for example, retired senior citizens). Today, such assumptions are increasingly challenged. Whereas welfare society:

> ... imagined [as] a collective enterprise in which workers and non-workers make their respective contributions ... many of these assumptions about the specifically *social* obligations and consequent rights of the citizen no longer apply in the active society.... The active society makes us all workers. (Walters, 1997, pp 223-4; emphasis in original)

Activity in the PLM, therefore, is seen both as *the* badge of individual integrity and also the only way for governments to address poverty. In contrast, policies that seek merely to improve public welfare benefits are seen as entrenching welfare dependency. The state should equip those outside the PLM to embrace change, to actively manage the risks and challenges that confront them by providing education and (re)training as required. If necessary, reluctant individuals should be forced into activity by the application of benefit sanctions. Only those who 'take charge' of their own lives are deemed to be responsible 'active' citizens (Wetherly, 2001).

This is certainly an agenda that Giddens and New Labour have been keen to endorse and such ideas enjoy more extensive support. Increasingly, they inform policy across Europe (Lødemel and Trickey, 2000; van Oorschot, 2000) and in the US (Prideaux, 2001; Deacon, 2002). Also, when tracing three contrasting attempts to rework welfare in the face of contemporary social change (that is, the New Right, New Labour and new social and welfare movements), Williams (1999) notes that, while the three use various approaches and have different end results in mind, they are all looking to encourage and endorse the 'active welfare subject'. Such an approach obviously has its attractions and it would be too simplistic to see people as passive victims of circumstance and/or oppressive social structures. Nonetheless, as critics point out, it is not without its pitfalls. As Wetherly (2001) notes, on one level 'active society'/'active welfare' theories and policies are to be commended because they counter the negative image of welfare claimants as powerless victims. However, he then goes on to state that they are also inadequate because the risks that individuals confront are "structural in origin" (Wetherly, 2001, p 164). While 'third way' type welfare policies centred on equality of opportunity may help certain individuals to make more of themselves and may well be positive for some, they fail to engage in any meaningful way with the *structural* causes of unemployment and poverty. The 'active society' approach 'de-socialises' the causes of poverty and individualises the problem of unemployment. A clear example may be seen in Chapter Eight's account of the way the victims of structural unemployment are reconstituted as individual 'jobseekers'. Others who are reliant on public welfare benefits are seen as inactive dependants who passively rely on public handouts as a result of either idleness or bad management of the risks that confront them (Walters, 1997). They are seen, therefore, as lacking any legitimate claim to collective support. Where once ideas of social justice and legitimacy were used to endorse claims to public welfare, they are now often used to deny such claims (Bauman, 1998).

Agents in action: principles, moral judgements and meeting needs

The discussions here draw on two qualitative studies with different types of welfare users. In many ways, this chapter is motivated by nagging questions concerned with the theorisation of agency and dependency in current welfare debates and how different users, in different settings, made sense of such questions and also actually set about meeting their own needs. As Beresford (2001) points out, we are all welfare service users but in different ways, and we might therefore expect service user discourses to be no different than popular discourses discussed in Chapter Four of this book. However, routine visits to an NHS doctor or attending a state school are not the same as being a disabled person who is unable to control their personal care package, or living a hand-to-mouth existence on benefits. Certain users encounter "long-term regulatory, intimate and segregating contact with welfare services" which regularly result in them experiencing "stigma, discrimination, poverty and exclusion" (Beresford, 2001, p 507). Overall, the respondents in the first study (Dwyer, 2000a, 2002) were people at the sharp end of British public welfare provision who were often heavily reliant on social welfare benefits for their day-to-day survival (Box 7.1).

Box 7.1: Outline of study with British welfare users

Ten focus groups (FGs) were convened for the purposes of the study:

FG 1 Benefit claimants and a worker   (6 men, 3 women)
FG 2 Residents association   (1 man, 5 women)
FG 3 Disabled benefit claimants   (6 men, 2 women)
FG 4 Senior citizens   (4 men, 2 women)
FG 5 Lone parents   (1 man, 4 women)
FG 6 Local charity group   (3 men, 1 woman)
FG 7 Women benefit claimants   (8 women)
FG 8 Informal mosque group   (5 men)
FG 9 Asian JSA claimants   (10 men)
FG 10 Muslim/Pakistani women   (8 women)

Sixty-nine respondents took part in the research. Of these, 36 were men and 33 women, with ages ranging between 19 and 80 years of age. Forty-three of the respondents could best be described as white, 23 as Asian and a further three as African-Caribbean. Ten respondents were in work (five full-time and five part-time) and a further eight respondents were largely dependent on various retirement pensions for their upkeep. Fifty-nine of those involved were outside the paid labour market at the time of the study and 17 people (16 of whom were female) identified themselves as having caring responsibilities within a family. Those respondents without paid work (excepting the retired pensioners noted earlier) were reliant on a range of state benefits, which included Jobseeker's Allowance (JSA), various disability benefits, a war pension, and income support. The focus group interviews took place between March and October 1997 at various locations around central Bradford, Yorkshire, England (for further details see Dwyer, 2000a, appendix).

The second study (Dwyer, 2000b, 2001; Ackers and Dwyer, 2002) focused on retired nationals from six EU member states who had, at various times, migrated internationally within the EU. Generally, they were more affluent than the respondents in the first study and around a third had taken early retirement. Many had quite substantial occupational pensions and a good number who had no doubt benefited from various occupational and fiscal welfare arrangements were able to call upon considerable personal wealth and assets as and when required (Box 7.2).

Box 7.2: Outline of international retirement migration in the EU study

The research objectives of this study demanded a broad approach encapsulating the experiences of the range of international retirement migrants (post-retirement migrants, returning workers, and returning retirees) from across the EU. Locations were as follows:

- *Greece:* mainly Athens and the island of Corfu, with a small number from Macedonia in northern Greece;
- *Italy:* Trieste and the surrounding rural area; also around Lake Garda;
- *Portugal:* Lisbon and the municipalities of Sintra and Caiscais (historic resort areas south of Lisbon);
- *Sweden:* the whole country;
- *UK:* England and Wales;
- *Republic of Ireland:* Dublin and County Roscommon.

A purposive non-random, sampling technique was adopted and interviews were carried out during 1998/99. A total of 210 semi-structured qualitative interviews were held; 100 with post-retirement migrants living in host EU countries and 110 with returnees who were resident in their country of origin (see Ackers and Dwyer, 2002, appendix, for further details).

Although the two studies engaged with two essentially different groups of users, they did share some common ground. First, the overwhelming majority of respondents in both studies were located outside the PLM, but usually for very different reasons. Second, all the respondents, were in their own ways and in a variety of settings, actively trying to engage with various welfare institutions to maximise the satisfaction of their needs at any given time. The ways in which they did this, and also the ways in which they looked to legitimise their own claims, and the claims of others, to public welfare, are outlined later in this chapter. They are important because they help to illustrate many of the problems and limitations of the welfare reforms currently being mapped out.

Principles of welfare and inclusion/exclusion

As Taylor-Gooby (1998, p 39) states, "social justice is concerned with who ought to get what". The following discussion highlights the diverse and often contradictory ways (see Dean, 1998, 2000) in which respondents seek to resolve an issue at the heart of any notion of social justice; that is to say, the principles that underpin rights to access public welfare provisions. In the first study (Dwyer, 2000a, 2002), while the respondents did not categorically speak in terms of the principles that underpinned their views, analysis of the interviews revealed that they regularly made implicit references to three differing principles when justifying rights to welfare. Interpreting them in their context, I would categorise them as a *universal* principle, a *contributory* principle, and a *social assistance* principle. Let us take, as an example, discussions on a right to healthcare. Primarily, such a right was justified according to the first two principles of universalism and contribution. The former, as the following quotation illustrates, has at its core a universal right to treatment in which the needs of an individual override issues of past contribution (the names given to respondents are not their real names):

> I was brought up to believe that the Health Service should be a universal service ... available to those who require those services, not dependent on their income; it should be dependent upon need. (David, Benefit claimants focus group)

When invoking a contributory principle, users emphasised the previous payment of financial contributions and an understanding that in agreeing to fund collective health provision individuals then had a right to access such services. For example:

> I have worked all my life so I have paid in all my life. (Linda, Women claimants focus group)

A number of respondents approved of a social assistance principle and the application of a means test, with tapered and or exempted contributions, in certain areas of public health provision. For example:

> Sorry but I have to say this before I explode. I have to pay £5.50 for my prescriptions and I cannot afford to go to the dentist.... I don't mind having to pay but there should be a grading system and I think that £5.50 for somebody on £20,000 a year is all right but we as people who are on a minimum wage should pay something like £2.50.... We are not all on the same pay but they seem to think that everybody has to pay exactly the same, and it is wrong. (Millie, Residents focus group)

It should come as no surprise that users made regular references that reflect these three differing principles as much public welfare provision has been delivered according to such rules.

A central element of the research was also to explore the opinions of users on a fourth principle, the principle of *conditionality*. This approach, which explicitly links access to welfare rights and entitlement to compulsory duties or approved patterns of behaviour, is central to the active welfare reforms being mapped out. This principle was perhaps the most controversial of all with approval or disapproval among the respondents varying dependent upon the context and manner in which it was applied. However, even in a sample dominated by people who were reliant on social welfare benefits, a little over 50% supported linking rights to unemployment benefits to compulsory behavioural and/or work or training conditions. These respondents believed it was vital that people made a contribution in return for benefit. Were they unwilling to do so, benefit sanctions were deemed to be reasonable:

> There are a lot of people who don't work and I don't see why we who have worked all our lives, who have paid our dues ... why these young ones should not put their bit into community work. (Jane, Senior citizens focus group)

> There is nothing wrong with having to do something to get your money ...
> and if that means you have a kick up the behind from the state, then so be it.
> (Jarvid, Informal mosque group)

Throughout the study, this idea of individual contribution is the most prevalent principle used to justify the inclusion or exclusion of individuals from publicly provided welfare. It was particularly strong among those who endorsed a highly conditional and exclusive view of welfare citizenship. They believed that individuals who they deem to be unwilling, or in certain cases unable, to contribute to the common good should be denied access to welfare rights; the indolent because they will not contribute via paid work, and those beyond the nation's boundaries because they have not contributed. In short, these respondents are making essentially moral judgements about those who are passive dependants and those who are active agents.

The judgements noted earlier are not, of course, confined to the respondents in one study. They chime with the findings reported in Chapter Four of this book and, for example, with findings in the Netherlands by van Oorschot (2000), who points out that there appears to be a sort of hierarchy of legitimacy in the 'deservingness criteria' used by the public when appraising various demands for collective support from different individuals and groups. In rank order (from most deserving of support), this runs as follows:

1) senior citizens;
2) sick and disabled people;
3) families with children in need whose provider(s) are unemployed;
4) those on social assistance.

In relation to his Dutch survey van Oorschot (2000, p 43) concludes that:

> When confronted with somebody asking for their support the Dutch public
> is likely to ask first: Why are they needy?, Are you one of us?, and what have
> you done or can you do for us?

In asking such questions and asserting differing principles, the public, academics and politicians are defining the rules of inclusion and exclusion. These principles matter because how and where they are applied is often the decisive factor in the type of welfare system that develops. They are also central to decisions about why and how the welfare needs of certain groups are prioritised, while simultaneously others are inadequately recognised or ignored. As Mullard succinctly puts it, "they provide the limits to what's possible" (2002, p 562).

Social divisions, welfare agency and visibility

One of the primary concerns of those who extol the virtues of active welfare policies is to reduce 'welfare dependency' by encouraging individuals actively to help themselves to become, as we noted earlier, 'responsible risk takers' (Giddens, 1998). The emphasis on responsibility here is significant. In the new positive welfare society, it is not enough for a person to be actively engaged with the risks and choices that confront them. It is also necessary that any such actions are deemed to be socially acceptable. A consideration of various types of agency using examples drawn from the two qualitative studies cited illustrates that such judgements are rarely straightforward:

> Well, how can you be responsible on a low income? You have got to dodge and be a deviant to survive haven't you? [Laughs] I have been in the past to survive.... I mean there is deviants in all walks of life – look at your millionaires, your tax evaders. We just try it on to know that we can put food in the kids' mouths, put clothes on their backs. Personally, I would say with children, because I've had them and I've been there, my money would never stretch out from Monday to Monday, it would never ever stretch out so I was one of those that was deviant to survive. I'm not saying everybody is but a lot are. I would get a little job here, get a little job there, or do a bit of shoplifting. It's survival, isn't it? (Molly, Lone parents focus group)

Molly argues that some lone parents, including herself, have effectively been forced to behave in what many would view as an 'irresponsible' manner because of inadequate social benefits. Interestingly, she also draws a parallel with the tax evasion of the extremely wealthy, a type of irresponsible behaviour that is often judged to be less damaging than shoplifting or benefit fraud. It could also be argued that, although Molly is acting illegally, she is essentially acting in a responsible manner; as a lone mother she is using the means at her disposal in order to ensure that her children are fed and clothed. Whether we view Molly's behaviour as responsible or irresponsible depends upon the particular moral perspective we bring to bear in judging her behaviour. Nonetheless, she is an active welfare subject confronting and managing the welfare needs of her family (Dwyer, 2000a). Evidence from other studies suggests that many of those dependent upon inadequate social benefits perceive such behaviour to be both rational and/or morally acceptable given their day-to-day struggle to make ends meet (see Dean and Melrose, 1997; Dean, 1998, 2000).

Now consider the following examples taken from qualitative research exploring the international migratory movements of retired European citizens within the EU (Dwyer, 2000b, 2001; Ackers and Dwyer, 2002). Initially, many retired EU migrants were actively seeking to maximise their assets and the enjoyment of their later years by relocating in retirement:

> I'm better off here in with this pension I can manage twice as well as in France. (French man living in Corfu)

I wouldn't call us tax dodgers, but of course it's a great advantage. In the case of his pension I think we are paying 20% less. (Swedish woman living in France, referring to her husband's pension)

Putting together a package of welfare services that met what they considered to be their personal requirements and needs was also an important element in these respondents' migratory decisions and subsequent movements, both permanent and temporary. Many were resourceful in getting the best welfare deal for themselves:

One thing was my wife's health – her arthritis improved greatly because of the sun and the dry climate but it started getting worse again, and we realised we wouldn't be able to afford the proper treatment for it in Greece, so we had to re-establish ourselves with an address in England so we could then become recognised by the NHS. We went to live with my stepdaughter in Bristol. We wrote to everybody saying we are back, officially we are now English residents. (English returnee)

A number of Southern European respondents who were permanently resident in their country of origin at the time of interview were also keen to 'work the system' in order to continue to access what they perceive to be the better public healthcare provisions of their previous host country:

I have medical care here but officially I do not appear as a permanent resident in Greece. I haven't transferred my rights from Germany. My children live in Germany so officially I appear as living with them there. Sometimes I go and visit them for a couple of months.... When I return from Germany I get a document which entitles me to medical care here. I also have the IKA insurance but I don't use it. I go to Germany for my check-ups. I have been doing this for 13 years now.

Respondents were not averse to bending the rules if or when altered circumstances demanded such action. If detrimental changes to their medical or financial circumstances indicated that further movement would enable them to better meet their changed circumstances, respondents would pursue their goal single-mindedly. In the words of one respondent:

When you move abroad, you have to be curious and daring, but when it comes to returning to your home country you have to be very calculating and well organised. It's a kind of conflict I suppose. (Swedish returnee)

Respondents, generally, are creative in the way they go about managing their welfare in order to maximise its potential and secure the best deal for themselves. Some will become officially resident in a host country if it is in their best interests while others, who to all intents and purposes are resident in host countries, decline to formally declare residence and retain bank accounts and/ or property and assets in their country of origin, or elsewhere, if such arrangements best suit their needs. They are not averse to manipulating tax and residency regulations for their own benefit. While, to some extent, these migrants are operating in the 'shadows' of the law, the divide between benefit shopping/welfare tourism and 'reflexive'/'active' citizenship of the kind envisaged by Giddens (1994) would seem to be finely drawn.

How do the illustrative examples drawn from the two qualitative studies add to our understanding of active/'third way' type welfare policies and in particular the ways in which dependency and agency are theorised? The first point to note is that of a common dependency on public welfare in very different settings. This runs counter to assumptions that underpin 'third way' theories which view welfare dependency in very narrow terms; that is, as dependency on social welfare benefits. Second, many people are actively engaged in managing the risks that confront them. They are not passive spectators of formal rights and policies. Both Molly and the respondents in the migration study are all seeking to play the welfare game and attempting to maximise their well-being. Why then, if we are all dependent upon public welfare and we are all in a variety of ways actively trying to get the best deal for ourselves, are only certain types of welfare dependency and risk management considered to be irresponsible? The insights here of Titmuss (1958) and others (Sinfield, 1978; Rose, 1981; Mann, 1992, 1998, 2001) who have developed his 'social division of welfare' (SDW) thesis are relevant.

In his essay, 'The social division of welfare', Titmuss (1958) argues that the state has a duty to meet the varying needs of its citizens. This it attempts to do, not with a single approach, but rather through three parallel systems of welfare: 'social', 'fiscal' and 'occupational', each of which must be considered in any discussion of the welfare state. 'Social welfare' consists of the publicly provided funds and services (social security benefits, local authority housing, the NHS, personal social services, and so on) that are often the single focus of dispute when the welfare state is discussed. In addition, Titmuss emphasises the importance of 'fiscal welfare' (tax allowances and relief) and also 'occupational welfare' – the perks derived from advantageous employment in the labour market (pensions and fringe benefits such as cars, meals, private health schemes, and so on). The healthcare, education, social services and other wide-ranging and significant benefits that the welfare state provides help to meet the varying needs of many different individuals and groups. By redefining welfare in a wider context, Titmuss illustrates that differing welfare provisions, fully sanctioned by the state, are delivered to different groups within British society and that the middle classes gain substantially from the public welfare in the wider sense.

By focusing their attention almost exclusively on Titmuss' 'social' component, it has been easy for certain politicians and commentators to set a narrow agenda when debating welfare (Mann, 1998). This agenda, which concentrates on both the pressing need to reduce the social security budget and the necessity to control and re-moralise members of a welfare dependent and deviant 'underclass', is a central feature of active/'third way' type theories. Shifts in welfare policy noted by Taylor-Gooby (1993, p 467) are now essential components of the new welfare settlement:

> If the trend in relation to mass welfare provision in areas such as health, social care, and pensions is greater selectivity coupled with shifts in the welfare mix in the direction of a pluralism in service delivery, policy for the new poor has moved in the reverse direction. The keynote here has been a strengthening of the apparatus designed to control the behaviour of people of working age who are marginal to the labour market.

Organisational changes in the delivery of public welfare and the emergence of the selective application of a principle of conditionality have undermined any previous notion of common citizenship that the SDW thesis implied. Against this backdrop, it becomes easier for those who already enjoy substantial, but relatively concealed, benefits from social (the public healthcare and education sectors), occupational and fiscal welfare to denounce those with the most visible claims (that is, those who rely on social welfare benefits) as passive welfare dependants. Thus:

> Inequality in the visibility of benefits is an important and integral part of the social division of welfare. The hierarchy of benefits moreover is clearly considerable providing very different amounts, under a wide range of conditions that may reinforce or strip the recipients of their status. (Sinfield, 1978, pp 136-7)

'Third way' welfare policies fail adequately to theorise welfare dependency and individual responsibility. The dependency of the majority enjoying the benefits of occupational and fiscal welfare, "which they have done nothing to earn" (Goodin, 2000, p 13), is basically ignored. The dependency of a minority reliant on meagre social welfare benefits is used to castigate claimants as irresponsible and undeserving of support presumably because they will not help themselves by engaging in the PLM. Such approaches, that legitimise certain claims to welfare by prioritising crude ideas of claim and contribution and moralistic ideas of individual agency and responsibility, are flawed.

Vincent (1996) reminds us that rich and poor are actively engaged in managing their risks, but that wealthy citizens are more effective in ensuring they get what they want due to the advantages they have accrued in the past. It is not just the retired EU migrants noted above who exploit a lack of visibility and/or their assets and the ability to relocate to maximise the benefits that public welfare may offer. The promotion of themes like opportunity and choice, central to ongoing welfare reforms, reaffirm more generally the advantage of more affluent citizens who use their economic and social capital to relocate to areas with the best schools, childcare, and healthcare facilities. It is unlikely

that those involved will be denounced as irresponsible, despite the fact that their active agency, their exercising of choice, compounds the marginalisation of "worst off citizens [who are] left in districts with the worst public services, as well as highest rates of crime, drug use, violence and other social problems" (Jordan, 2001, p 529). Against this backdrop of increased marginalisation and the 'enforcement ethos' of various 'new deals', those at the sharp end of public welfare are active themselves in using a variety of methods, including claiming social security while working, to ensure that their needs are met (Jordan, 2001). The key question is, 'Who are the responsible, reflexive citizens, and who are the calculating, irresponsible, self-interested welfare dependants?'

Across Europe, less universal and more conditional and selective welfare arrangements are being put in place (van Oorschot, 2000) and it is increasingly difficult for individuals and groups to have their claims to welfare recognised as deserving of public support. Contemporary academics, politicians and users alike all make judgements about who has, or does not have, a legitimate claim to public welfare and why one claim is more deserving than another. As active/ 'third way' welfare starts to dominate, principles of need and entitlement become marginal and notions of desert and individual responsibility start to dictate our deliberations. Such ideas are poorly suited to the development of systems of public welfare that will best meet the needs of marginalised and disadvantaged groups. In reality, who gets what from the welfare state, and when and how they get it, has little to do with personal responsibility and dessert. If necessary, people will mobilise various 'deservingness criteria' (van Oorschot, 2001) to make or validate a claim for public welfare services or benefits even though they may in the past have previously spent a lot of time and energy trying to minimise their contributions to collective welfare (White, 2000). It is often the most skilful operators, rather than the most deserving claimants, who operate most successfully within the maze of rights, rules and administrative discretion (Adler, 1997) that make up contemporary welfare states.

A more sophisticated understanding of agency is required than the one offered by Giddens and 'third way' supporters. As people are confronted with the realities of social change and the risks that it entails they are willing to take chances. They will consider certain actions on the boundaries of formal legality as legitimate because they offer the best way for them to meet their needs within a real situation. As Vobruba (2000, pp 608-11) notes:

> With the widening gap between institutionalised normality and real living conditions some kinds of life chances emerge that might be illegal but are seen as legitimate by the people in question ... thus people's strategies for coming to terms with reality collide with official offers of inclusion.

Empirical evidence suggests that the majority of those of working age who are reliant on social benefits are as keen as the rest of the population to engage with the PLM and thus meet their wider responsibilities (Bryson, 1997; Dean, 1998, 2000; Dwyer, 2000a). Similarly, Chapter Nine of this book argues that a lack of required council tax payments was indicative of people trying to cope with poverty rather than a deficit of citizen responsibility. In their own ways and from different positions within our highly stratified and unequal societies, everybody (with varying degrees of success) is trying to secure the best welfare deal for themselves. Recent social, political and economic changes mean that most citizens are effectively pursuing either 'proactive' or 'defensive' strategies in relation to their welfare needs at any one time. These are two different types of activity:

> The distinction lies between those whose power location creates an 'ability' to intervene in ways that can transform their position in a particular area of the public sphere, and those lacking access to relevant power networks who find themselves engaged in efforts … simply to preserve existing interests and entitlements. (Ellison, 2000, para 1.4)

As Taylor-Gooby (2000, 2001) notes, 'risk' is differentially experienced by different social groups in contemporary society. Active/'third way' welfare works to the advantage of more privileged citizens and to the detriment of vulnerable groups. Social/economic divisions still matter in relation to welfare risks and an individual's ability to manage them.

Conclusion: positive ways forward

It is not the intention of this chapter to criticise or condemn the various tactics used by different groups of welfare service users to ensure that their needs are met. We are all dependent on public welfare systems at various times throughout our lives. It is important that we assert more sophisticated understandings of agency and welfare dependency than those currently in vogue. As theorists concerned with the SDW point out, narrow conceptions of social rights/ responsibilities and dependency are wrong. Furthermore, the simplistic dichotomy between two ideal types – the independent, responsible, active, (full-time) paid worker and the irresponsible, passive, welfare dependant who do not engage with the PLM – at the heart of many current welfare reforms fails to recognise the more complex social reality in two ways. First, it ignores the extent to which a functioning market economy and formal public welfare systems depend upon gendered, informal welfare for their continued successful operation. Second, the dichotomy ignores the extent to which many so-called dependants assume such burdens of informal care yet remain unrecognised and undervalued (Rose, 1981; Lister, 1997; 1990). Active/'third way' theories, which dominate contemporary welfare reforms, are built around the principle of highly conditional social welfare rights and limited notions of socially valuable contribution and agency. They lead us towards exclusive and coercive welfare systems in the future. It is important to recognise the limited potential of such approaches for meeting the needs of marginalised social groups (see Dean, 2000; Taylor-Gooby, 2000). Welfare-to-work policies, so often identified as being of central importance, appear better at meeting the requirements of industry and capital rather than poor citizens (Peck, 2001; Prideaux, 2001).

Given the serious shortcomings of active/'third way' welfare outlined in this chapter, how then do we move forward positively in relation to welfare reform? Clearly, it would be as wrong to view the PWWS as a golden age to be recaptured. Social change and the well-documented shortcomings of past policies make such an aim undesirable and inappropriate. Today, welfare dependency is narrowly defined by many as a stigmatising signal of individual failure (Batsleer and Humphries, 2000). This view needs to be countered. Simplistic debates that contrast dependence and independence are flawed: we are all socially interdependent. Our very sense of self, who we are, is constructed over time through our links and relationships with other human beings. We all exercise choice and agency in relation to welfare against the backdrop of the complex and changing welfare institutions. These may provide both opportunities and constraints to particular groups at different times (Twine, 1994).

It has been suggested that in the UK, New Labour's 'third way' has seen the introduction of a range of policies some of which "attempt to level the playing field and some of which are designed to activate the player" (Deacon, 2002, p 117). Supporters of 'third way' welfare such as Deacon, however, also recognise that in spite of recent significant commitments to fund healthcare and education through increased National Insurance contributions (see Taylor-Gooby et al, 2002, for details), not enough emphasis has been placed on tackling existing, unacceptable material inequalities. Greater levels of economic redistribution in favour of poor citizens must be a central feature of future welfare policy, because as Twine (1994, p 12) notes, "redistributing resources also redistributes freedom and choice". The promotion of policies that prioritise the notion of *interdependence* also need to be to the fore, not least as a counter to the fallacy of the celebrated, independent, self-reliant citizen. As Williams (1999, p 667) states:

> We need to recognise that we are all *necessarily* dependent on others, but at the same time challenge the institutions, structures and social relations which render some groups *unnecessarily* dependent.

This may be hard for some people to accept because it means we are faced with the reality that our progress, or elevated social status, is often achieved with the help, or at the expense, of others. It may well be time to prioritise values such as need and interdependence when theorising welfare. Positive welfare will only become a future reality if academics, politicians and users adequately acknowledge that the best starting point for meeting the diversity of needs that exist in modern societies is recognition of 'our common humanity' (Harris, 2002).

References

Ackers, L. and Dwyer, P. (2002) *Senior citizenship? Retirement, migration and welfare in the European Union*, Bristol: The Policy Press.

Adler, M. (1997) *Welfare rights, rules and discretion: All for one or one for all*, Edinburgh: New Waverley Paper SP 12, Department of Social Policy, University of Edinburgh.

Batsleer, J. and Humphries, B. (2000) 'Welfare, exclusion and political agency', in J. Batsleer and B. Humphries (eds) *Welfare, exclusion and political agency*, London: Routledge.

Bauman, Z. (1998) *Work, consumerism and the new poor*, Buckingham: Open University Press.

Beresford, P. (2001) 'Service users, social policy and the future of welfare', *Critical Social Policy*, vol 21, no 4, pp 495-512.

Blair, T. (1998) *The third way: New politics for a new century*, Fabian Society Pamphlet no 588, London: The Fabian Society.

Blair, T. (1995) *Let us face the future: The 1945 anniversary lecture*, London: The Fabian Society.

Bryson C. (1997) 'Benefit claimants: villains or victims?', in R. Jowell et al (eds) *British social attitude: The 14th report. The end of Conservative values?*, Aldershot: Ashgate/Social and Community Planning Research.

Deacon, A. (2002) *Perspectives on welfare: Ideas, ideologies and policy debates*, Buckingham: Open University Press.

Dean, H. (2000) 'Managing risk by controlling behaviour: social security administration and the erosion of citizenship', in P. Taylor-Gooby (ed) *Risk, trust and welfare*, Basingstoke: Palgrave/Macmillan.

Dean, H. (1998) 'Benefit fraud and citizenship', in P. Taylor-Gooby (ed) *Choice and public policy: The limits to welfare markets*, Basingstoke: Macmillan.

Dean, H. and Melrose, M. (1997) 'Managing discord: fraud and resistance in the social security system', *Social Policy and Administration*, vol 31, no 2, pp 103-18.

Dwyer, P. (1998) 'Conditional citizens? Welfare rights and responsibilities in the late 1990s', *Critical Social Policy*, vol 18, no 4, pp 519-43.

Dwyer, P. (2000a) *Welfare rights and responsibilities: Contesting social citizenship*, Bristol: The Policy Press.

Dwyer, P. (2000b) 'Movements to some purpose? An exploration of international retirement migration in the European Union', *Education and Ageing*, vol 15, no 3, pp 253-77.

Dwyer, P. (2001) 'Retired EU migrants, healthcare rights and European social citizenship', *Journal of Social Welfare and Family Law*, vol 23, no 3, pp 311-27.

Dwyer, P. (2002) 'Making sense of social citizenship: some user views on welfare rights and responsibilities', *Critical Social Policy*, vol 22, no 2, pp 273-99.

Ellison, N. (2000) 'Proactive and defensive engagement: social citizenship in a changing public sphere', *Sociological Research Online*, vol 5, no 3 (www.socresonline.org.uk/5/3/ellison.html 22/7/02).

Faulks, K. (2000) *Citizenship*, London: Routledge.

Giddens, A. (1994) *Beyond left and right: The future of radical politics*, Cambridge: Polity Press.

Giddens, A. (1998) *The third way: The renewal of social democracy*, Cambridge: Polity Press.

Goodin, R.E. (2000) 'Principles of welfare reform: the OECD experience', Paper presented to a conference 'Welfare Reform', Melbourne Institute, November.

Harris, P. (2002) 'Welfare rewritten: change and interlay in social and economic accounts', *Journal of Social Policy*, vol 31, no 3, pp 377-98.

Jordan, B. (2001) 'Tough love: social work, social exclusion and the Third Way', *British Journal of Social Work*, vol 31, pp 527-46.

Lister, R. (1990) 'Women, economic dependency and citizenship', *Journal of Social Policy*, vol 19, no 4, pp 445-67.

Lister, R. (1997) *Citizenship: Feminist perspectives*, Basingstoke: Macmillan.

Lødemel, I. and Trickey, H. (2000) *'An offer you can't refuse'. Workfare in international perspective*, Bristol: The Policy Press.

Mann, K. (2001) *Approaching retirement: Social divisions, welfare and exclusion*, Bristol: The Policy Press.

Mann, K. (1998) 'Lamppost modernism: traditional and critical social policy?' *Critical Social Policy*, vol 18, no 1, pp 77-102.

Mann, K. (1992) *The making of an English 'underclass'*, Buckingham: Open University Press.

Mullard, M. (2002) Book review of R.F. Drake, 'The principles of social policy', *Journal of Social Policy*, vol 31, no 3, p 562.

Orton, M. (2002) 'Why do people have council tax debts? – Citizenship, responsibility and poverty', Paper presented to the annual conference of the Social Policy Association, University of Teeside, Middlesborough, July.

Peck, J. (2001) 'Job Alert! Shifts, spins and statistics in welfare to work policy', *Benefits*, Issue 30, pp 11-15.

Prideaux, S. (2001) 'New Labour, old functionalism? The underlying contradictions of welfare reform in the UK and the US', *Social Policy and Administration*, vol 35, no 1, pp 85-115.

Rose, H. (1981) 'Rereading Titmuss: the sexual division of welfare', *Journal of Social Policy*, vol 10, no 4, pp 477-502.

Sinfield, A. (1978) 'Analyses in the social division of welfare', *Journal of Social Policy*, vol 7, no 2, pp 129-56.

Taylor-Gooby, P. (1993) 'Citizenship, dependency and the welfare mix: problems of inclusion and exclusion', *International Journal of Health Services*, vol 23, no 3, pp 455-74.

Taylor-Gooby, P. (1998) 'Equality, rights and social justice', in P. Alcock, A. Erskine and M. May (eds) *The student's companion to social policy*, Oxford: Blackwell/SPA.

Taylor-Gooby, P. (2000) 'Risk and welfare', in P. Taylor-Gooby (ed) *Risk, trust and welfare*, Basingstoke: Palgrave/Macmillan.

Taylor-Gooby, P. (2001) 'Risk, contingency and the Third Way: evidence from the BHPS and qualitative studies', *Social Policy and Administration*, vol 35, no 2, pp 195-211.

Taylor-Gooby, P., Hastie, C. and Bromley, C. (2002) 'New Labour = new taxes + world class NHS – do voters approve?', Paper presented to the annual conference of the Social Policy Association, University of Teeside, Middlesborough, July.

Titmuss, R.M. (1958) 'The social division of welfare', in R.M. Titmuss, *Essays on the welfare state*, London: Allen and Unwin.

Twine, F. (1994) *Citizenship and social rights: The interdependence of self and society*, London: Sage Publications.

van Oorschot, W. (2000) 'Who should get what and why? On deservingness and the conditionality of solidarity among the public', *Policy & Politics*, vol 28, no 1, pp 33-48.

Vincent, D. (1996) *Poor citizens: The state and the poor in 20th century Britain*, London: Longman.

Vobruba, G. (2000) 'Actors in processes of inclusion and exclusion: towards a dynamic approach', *Social Policy and Administration*, vol 34, no 5, pp 601-13.

Walters, W. (1997) 'The active society: new designs for social policy', *Policy & Politics*, vol 25, no 3, pp 221-34.

Wetherly, P. (2001) 'The reform of welfare and the way we live now: a critique of Giddens and the Third Way', *Contemporary Politics*, vol 7, no 2, pp 149-70.

White, S. (2000) 'Review article: social rights and social contract – political theory and the new welfare politics', *British Journal of Political Science*, no 30, pp 507-32.

Williams, F. (1999) 'Good enough principles for welfare', *Journal of Social Policy*, vol 28, no 4, pp 667-88.

Williams, F. (1992) 'Somewhere over the rainbow: universalism and diversity in social policy', in N. Manning and R. Page (eds) *Social Policy Review 4*, Canterbury: Social Policy Association.

EIGHT

Ethical techniques of the self and the 'good jobseeker'

Ruth Rogers

Introduction

Chapter Three of this book has already discussed the different ways in which governmental press releases may 'constitute' the citizen. In Chapter Six, I have with Hartley Dean already discussed how the information and knowledge of benefits administrators affords them the ability, in certain ways, to transform or 'reconstitute' the social security claimant. One of the time-honoured ways in which benefits claimants have been understood and managed has been by partitioning them between deserving and undeserving cases. Through a textual analysis of two British government documents, this chapter looks at how governmental discourse both addresses and manages two different types of unemployed person or 'jobseeker' (here referred to as the 'good jobseeker' and the 'deviant jobseeker'). It is argued that although governmental discourse about unemployment requires jobseekers to abide by the strict market ethic of employability, flexibility and continuous learning, they are afforded only limited rights. This chapter briefly outlines the current political context surrounding unemployment policy in Britain and the theoretical background to the analysis, and then offers a commentary upon the two documents.

Choice of documents

The two documents chosen for analysis are *The job kit: Your job search guide* (DfEE, 1998a) and *Job hunting: A guide for managers, executives, professionals, new graduates* (DfEE, 1998b). Both of these documents are, in theory, readily available to jobseekers and are concerned to offer help and advice with job seeking, such as how to write a curriculum vitae (CV) and covering letter, and how to perform at an interview. Both documents are relatively lengthy A4 booklets (approximately 70 and 50 pages respectively), with a fairly 'glossy' presentation.

One of the primary distinctions between *Job hunting* and *The job kit* is the fact that they are directed at a very different reader. For example, *Job hunting* assumes a far higher level of competency from its readers, and also affords them a far greater degree of autonomy in managing their own time. Furthermore, the document assumes that its readers are to a large extent already in control of their status and need only basic advice and information. This contrasts sharply with the various modes of governance found within *The job kit*, which acts as a strong disciplinary mechanism. Here, the implication is that the target readers are potentially hostile or 'deviant', with few employment skills, little experience, and as such, are in far greater need of guidance and direction. Consequently, they are afforded far less freedom and autonomy in terms of how they manage their time and conduct their job-seeking duties.

Significantly, despite these differing degrees of autonomy afforded to the different types of reader, both types, nonetheless, are encouraged to be equally enterprising and professional in their *approach* to job seeking. This translates into a clear discrepancy between the various rights and responsibilities of the readers. Although they have the same responsibilities to market themselves, find employment and adopt certain ethical values, they are not afforded the same rights. It is for this reason that *The job kit* will be the main focus of this chapter, while *Job hunting* will be considered primarily for comparative purposes.

Earlier versions of the documents had first been published in 1995 and changed only incrementally following the election of a New Labour government. Nonetheless, the context in which the documents could be promoted and interpreted clearly changed as New Labour developed its distinctive welfare-to-work approach. Although the government department originally responsible for the document has since merged with another, to create the Department for Work and Pensions (DWP), the advice published for jobseekers, for example through the DWP's website, appears to be substantially, if not exactly, the same.

Political context – significance of the Jobseeker's Allowance and New Deal

The introduction in 1996 under a Conservative government of the Jobseeker's Allowance (JSA) and, from 1997 onwards, of the New Labour government's various New Deal programmes, were intended on the one hand to reduce unemployment and, on the other, to achieve closer monitoring and policing of the unemployed. The effect constituted a general shift away from the preconceived notions of the welfare state and, especially under New Labour, this reflected a concern to alter the way in which unemployment and the role of social security is perceived; from unemployment as a way of life and social security as an alternative to employment, towards unemployment as a transitory period, in which benefit is provided as the final option and only for very brief spells between periods of employment. With this, the JSA and New Deal may be seen to epitomise a central shift within British social security discourse and a redefinition of the terms on which unemployment is to be experienced. It is not simply that unemployment has been subject to new forms of government; it is more that the notion of unemployment, as a problem (be it economic or social), has been redefined, such that the concern of government now is in many ways not unemployment per se, but 'employability'. Under New Labour's 'third way' (see, for example, Giddens, 1998; see also Chapter Seven of this book), the individualist notion of self-help has taken on new forms, in that the government's chief concern is not about creating new jobs by improving the functioning of the market, but increasing the employability of the workforce. Following this shift, the discourse of the 'jobseeker' now prescribes what a jobseeker should be, how s/he should perform and conduct her/himself. With this, the governance of unemployed people focuses not only on the employability of the workforce, but also on managing the conduct of jobseekers with regard to their appearance, behaviour and attitudes.

A key feature of this shift in the management of unemployment concerns the new demands placed on jobseekers to reconstruct their own identities based around notions of entrepreneurialism, in that all those capable of work are now obliged to reconstruct themselves in terms of the discourse of enterprise and marketability. This notion of 'enterprise' encompasses an "array of rules for the conduct of one's everyday existence" such as "energy, initiative, ambition, calculation and personal responsibility" (Rose, 1992, p 146) and is promoted through policy objectives and initiatives described in such key phrases as "fully flexible labour force", "framework for learning", "individual learning accounts", "lifelong learning", "knowledge driven economy", and "zero tolerance of underachievement" (Labour Party, 1997c, 1997d; Cabinet Office, 1999). It is argued that, in many ways, the act of job seeking has become 'professionalised'. The act is constituted almost as a 'job' in its own right, since 'good job seeking' requires individuals to be enterprising, flexible, and highly motivated, and to regard their job seeking with the same determination and rigour that one would a professional career. This chapter is concerned with the implications this has for both the construction and management of the 'jobseeker'.

Theoretical background

Ethics of the self

The theoretical basis behind my textual analysis of the documents owes much to Foucault's (1998) conception of governance and surveillance and his work on the technologies of self. It is concerned with the prescriptive codes of conduct found within the discourse of the documents, such as what sort of person a 'jobseeker' should be, how s/he should perform and conduct her/himself. Following Foucault, what is of interest here is the way in which these technologies of self serve to modify individuals, in that they require individuals not only to develop certain practical skills, but also to adopt certain 'attitudes' (Foucault, 1988, p 18).

For example, the two documents chosen for analysis both operate from within a confessional discourse, in that they emphasise the importance of evaluating and re-evaluating oneself in terms of performance, skills and flexibility (Foucault, 1979). The documents also make frequent reference to the role and importance of the CV, previously identified as "one of the great confessional texts of our age, matching the diary, the psychoanalytical session and the religious confession in significance" (Metcalfe, 1992, p 620; Miller and Morgan, 1993; Dean, 2003). Careers guidance publications have long claimed that "The first stage in job-hunting is 'know thyself'" (Roberts et al, 1989, p 2, cited in Metcalfe, 1992, p 627). This confessional mode of governance, stressing the importance on providing young people with the ability to identify their positive characteristics and to match their skills to a job, is seen as essential to the development of individuals' identities and in providing them with a positive self-image.

To illustrate further, Foucault has argued that there are three modes of governance (or 'techniques of regulation'). The first of these entails 'disciplinary techniques of objectification'. This is exercised through experts or professionals, who 'gaze' upon a 'passive' population, whose members are considered 'objects' of the discourse, referred to in the power–knowledge dichotomy as a technology of power. The second mode of governance is referred to as the 'disciplinary techniques of subjectification'. Although related to the first mode, it entails an extension through the confessional process, whereby experts or professionals now acquire a certain knowledge of the individuals concerned. Here, the subjected individuals begin to adopt the discourse, which they use to inform their own technology of self and with this, they become, not passive objects, but active '*subjects*' of the discourse. The third and final level entails 'ethical techniques of the self', whereby individuals, having made themselves an active subject of the discourse, can choose to do so without the use of the expert or professional. They can adopt or reject certain elements of the discourse and administer their own governance without the aid of an external power. For example, Foucault (1988, p 18) claimed that the "technologies of the self":

> permit individuals to effect by their own means or with the help of others a certain number of operations on their own bodies and souls, thoughts, conduct and way of being.

This distinction, however, between technologies of the self and technologies of power should not be overstated, as active subjects of the discourse always remain to some extent defined by technologies of power and can never be entirely divorced from governmental techniques in that, although the essential element to the techniques of the self is that the subject must regulate her/himself (Leonard, 1997, p 42), the existence of an external governing body will invariably remain (Foucault, 1988). Consequently, rather than focusing solely on the coercive and punitive measures intrinsic to this shift in policy, it is important to remember that the essential element to the techniques of the self as a mode of governance is that the targets are in charge of their own governance:

> Governance in this case is something we do to ourselves, not something done to us by those in power. (Cruikshank, 1996, p 235; see also Foucault, 1988; Rose, 1989; Burchell, 1996)

The 'implied reader' and the 'target reader'

One of the areas of interest in relation to the documents I discuss here is the relationship between what are referred to as the 'target reader' and the 'implied reader'. It may be argued that all texts articulate an 'implied reader', with whom the actual reader is invited to identify, and which to some extent predetermines how they respond to the text (Iser, 1974, p 34). Iser claims that within *any* given text it is possible to identify the narrator, the characters, the plot and the 'implied reader' and it is argued that both *The job kit* and *Job hunting* articulate an 'implied reader', referred to here as the 'good jobseeker'. This 'good jobseeker' is portrayed as being well organised, competent, hard working, adaptable, highly motivated: in short, professional or businesslike (DfEE, 1998a, 1998b). It is argued that one effect of this presentation of the 'good jobseeker' through the 'implied reader' is that the 'actual reader' is encouraged to identify and aspire to this and consequently, the number of possible responses the reader can make to the text are to some extent predetermined.

However, I argue that the 'target reader' of *The job kit* is an individual who actually possesses very few of these qualities. Furthermore, *The job kit* is not targeted at a generic jobseeker, but at the 'hostile' or 'deviant jobseeker', in that the text is specifically targeted at those jobseekers who are not 'enterprising', 'professional' or 'determined'. This distinction clearly highlights the ethical mechanism inherent in the relationship between text and reader, in that the implied reader comprises the source of ethical authority with which any actual reader who possesses these qualities is invited to identify, and to which any actual reader who does not possess these qualities is encouraged to aspire.

The texts

Job hunting

Throughout the text of *Job hunting*, which as its subtitle attests is expressly addressed to "managers, professionals, executives and new graduates", there is every indication that the target reader is an individual who is to a large extent in control of her/his employment status and appreciates the need to secure paid employment as soon as possible. The illustrations of the sorts of jobs the jobseeker may have had or may be looking for indicate that this jobseeker is skilled and experienced in her/his field and requires only light guidance and information. For example, the text gives examples of possible positions such as "senior purchasing executive" or "purchasing and materials manager" (DfEE, 1998b, p 17). The document also advises jobseekers what to do regarding any mortgage they may have or how to arrange a funding reassessment if they have a son or daughter studying at university (DfEE, 1998b, p 5). The document anticipates that unemployment may have come to the reader as "a shock", that the jobseeker may be "unused to the business of changing jobs", and that s/he may be on the employment market "through no choice of [her/his] own"

(DfEE, 1998b, p 4). The document then goes on to offer guidance and advice on how emotionally to deal with the prospect of unemployment, the indication being that the jobseeker has probably spent most of her/his working life in productive paid employment.

Significantly, within *Job hunting* jobseekers are by inference allowed the right to demand a certain level of salary and to reject certain jobs they may consider inappropriate. For example, jobseekers are invited to think "what level of responsibility [they are] aiming for?"; whether they are "more interested in personal performance or in administration, management or leadership?"; or whether they "want to practice a specialism, perhaps to act as a staff adviser or to be a manager with line responsibility?" (DfEE, 1998b, p 7). Similarly, when asked to reassess their job-seeking performance, the document asks jobseekers to think about how many job offers they have had and, where appropriate, what their reasons were for not accepting them (DfEE, 1998b, p 29). Also, when discussing the purpose of the job interview, the document claims that it is "your chance to find out more about the job", suggesting the jobseeker finds out "more about the product or service and its market and [discusses] training and career prospects within the organisation" (DfEE, 1998b, p 23).

The significance of this does not become clear until this level of autonomy is compared with that afforded the 'good jobseeker' articulated within *The job kit*, in that this jobseeker is not afforded *any* right to refuse employment, and the purpose of the interview is to convince the interviewer to give the jobseeker a job, rather than to assess the suitability of the position. Similarly, *Job hunting* explains the jobseeker should "Set aside time – every day, or every other day, and set targets of job leads to be followed up each day or week" (DfEE, 1998b, p 8), which contrasts sharply with the advice offered in *The job kit*, involving a far more complex and technical detailing of specific tasks the jobseeker should be active in, providing a list of set tasks for Monday through to Saturday. Thus, the reader of *Job hunting* is articulated as being largely in control of her/his own employability, as self-sufficient and as such is excused from much of the disciplinary discourse directed at the jobseeker through *The job kit*. However, although the target readers of the two documents are clearly distinct from one another, their articulated 'acceptable' modes of behaviour, attitudes to work and motivational skills are largely indistinguishable. Consequently, I would argue, the jobseeker is encouraged to aspire to a managerial (or what I would term 'professionalised') discourse of employability regardless of her/his class or occupational status, although this does not necessarily guarantee her/his entitlement to the same level of 'rights'. Just as managerialism is displacing bureau-professionalism in the realm of public service provision (Clarke and Newman, 1997), it is clear that managerial values of business-professionalism – good organisation, adaptability, hard work, conscientiousness, reliability, good communication – are valorised in the discourses directed to jobseekers.

The job kit

As I have indicated, in *The job kit* there is a distinction between the target reader and the implied reader: it is clear that, while the document implies a reader who is highly motivated and 'professional' in the way s/he approaches her/his job-seeking activities, there is every indication that the target reader is someone who is lacking in these skills and in need of "character improvement" (Blair, 1996). The examples given in *The job kit* of realistic attainable employment positions are predominantly from the low- or semi-skilled employment sector (including local shop work, child-minding, mothers' helps, gardening, catering assistant, machine worker; DfEE, 1998a, pp 10, 12, 23-4, 36), indicating that the target readership may have spent sizeable amounts of time involved predominantly in low-skilled, low-paid, often temporary and insecure employment. In addition to this, *The job kit* suggests that jobseekers could find employment vacancies by looking at advertisements in local shop windows (DfEE, 1998a, p 12). Thus, while the text articulates a 'good jobseeker' who is enterprising and professional, there is at the same time the suggestion that the actual 'target reader' is a jobseeker who is neither distinctively enterprising nor professional. The indication is that *The job kit* is not targeted at *all* jobseekers, but at those jobseekers who are considered to be failing in their job-seeking roles and who are less likely to find employment independently.

Second, the text employs a simplistic and often patronising language and style indicating its readership may be assumed to have a relatively limited level of educational attainment. This is amplified by the adoption of an extremely informal, often colloquial discourse, which affords the text a 'mentoring' quality that presupposes a lack of self-confidence and a limited knowledge of effective and efficient job seeking (Fairclough, 1992, p 204). The implication is that the reader is assumed to be in need of in-depth support and advice, and perhaps incapable of developing effective job-seeking skills independently. As well as directing attention towards those jobseekers who may be considered limited in employment skills and experience, *The job kit* also presupposes low self-esteem and limited knowledge on the part of its target readership in some of the basics of effective job seeking.

Cruikshank (1996, p 233) argues that attempts such as this to promote self-esteem constitute a new "mode of governing the self" and a "practical and productive technology available for the production of certain kinds of selves". This emerges directly from the confessional and disciplinary discourse, as it is argued that those who attempt to improve their self-esteem (or "undergo 'revolution from within'"), "are citizens doing the right thing; they join programmes, volunteer, but most importantly, work on and improve their self-image" (ibid). Self-esteem is "technology of citizenship and self-government for evaluating and acting upon ourselves so that the police, the guards and the doctors do not have to" (Cruikshank, 1996, p 234). Cruikshank also argues that self-esteem is a 'social goal' that enhances society in that the relationship we have to ourselves is directly related to responsible citizenship, which depends on 'personal and social responsibility'. Those who fail to link their "personal fulfilment to social reform are lumped together as social problems, are diagnosed as 'lacking self-esteem' and are charged with 'antisocial behaviour'" (Cruikshank, 1996, p 234). From this, a jobseeker without self-esteem is a jobseeker lacking the ability to manage her/his job-seeking activities efficiently. This adds weight to the two primary arguments. First, that the document specifically targets a 'deviant jobseeker', who is either relatively unskilled and inexperienced, unwilling to take the necessary steps to secure employment, or lacking appropriate self-esteem. Second, that there is a clear distinction between the target reader and the implied reader as it is essential to the structure of the text that the reader aspires to the identity of the 'good jobseeker', who is not only professional and enterprising, but also highly confident. This implied reader functions as the ethical mechanism that enables the text to prescribe the conduct of the 'actual' reader. This analysis now focuses more closely on the 'good jobseeker' and the ethical significance it has for the construction of the actual reader.

Definitions of a 'good jobseeker'

The job kit prescribes the conduct of the jobseeker through a detailed illustration of the various activities the jobseeker is encouraged to perform. With this, there emerges from the text a very clear image of the 'good jobseeker', including the sorts of activities the 'good jobseeker' should be involved in and the sorts of attitudes the 'good jobseeker' is expected to adopt. As such, a 'good jobseeker' is not simply required to perform certain practical activities, but more importantly, to adopt 'certain attitudes' (see Foucault, 1988). This section attempts to identify precisely the various and sometimes contradictory articulations of the 'good jobseeker' in terms of the identities s/he is invited to adopt and the techniques of the self s/he is invited to perform. This section will focus on the ways in which the 'good jobseeker' is invited to be 'professional' (in the sense I have outlined earlier in this chapter) and highly organised; highly motivated and flexible; while also being reserved and possessing relatively modest demands.

The 'good jobseeker' is professional and highly organised

The significance of business-professionalism is central to *The job kit*, as one of the key characteristics of the 'good jobseeker' is the ability to adopt a professional and organised approach to job seeking. Significantly, the text turns the act of job seeking into a highly complex 'professional' project, dependent upon effective targeting and requiring a high degree of organisation and political acumen. Similarly, well-organised administration is presented as being essential to effective job seeking, and in order to become a 'good jobseeker', one is obliged to adopt a professional approach to one's own management by becoming highly organised and efficient and keeping a constant record of one's job-seeking activities and their outcomes.

There are many instances in the text where the jobseeker is encouraged to become highly organised and is reminded of the advantages of keeping a close record of progress and following designated action plans. It is also suggested that efficient job seeking involves entering the details of all job-search activities into a carefully constructed chart, the 'Jobseeker's Log' (DfEE, 1998a, pp 17-18). *The job kit* goes into step-by-step detail as to the appropriate 'action plan' a 'good jobseeker' should adopt, stating that "you can't just 'look for a job'" (DfEE, 1998a, p 4), and that you need to "work to a plan" (DfEE, 1998a, p 7). *The job kit* also outlines a clear weekly timetable for the jobseeker to follow, including recommended day-to-day activities from Monday through to Sunday. For example, it is suggested the jobseeker on Monday visits the Jobcentre and produces letters of application; on Tuesday, follows up promising leads gained earlier in the week by telephone or in person; Wednesday, visits both the Jobcentre and employment agencies; Thursday, reads the situations vacant in newspapers and identifies suitable jobs; Friday, replies to these advertisements, arranges interviews and returns to the Jobcentre for the third time; Saturday, visits the library or any other sources of further information regarding potential employment positions; and finally, on Sunday, the jobseeker has a 'day off' (DfEE, 1998a, pp 7-8). This is of particular significance in that the elaborate detail offered in the weekly plan clearly articulates a 'good jobseeker' who is very much in control of her/his own governance and self-management and importantly, thoroughly 'active' in her/his approach to job seeking. With this, the very act of job seeking is portrayed as being a form of employment in itself, in that it occupies such a large amount of the jobseeker's time. This, in turn, has strong ethical significance for the text in that the 'good jobseeker' is obliged to redefine her/himself in terms of this professional, active discourse, while alternative, less active forms of discourse are illegitimate.

Jobseekers are also encouraged to become highly resourceful and strategic in their job-seeking techniques. When looking for work in local or national newspapers, the jobseeker is encouraged to carefully study news articles as well as the situations vacant, because they often provide information regarding new firms that may be moving to the area, firms that have recently won contracts, or firms that may be planning on expanding their business and looking for employees (DfEE, 1998a, p 9). The jobseeker is also told to read through any other newspaper advertisements, as they may offer contacts or other sources of information about a company, and that this is "useful when making a call to see if they have any jobs" (DfEE, 1998a, p 9). This presents the value of making speculative phone calls to companies regarding employment opportunities as self-evident and an essential element to the activities of a highly motivated jobseeker. *The job kit* encourages the jobseeker to use the local library as a resource for finding out possible employment opportunities, suggesting s/he should "Find out what's going on in your local area – you might uncover some job leads" (DfEE, 1998a, p 13). The significance here is that it is clear the 'good jobseeker' must occupy her/himself with far more than simply looking at the job advertisements in either the Jobcentre or newspapers in order to fulfil the demands as set out by *The job kit*. Instead, jobseekers must adopt a far more extensive and thoroughly enterprising approach to job seeking and their job seeking time must include active research into the local area and constant inquiry into new job-seeking techniques.

The job kit also suggests 'word of mouth' as a job-seeking technique and strongly encourages the jobseeker to discuss any possible employment openings with relatives or friends. Significantly, this technique is referred to in *The job kit* by the managerial term 'networking', and is presented as a highly organised and coordinated activity. For example, clearly ordered, step-by-step instructions are provided concerning how one should organise oneself while 'networking', under clear, bold subheadings such as: "THINK?"; "PLAN"; "DO" and "THEN" (DfEE, 1998a, pp 13-14). With this, jobseekers are encouraged to plan in advance how they will address colleagues and what information they will both ask for and provide, identifying exactly how the colleagues can be of assistance, precisely what kind of work the jobseeker is looking for and what skills they have (DfEE, 1998a, p 14). The significance of referring to 'word of mouth' through the professionalised discursive term 'networking', is that the act of asking friends or relatives about employment openings is reconstructed as an enterprising and professional extension of efficient job seeking rather than a potentially embarrassing or humiliating task of contacting old acquaintances and requesting help. Thus, the text places into the margins the possibility that being a 'jobseeker' may not be entirely 'professional', but may involve having to perform demeaning and undignified tasks (Derrida, 1972; Billig, 1990).

This importance on maintaining the business-professionalism of the jobseeker is further reflected when *The job kit* asks the jobseeker if they have taken any of a list of measures to secure employment. The list includes things such as whether or not they have a CV and how often they attend the Jobcentre. Jobseekers are then asked to 'grade' themselves depending on how many measures they have already taken. One of the measures is "Do you read daily newspapers (local and national), trade magazines and journals for the job information and vacancies? Do you know where to find copies if you don't want to buy them?" (DfEE, 1998a, p 4). There is significance here in the phrase 'don't want to buy'. It is essential to the authority of the text at this stage that the jobseeker is articulated as professional, and it is the statement 'don't want to buy' that allows this notion of professionalism to be maintained. Conversely, if the document were to suggest that the jobseeker could not *afford* to buy the newspapers, as might well be the case given the severe financial constraints associated with being on JSA, the 'professionalism' of the jobseeker would have been undermined. However, the text marginalises those images of unemployment that are associated with poverty and deprivation, replacing them with more dynamic images concerning 'enterprise' and 'professionalism'.

The 'good jobseeker' is highly motivated and flexible

In order to become a 'good jobseeker', the jobseeker also has to be thoroughly determined and enthusiastic in all approaches to employment. This extends beyond the willingness to adopt as many job-seeking techniques as possible and includes having unwavering enthusiasm for job-seeking activities and being highly flexible with regard to what s/he is prepared to do in order to secure employment.

In terms of motivation and enthusiasm, *The job kit* explains that some employers do not even reply to job applications or letters, but in spite of this, the jobseeker must not "become disheartened" and must "keep trying" (DfEE, 1998a, p 8). It is claimed that instead of employers offering a job, they sometimes agree to keep details on file. In the event of this, the jobseeker is told not to think of it as a 'brush-off', but to remember that "you're a step closer to getting a job than before you started" (DfEE, 1998a, p 8). With this, the 'good jobseeker' is not afforded the right to become dispirited with unsuccessful job seeking, but is required to be constantly motivated and encouraged to seek out as many job-seeking techniques as possible, and to pursue them with the same vigour and enthusiasm, regardless of rejections.

As well as remaining enthusiastic in her/his job seeking, the 'good jobseeker' must be highly flexible in her/his approach to both job seeking *and* employment. *The job kit* offers a number of sample covering letters and application forms which are designed to help the jobseeker "write better letters" (DfEE, 1998a, p 28). With this, the jobseeker is strongly encouraged to learn from and, wherever possible, to replicate the contents and presentation of these samples. For example, one of the sample letters declares that the jobseeker is prepared to work Saturdays "on a rota basis", has her/his own transport, is available for interview "at any time", and could "start immediately" (DfEE, 1998a, p 31). In the next sample letter, the jobseeker claims to be available to work "full-time including evenings and weekends if required", and to be available for interview "at your convenience" (DfEE, 1998a, p 32). Similarly, the sample application form declares that the jobseeker is willing to work extra hours, is able to start work "straight away", and has a clean driving licence and own transport (DfEE, 1998a, p 38). This is essential to the ethical construction of the jobseeker, as readers of *The job kit* are explicitly encouraged to use the sample application form and covering letters as a direct guide for their own job applications and with this are clearly encouraged to adopt the same qualities of flexibility and adaptability with regard to employment.

The jobseeker is also encouraged to increase flexibility by considering voluntary work as well as paid work, or by seeking out employment further afield and even abroad. *The job kit* claims that voluntary work can be a "chance to use your existing skills, gain experience, develop new interests and get training in new areas of work", that "It could sometimes lead to a paid job", and that it "Looks good on a CV too" (DfEE, 1998a, p 11). *The job kit* reminds the jobseeker that Jobcentres display full-time, permanent, part-time and temporary vacancies in the local and adjoining areas and that they can also provide help when looking for jobs in other parts of the country and abroad (DfEE, 1998a, p 9). Later in the document, jobseekers are invited to "take stock" of their job-seeking progress and think about whether they are "*really* keeping [their] options open" regarding what work they have been prepared to look for (DfEE, 1998a, p 58). The jobseeker is then invited to think about whether s/he could "move away and look for work in another area (or abroad)"; consider "voluntary work"; or consider looking for "one, maybe two, part-time jobs" (DfEE, 1998a, p 58). *The job kit* concludes by devoting two sections to discussing the advantages of working abroad and voluntary work (DfEE, 1998a, pp 62-63).

The 'good jobseeker' is reserved

Throughout the document, the 'good jobseeker' is identified as enterprising, professional, highly motivated and resourceful. However, in contrast to this, s/he is also encouraged to be reserved and exhibit only relatively modest needs. With this, the primary motivation of the jobseeker is to find employment as quickly as possible and the sense of urgency that surrounds this is seen to far outweigh any concern the jobseeker may or may not have regarding the type of work, quality of work, or level of pay. This articulation of the 'good jobseeker' is clearly represented towards the end of the document, where the jobseeker is advised on how to behave at an interview. The document informs the jobseeker that, at the end of the interview, it is normal procedure for the interviewees to be asked if they have any questions they would like to ask the interviewer. With this, the jobseeker is provided with a list of suitable questions s/he may like to use, such as; "Who would I report to?", "What will my first job be?", "What training will I have, if any?" and "Does the company carry out job reviews?" (DfEE, 1998a, p 46). Interestingly, these questions are not seen to represent a genuine concern on the part of the jobseeker as to the suitability of the employer, but instead are in place in order to enhance the jobseeker's interview performance by demonstrating to the interviewer that they are enthusiastic about the job. For example, *The job kit* states that the jobseeker should ask questions, because "Asking questions, but not too many, can show you are interested" (DfEE, 1998a, p 46). With this, the document thoroughly marginalises the idea that the jobseeker may want to use the interview in order to ascertain the suitability of the employer. The ethical techniques entailed for the jobseeker relate not to "an ethos of creativity and development", but "new sets of tricks in order to be competitive" (Standing, 2002, p 172). What is more, the ethics of the jobseeker do not permit the luxury of being able to choose which jobs may or may not be suitable, since this is clearly a privilege only afforded to those already in employment (or to a more limited extent, as was seen in *Job hunting*, those with managerial or professional experience or higher qualifications). Despite the emphasis within the discourse of unemployment on the exchange of rights and responsibilities, those rights do not appear to extend past the right to 'access' employment and certainly do not include the right to reject it.

This theme emerges elsewhere in the document as it becomes clear that the only legitimate objective for the jobseeker is to become engaged in work, be it paid work, voluntary work, or part-time work and with this, any technical or logistical issues concerning the nature or quality of work are thoroughly marginalised. For example, throughout the document, a considerable amount of advice is offered concerning how the jobseeker should identify their basic skills, how they can efficiently manage their job-seeking time, how they should construct a CV or a covering letter and how they should perform at an interview. However, distinctly absent from *The job kit* is any advice concerning how the jobseeker should identify those jobs that they may be suitable for, or how they should isolate those jobs they may prefer. Emphasis is constantly directed at adaptability and how the jobseeker can adapt their skills to fit the job. *The job kit* asks, "How can you best fit your skills to match the job?" (DfEE, 1998a, p 40). It enjoins the reader "Be positive and emphasise why you are *perfect* for the job" (DfEE, 1998a, p 29) and "Don't always rely on the job title being correct. Check the details. You may be able to do the sort of work required" (DfEE, 1998a, p 9). Thus, the emphasis is very much placed on ensuring the jobseeker is fully flexible and capable of adapting any skills they may have to fitting the requirements of a variety of employment positions rather than carefully selecting a smaller number of perhaps more suitable positions.

This emphasis on the centrality of employment is clearly represented in the following quotations. In the section concerning appropriate interview techniques, *The job kit* suggests a number of questions the jobseeker may be asked at the interview, and a number of possible answers the jobseeker may want to give. In response to the question, "Why have you had so many jobs?", it is suggested the jobseeker simply emphasise how s/he "would rather be in work than out of work" (DfEE, 1998a, p 42). This further illustrates the argument that the jobseeker's primary need is simply to be 'employed', regardless of the nature, quality or suitability of the employment. Similarly, *The job kit* advises jobseekers who are applying for jobs for which they are overqualified that if they are questioned at interview level about being overqualified, they can respond by emphasising that they are either (a) "looking for something fresh/new/different", or (b) that they "can take as well as give instructions" (DfEE, 1998a, p 44). This suggested question is simply one out of 20 and the fact that the jobseeker may apply for jobs they are overqualified for is not emphasised in the text as being of any particular significance. It is portrayed as being little more than an acceptable and even expected element of every jobseeker's duty. Also significant is the position of this question in the text. The questions preceding this one are "Aren't you (a) too young, or (b) too old?" and, preceding that, "Why have you had (a) so many jobs, or (b) only one job?" (DfEE, 1998a, p 43). In contrast, the question 'Aren't you overqualified?' (p 43) is quite distinct by the absence of 'Aren't you *under*qualified?'. This again adds weight to the argument that the objectives of the 'good jobseeker' cannot and should not extend beyond the need to find employment as quickly as possible, which invariably involves the lowering of demands and expectations on the part of the jobseeker in question.

There are also a number of instances of authoritative discourse as the jobseeker is told precisely how to conduct her/himself at the interview. At the interview, the jobseeker is told "DO NOT sit until invited"; "fidget and slouch in the chair"; "smoke"; "swear (even mildly)"; "criticise former employers"; "interrupt"; "draw attention to your weaknesses"; or "go over the top – stay calm and stick to the facts" (DfEE, 1998a, p 50). Also, if the jobseeker is asked when s/he is available to start work, s/he is instructed to simply answer, "As soon as possible!" and clearly told, "Do not put any barriers in the way" (DfEE, 1998a, p 46). The significance lies in the use of the phrase 'Do not' as it is quite distinct from the more colloquial discursive style that has been used so far in the text. For example, throughout the document, 'Don't' has been used 24 times compared to 'Do not', which has been used only twice. This commanding tone strongly emphasises the fact that the jobseekers are almost completely defined by their responsibility to find work as soon as possible and must not conduct themselves in a way that may even slightly jeopardise that responsibility.

Conclusion

The emphasis on the enhancement of skills and individual responsibility encouraged by New Labour can be traced back to policies previously pursued in the 1980s and 1990s under Conservative governments. However, there has been a notable shift in emphasis towards the ideal of self-help within the Labour Party since approximately 1995, and Labour now argue that, when individuals are offered employment and training, they have a reciprocal duty to take them up and that this is "empowerment not punishment" (Labour Party, 1997a, p 17). In response to current fears concerning job insecurity and the demise of a 'job for life', New Labour have attempted to reconstruct the issue of job security not as a structural feature of the economy and the labour market, but as a problem determined by the conduct of the individual. Labour's language of opportunity has changed job security into something that is seen to be achieved through individual efficiency and 'lifelong learning'; they had sought to establish 'individual learning accounts' and continue to emphasise that "the young unemployed have a responsibility to seek work, accept reasonable opportunities and upgrade their skills" (Labour Party, 1996, cited in Levitas, 1998, p 121). Security has now "been constructed as something individuals achieve through employability and individual obligation" (Levitas, 1998, p 121). It appears to be the policy of the government to assume that individuals have the responsibility and potential to acquire new skills and upgrade old ones in a constant effort to make themselves more employable. Hitherto, social policy measures employed by Labour were concerned with alleviating poverty whereas now they are centred around a far more 'active' approach to preventing poverty, as well as promoting opportunity and potential (Walker, 1999).

For New Labour, the exchange of rights and responsibilities is essential for an inclusive society, and citizenship is entirely conditional on individuals fulfilling their duties. They argue that "Rights and responsibilities must go hand in hand" (Labour Party, 1997b, p 18); for "A hand up not a hand out" (National Policy Forum Report, 1999, p 95); that "The contract is simple: quality opportunities for real responsibility" and "'Something for something' is the foundation" (Labour Party, 2001, p 26). However, this chapter has argued that, although New Labour place strong emphasis on the relationship between rights and responsibilities and require jobseekers to adopt the same market ethic and abide by the same ethical codes as somebody who is currently employed, jobseekers are *not* entitled to the same rights as their working counterparts. Furthermore, these new demands placed on jobseekers to be 'active' in their job seeking, as well as being 'enterprising' and 'industrious' are not uniformly applied and there is far closer targeting of those individuals seen to be in need of 'character improvement'. This is reflected in the way in which *The job kit* does not appear to be directed at *all* jobseekers, but at the 'hard-to-reach' jobseeker; the implicitly 'deviant jobseeker'. This targeted approach is consistent with the way New Labour governments have targeted problematic neighbourhoods, on the one hand (through Employment Zones, Education Action Zones, Health Action Zones, Sure Start and New Deal for Communities), and problematic individuals on the other (through the Social Exclusion Unit and other initiatives focused, for example, on rough sleepers, pregnant teenagers, school truants, young people not in employment, education and training, and, most seriously, upon antisocial behaviour). This is the context in which *The job kit* targets a very specific sort of jobseeker.

Regardless of how realistic it is to expect this jobseeker to secure meaningful paid employment, s/he is still compelled to adopt the same market ethic of enterprise, employability, flexibility and professionalism as well as being 'competent', 'adaptable', 'hardworking', 'conscientious' and 'reliable'. Jobseekers are given the sole responsibility for their job-seeking success, in that the only legitimate explanation for a failure to secure employment is the jobseekers' employability. Furthermore, there is an absence of *any* guidance concerning the sorts of jobs the jobseeker should apply for or that might be more suitable for them, or any reference or acknowledgement of other factors that may contribute to a jobseeker's lack of success. This, in many ways may reflect the reality that supply-side employment policies by themselves can do little to ensure material social inclusion through labour market participation, but that it may yet be possible to produce subjects who make the correct ethical response to the dominant policy discourse and who can be encouraged to align their own desires and sense of self-realisation to those of the 'third way'.

References

Billig, M. (1990) 'Rhetoric and social psychology', in I. Parker and J. Shorter (eds) *Deconstructing social psychology*, London: Routledge.

Blair, T. (1996) 'Faith in the city: Ten years on', speech at Southwark Cathedral, 29 January.

Burchell, G. (1996) 'Liberal government and techniques of the self', in A. Barry, T. Osborne and N. Rose (eds) *Foucault and political reason*, London: UCL Press.

Cabinet Office (1999) *The government's annual report 1998/99*, London: The Stationery Office.

Clarke, J. and Newman, J. (1997) *The managerial state*, London: Sage Publications.

Cruikshank, B. (1996) 'Revolutions within: self-government and self-esteem', in A. Barry, T. Osborne and N. Rose (eds) *Foucault and political reason*, London: UCL Press.

Dean, H. (2003) 'Re-conceptualising welfare to work for people with multiple problems and needs', *Journal of Social Policy*, vol 32, no 3, pp 441-59.

Derrida J. (1972) *Dissemination*, London: Athlone Press.

DfEE (Department for Education and Employment) (1998a) *The job kit: Your job search guide*, London: Employment Service on behalf of DfEE.

DfEE (1998b) *Job hunting: A guide for managers, executives, professionals, new graduates*, London: Employment Service on behalf of DfEE.

Fairclough, N. (1992) *Discourse and social change*, Cambridge: Polity Press.

Foucault, M. (1979) *The history of sexuality. Vol I*, London: Allen Lane.

Foucault, M. (1988) 'Technologies of the self', in L. Martin (ed) *Technologies of the self*, London: Tavistock.

Giddens, A. (1998) *The third way*, Cambridge: Polity.

Iser, W. (1974) *The implied reader: Patterns of communication in prose fiction from Bunyan to Beckett*, London: Johns Hopkins University Press.

Labour Party (1996) *Lifelong learning*, London: The Labour Party.

Labour Party (1997a) *Labour Party policy briefing*, London: The Labour Party.

Labour Party (1997b) *New Labour: Because Britain deserves better*, General Election Manifesto, London: The Labour Party.

Labour Party (1997c) *Building the future together: Labour's policies for partnership between government and the voluntary sector*, London: The Labour Party.

Labour Party (1997d) *Unemployment: The skills challenge*, London: Labour Research Department.

Labour Party (2001) *Ambitions for Britain*, General Election Manifesto, London: The Labour Party.

Leonard, P. (1997) *Postmodern welfare: Reconstructing an emancipatory project*, London: Sage Publications.

Levitas, R. (1998) *The inclusive society: Social exclusion and New Labour*, Basingstoke: Macmillan.

Metcalfe, A. (1992) 'The curriculum vitae: confessions of a wage-labourer', *Work, Employment and Society*, vol 6, no 4, pp 619-41.

Miller, N. and Morgan, D. (1993) 'Called to account: the CV as an autobiographical practice', *Sociology*, vol 27, no 1, pp 133-43.

National Policy Forum (1999) *Economy and social security*, London: National Policy Forum.

Roberts, L., Meager, L and Shields, L. (1989) *Applications and interviews*, London: Association of Graduate Careers Advisory Services.

Rose, N. (1989) *Governing the soul*, London: Routledge.

Standing, G. (2002) *Beyond the new paternalism*, London: Verso.

Walker, R. (1999) '"Welfare to work" *versus* poverty and family change: policy lessons from the USA', *Work, Employment and Society*, vol 13, no 3, pp 539-53.

NINE

New Labour, citizenship and responsibility: family, community and the obscuring of social relations

Michael Orton

The preceding chapters of this book have opened up discussion of political, popular, welfare provider and welfare user discourses of citizenship and responsibility. The particular concern of this chapter is with New Labour's 'third way' discourse of citizenship and responsibility in relation to family and community. It explores issues of responsibility, family and community by drawing on a UK-based qualitative study of a very particular sample, a group that could be characterised as 'irresponsible citizens'. While the primary concern is with New Labour, this is not to ignore the fact that New Labour's emphasis on responsibility can be located in the broader context of what I here describe as a dominant paradigm. The emphasis on responsibility in New Right and communitarian accounts of citizenship, such as those by Mead (1986) and Etzioni (1995) respectively, and in definitions of the 'third way' (see Giddens, 1994, 1998; Blair, 1998) is critically documented elsewhere (for example, Lister, 1997; Dean, 1999, 2002; Dean with Melrose, 1999; Dwyer, 2000). New Labour's discourse of responsibility, although contested, forms part of a broader view of citizenship which Jordan (1998) has described as the 'Blair/Clinton orthodoxy' and Standing (2002) as 'the new paternalism'. Themes of obligation in relation to family, community and work are central in this dominant paradigm, as is the implicit view of there being a contemporary deficit of responsibility. In particular, there is a belief that a welfare ethos exists which encourages the poor to avoid their obligations as citizens to be educated, to work, to support their families and to obey the law (Wilson, 1994). Hence, the interest in the research to which this chapter relates in a sample of ostensibly 'irresponsible citizens'.

The sample was made up of people who had received a court summons for non-payment of local taxation. During the late 1980s and early 1990s, the UK saw major changes to local taxation with the longstanding system of general rates, based on property values, being replaced in 1989/1990 by the community charge, based on individual residency (colloquially dubbed the 'poll tax'), which in turn was replaced in 1993 by council tax. Council tax, which is based on a combination of property values and individual residency, remains the contemporary system of local taxation used to finance services provided by municipal authorities. Council tax may not be based on such explicit notions of civic responsibility as its predecessor, poll tax, but it still represents a fundamental obligation with citizens contributing payments to finance the provision of local services (for a discussion of the relationship between poll tax and notions of citizenship, see Lister, 1990). Indeed, in accounts by commentators as diverse as Marshall (1963), Mead (1986) and Etzioni (1995), the payment of taxation is cited as a basic citizenship obligation. All those in the research were benefiting from local council services ranging from street lighting and refuse collection through to libraries, leisure facilities and schools. These citizens, however, had failed to contribute to the collective provision of those services through the payment of council tax. On the face of it, therefore, the people in the research constitute a sample who can stand accused of civic irresponsibility (for a discussion of the causes of non-payment, see Orton 2002).

The particular composition of the sample was central to the research. Much of the debate about citizenship is theoretical (Dwyer, 2000), but there have been some empirical studies of the experience of responsibility in communities (for example, MacKian, 1998) and the experience of responsibility in families, most notably by Finch and Mason (1993). Other studies (for example, Dean and Taylor-Gooby, 1992; Kempson et al, 1994; Middleton et al, 1997; Forrest and Kearns, 1999) can also be drawn upon. So the research here, in considering the experience of family and community, engages with similar issues to those that have informed other empirical research, and also studies which have considered popular discourses around citizenship (Dwyer, 1998, 2000; Dean with Melrose, 1999), but what is different is the apparent civic irresponsibility of the sample. This raises questions as to whether the research provided evidence different to that in other studies? Did interviewees' deficit of citizenship responsibility in not paying local taxation extend to family and community? Did these 'irresponsible citizens' employ different discourses to those found in other studies, and provide support for the dominant paradigm's assertion of a deficit of responsibility?

The first part of this chapter will consider 'family'. It will begin by examining New Labour's emphasis on responsibility in relation to family, contextualising this within the dominant paradigm, and then drawing on the research. The second part will turn to a consideration of 'community'. The chapter will then draw together themes that emerged in the research in relation both to family and community; issues about poverty and dependency, and dimensions of gender and care. In so doing, the discussion turns to whether New Labour's emphasis on responsibility obscures rather than illuminates our understanding both of the reality of the experience of family and community, and more fundamentally the nexus of responsibilities that exist between the state, family and community, particularly in the context of the shifts at the level of political economy that have taken place over the last quarter of a century. The chapter concludes by drawing on the research to posit ideas for a discourse of citizenship that would speak to the experience of those in the study.

Citizenship, responsibility and family

New Labour's emphasis on responsibility in relation to family can be seen in specific policy developments such as the 1999 Crime and Disorder Act, which empowered the courts to make parenting and child safety orders, directly enforcing parental responsibility (Driver and Martell, 2002). However, the connection between family and responsibility is made, not so much in relation to the identification of specific obligations, but at a more general level, and in particular in relation to the privileging of the nuclear family over other family forms. This can be seen in New Right accounts, for example Murray (1994, p 15) argues that "the traditional monogamous marriage with children is in reality, on average, in the long run, the most satisfying way to live a human life". In Etzioni's (1995) communitarian account, there is an acknowledgement of diversity, but this is quickly superseded by the expression of a strong preference for two (heterosexual) parent families and bemoaning a contemporary lack of established moral positions. Similarly, Giddens (1998, p 92) contends that "Recapturing the traditional family is a non-starter", but at the same time argues against the proliferation of family forms, citing evidence to support the claim that two parents are better than one, and divorce harms children. The argument, therefore, is not so much that there is a current deficit of responsibility within families, but that there is a need for re-emphasising the importance of the nuclear family form because the members of such families have traditionally accepted responsibility for caring for each other. As Carpenter (1994) argues, what is invoked is an image of an era when Victorian values reigned supreme and families looked after their own. It is through this generality that the family is made responsible for issues ranging from childhood delinquency to care for elderly people (Clarke et al, 2000).

New Labour's approach to family contains some welcome elements, such as the National Childcare Strategy (Williams, 2001) and greater support for all families with children (Driver and Martell, 2002), but this does not mean that the nuclear family is neglected. Support for the nuclear family can be seen in New Labour's rhetoric (Fairclough, 2000) and marriage is seen as a more desirable family form, one worthy of special efforts to protect it (Driver and Martell, 2002) – a policy objective that is already being vigorously pursued in the US (for example, Duerr Berrick, 2002). Indeed, New Labour's strategy for supporting families places special significance on "strengthening marriage" (Home Office, 1998, p 5) with it being argued that the nuclear family form should be at the heart of our society (Johnson, 1999). Despite some welcome elements in New Labour's approach to family, this is not what Silva and Smart (1999) argue should be a debate about what families 'do' as opposed to what form they take. There is certainly greater resonance with Lasch's (1995) idealised account of family rather than more radical views, for example the nuclear family as a specific social construct (Gittins, 1993) or the family as antisocial (Barrett and McIntosh, 1982). New Labour's approach does not acknowledge research demonstrating issues of inequalities within families, particularly gendered inequalities, which hide the unequal burden of poverty (Volger, 1994). Nor does New Labour's approach acknowledge studies demonstrating that while people do think in terms of responsibilities within families the idea that there are responsibilities associated with the family which people will automatically acknowledge, is not characteristic of contemporary family life (Finch and Mason, 1993; Finch, 1996).

Let us now turn to the research, drawing on interviews with 'irresponsible citizens' to examine their experience of responsibility in family and how this compares with the dominant paradigm.

Experiencing responsibility in families

The research involved in-depth interviews with 30 people who had received a court summons for non-payment of council tax. The research was conducted in one local authority area, an urban setting in the Midlands/North of England. Notwithstanding the emphasis on the nuclear family seen earlier, the research immediately found a diversity of family forms. Several of the interviewees were divorced and were now lone parents, living alone, or with new partners. Some couples were living together rather than being married. As Smith (1997, p 190) argues, family structures are changing and "we are living through an accelerated decomposition of the 'modern family'", with divorce and the number of children born outside marriage increasing, and the rate of marriage declining. In the sample, households consisting of a married couple with children were in a minority, reflecting contemporary social trends (for example, see National Statistics, 2001).

Social reality entails diversity, not the homogeneity of the nuclear family, but that is not to say that responsibility is not part of the experience of family. The research found both a breadth and depth to how family members help each other, with the relationship between parents and children providing the clearest examples. An illustrative example of the kind of complex networks of responsibility that exist in 'reconstructed' families was provided by Helen (all names are pseudonyms) as she explained:

> I had my first two children with my ex-husband ... things went wrong. I moved out and took the children. Then I met Kevin. He moved in ... and now we've had this new baby together.... My ex still has the two of them alternate weekends ... and he pays maintenance.

Helen, her ex-husband and her new partner had reached amicable arrangements, taking responsibility for the care and financial support of the three children involved, but not within the framework of the nuclear family form.

For the parents of young children the need for responsibility was seen as obvious and all-embracing. As John put it regarding his son, "At the end of the day he's only three so he can't look after himself so I've got to do it". Responsibility for young children was seen as covering every aspect of a child's needs. Angie and Josie, two lone parents who shared a house and were interviewed jointly, discussed the matter as follows:

Angie (A): It's 24 hours a day, isn't it. Seven days a week.

Josie (J): Clothing, feeding them, [giving them] security.

A: It's an awful lot. You don't know what you're going to get into until it happens. You have this picture of having kids and dressing them up....

J: Not any more!

The research also provided examples of responsibility within families beyond the parent–child relationship, but these still mainly revolved around childcare. There were a number of examples of grandparents caring for grandchildren, reflecting the very large volume of childcare now being provided by grandparents (Mooney et al, 2002; Wheelock and Jones, 2002). For example, Althea had a granddaughter with severe disabilities. Althea's daughter was the main carer but Althea regularly cared for her granddaughter as a way of providing respite. Another example of care beyond the parent–child relationship was provided by Josie (quoted earlier) who sometimes shared with her siblings and some cousins the after-school care of her own daughter and the children of these other family members.

An example of responsibility within families which was not based on childcare was provided by Phil and Alison. The couple's business had failed leaving them with multiple debts including mortgage arrears which had led to them being evicted from their home. The couple and their eight-year-old son were homeless. They were offered a flat on an unpopular council estate, but as Phil explained, "when Alison's dad heard where we were going to have to live, well ... he's a pensioner so he's got no money ... but he said 'Come and live with me, I've got three bedrooms'". This arrangement had already lasted for 18 months and Alison and Phil saw no sign of being able to move out in the near future. While it was Phil's father who was demonstrating familial responsibility, Alison and Phil accepted his generosity unquestioningly; it was a cultural expectation so far as they were concerned.

What is immediately apparent is that interviewees, despite their civic irresponsibility in relation to the non-payment of local taxation, expressed the same sense of responsibility in families as in other studies. The special status accorded to responsibilities between parents and children, the importance of family as a source of help and the involvement of kin beyond the nuclear family, are themes that resonate with findings from other research (for example, Finch and Mason, 1993; Kempson et al, 1994). What is striking about the quotations from these 'irresponsible citizens' is not that they are markedly different from respondents in other studies, but how similar they are. This can be seen further as the research is explored in more detail.

Family as a negative experience

The research found that responsibility was a real part of the experience of family but what was also demonstrated, in contrast to idealised views of family, was that the experience of family is not necessarily positive: the family can be the cause of problems. For example, Ian described why he had been unable to move direct from school to university, as he had planned, but had followed a more complex route into higher education:

> I left school because of family problems ... I didn't get on with my step-dad. I had to drop out in upper sixth ... I did all sorts of jobs.... I went back and did a foundation course. That's how I got back into it.

Sheila's story was harrowing:

> I've been here since 1966. I've been married twice. I came here with my first husband.... To cut a long story short, the marriage didn't turn out ... I got divorced. A couple of years after that I met my second husband. He was a widower. He had seven children. I went to live with him. The first two years things were going fine and then he started with his violence. I didn't know at first he was violent. One thing led to another. The same old story – next day it'd be 'I'm sorry'. Of course the way I'd been brought up was 'You make your bed, you lie on it', so of course I stuck with it. I brought the kids up and it just went from bad to worse. After 14 years he had a heart attack. We were living in rented accommodation. He said, 'We're not married. If anything happens to me the landlord could put you out', which he could. So we got married. On with the violence again. Bad to worse. Eventually I walked out on him. Ended up in a hostel for battered women. They were ever so good to me there.... They got me this flat. I've been on Income Support since.

Family as a place of danger for many women stands in stark contrast to the uncritical privileging of the nuclear family form. Murray (1994, p 16) acknowledges that "there is such a thing as spouse abuse", but any concern is immediately dismissed because Murray argues that "defined in any serious way, it is statistically uncommon", and any negativity is overwhelmed by Murray's praise of the nuclear family. But as Lister (1997, p 112) argues, "Where economic dependency deprives women of voice and closes off their exit, they can all too easily become trapped in violent and abusive relationships". The dominant paradigm appears to have little resemblance to the reality of this experience of family.

The apparently irresponsible citizens in the research did not provide evidence to support contentions of a deficit of responsibility in relation to family. They did express and experience responsibility within family. The research, however, leads us away from idealised accounts to the reality of people at the very least having a diversity of experience of family (Finch and Mason, 1993) and at worst violence within families being the 'raw end' of patriarchy (Gittins, 1993) and the nuclear family form as a particular, and negative, ideological construct (Barrett and McIntosh, 1982).

Let us now turn to interviewees' experience of community, beginning with a brief discussion of the debate about citizenship, responsibility and community.

Citizenship, responsibility and community

Community plays a similar role to family in providing a focus for the dominant paradigm's emphasis on responsibility, but in this case in relation to locality. Murray (1996, p 50) argues that communities should be given "a massive dose of self-government". However, the thrust of Murray's argument is more generally that communities reflect problems created by 'illegitimacy' (that is, births out of wedlock) and 'non-work' (that is, failure or refusal to participate in the labour market). It is in communitarian accounts that community is given centrality, with community being seen as the answer to problems. The notion of community as the means of resolving social ills is a dominant theme in Etzioni's (1995) account.

Blair makes extravagant claims about community; for example, that the "partnership between active government and an active community is key to our success as a nation in dealing with *everything* from social exclusion to poor literacy, crime to ill-health" (Blair, 2000, emphasis added). Community is important to New Labour in its approach to welfare, appealing to values of reciprocity, responsibility and mutuality drawn from the traditional community, recalling the 'model of small association' (Jordan, 1998). Locality is important in a whole plethora of area-based initiatives, ranging from Health Action Zones to the New Deal for Communities. Local authorities have taken up the principle of partnership, giving people in deprived areas a more active role in defining needs and service provision, and working with welfare agencies and collective actors in the informal economy. New Labour's version of responsibility and community thus extrapolates from the small-scale association of voluntary organisations and the like, and applies this to large-scale societies and the formal rights and duties of citizenship (Jordan with Jordan, 2000).

Despite the attention given to community, and the claims made about its importance, there is considerable confusion about what a community is (Levitas, 1998). Accounts such as those by Etzioni (1995) and Dennis (1997) include a clear element of nostalgia for a claimed period of stronger communities; but images of communities populated by nuclear families, close-knit contacts and voluntary groups, lead to the conclusion that "the rhetoric of community is all too often based upon archaic 'hand-me-down'" which fails to address the changing nature of social organisation (MacKian, 1998, p 47). Such nostalgic images sit uneasily with the pluralism of present-day communities and multiethnic societies (Jordan with Jordan, 2000). In defining responsibility within communities, it is voluntary work that is most commonly cited. For example, Etzioni is critical of the use of paid labour to do work that used to be done voluntarily, for example caring for elderly people, while Blair (2000) argues that it is voluntary work that underlines the "rebirth of ... community spirit". The importance New Labour attaches to formal volunteering is demonstrated through initiatives such as the active community awards and the Time Bank.

Again, this emphasis on the importance of community fails to acknowledge the reality of community as a fiercely contested concept. Williams (1989) argues that community takes little account of the extent to which conflicts of interest and ensuing relationships of power at the societal level, are reproduced at the local level, particularly in terms of class, 'race' and gender. Empirical studies have similarly found community to be the site of tensions (for example, see Forrest and Kearns, 1999). So, to return to the research, how did the 'irresponsible citizens' experience responsibility in community?

Experiencing responsibility within communities

Interviewees gave examples indicating a diverse range of involvement in community groups, churches, schools, workplace and friendship groups. For example, Jas was a member of a formal workplace group that arranged events for a children's charity. He dedicated several weekends each year to fundraising. Other people had very specific examples of community involvement. Anhil had established a position within the local Hindu community of giving advice to people considering setting up their own business. He also organised social events for the community. Several of the women in the research were involved in activities at their children's schools and/or nurseries. For example, Anjana said, "I go to help at parties at the nursery and stay for the afternoon".

For many interviewees, however, community was a vague concept which made sense only in talking about the local neighbourhood, with examples of community revolving around a sense of neighbourliness and providing assistance in ad hoc, informal ways. For example, Iqbal had recently mended a neighbour's tap so the neighbour avoided the cost of employing a plumber. Joe had a set of long ladders and explained: "If someone wants to borrow my ladders, save them buying a set, I don't mind them borrowing them". Responsibility expressed as care also featured. As Sue explained: "I take my ex-mother-in-law shopping two or three times a week.... She's 69". However, Angie's explanation of arrangements with her neighbour was a typical example of what several people said about simple ways neighbours help each other: "They have our key in case we're locked out and vice versa we've got their key. They'll take parcels in for us". This kind of informal activity is about people simply 'getting on' with the difficulties of everyday life and, although not constituting the formal voluntary work recognised by communitarians as indicating responsibility within communities, such activity makes up the majority of citizen involvement within the community (MacKian, 1998).

As with the experience of family, the experience of community was also not necessarily positive. Rather than geographic community as a place of support and help, Althea's experience of neighbourhood was as a place of racist hostility. Her experience of racist neighbours was a far cry from communitarian imagery:

> One next door neighbour was great. Me and my children were always welcome there. The other one ignores me. The nice neighbour has gone now and the new one is as bad as the other side. I don't think they like black people.

Another interviewee, Mo, described his experience of his local community as follows:

> You do get hassle.... We got burgled when we were asleep in bed.... I'd love to buy a big house somewhere really nice, where people can't come near it.

Mo was not looking to communitarian images of a strong community to resolve problems; rather, it was an escape from community that he wanted.

So, just as the research did not provide evidence to support contentions of a deficit of responsibility in relation to family, nor did the civic irresponsibility of those in the research mean they did not express and experience responsibility within community. The experience of those in the research was again comparable with other studies which have found that friends can act as a key source of support in coping with problems (Wood and Vamplew, 1999), and local neighbourhoods can remain central to people's lives, but degrees of attachment vary (Cattell and Evans, 1999) and women are often the mainstays of community through networks developed in caring for children and other family members (Andersen et al, 1999).

The reality of interviewees' experience was, however, very different to nostalgic and idealised images of community. As with the experience of family, interviewees' experience of community did not reflect New Right, communitarian or 'third way' accounts. The experience of family and community was in fact underpinned by a very different set of issues; issues of poverty and dependency, and care and gender, to which we will now turn.

Poverty and dependency

Poverty was a central issue for interviewees, and one that permeated the experience of family and community. For example, bringing up children is hard, but the level of difficulty is intensified when parents are on a low income. Accounts of women going without in order to put their children's needs first are well documented (for example, Middleton et al, 1997; Goode et al, 1998) and this was an issue in the research. Sue, who had two sons and was in receipt of Income Support, explained:

> I never hardly buy myself new clothes. The boys don't go without – I go
> without myself.

The considerable extent of responsibility within families has been demonstrated,
but the research also found that the ability of family members to help each
other is dependent upon the resources available to them. To use the example
of Sue again, she described the help she received from her mother as follows:

> I never come back from mum's without something, even if it's cakes, yoghurts,
> anything. She lets me have all she can but she can't really manage it. She's
> a pensioner.

Sue's very low income meant she was grateful for this help, but the level of that
help was limited by her mother's own poverty.

Poverty was also relevant to the experience of community. For example,
Rose talked positively about how her neighbours helped each other. She gave
an example of how she had run out of tea bags so asked a neighbour for one.
Instead, the neighbour gave a whole bag full. As Rose explained:

> When I bought a box I offered her them back. She said 'Oh no'. That's
> what they're like [around here]. If they've got it, they'll lend it you.

That giving a few tea bags is seen as generosity is in reality a mark of poverty
and the limits, not the extent, of community support. And Rose reinforced
this point when she said of her neighbours: "They won't lend you money –
nobody's got any!"

Even where help was available, it did not necessarily tackle the problems
people faced in coping. As Janardan put it: "I could borrow money from
friends or relatives but I would just have to repay it – I would just be putting
myself into more debt, more problems than you already have". Family and
community could not solve the poverty that people faced.

Poverty was linked to the issue of dependency. The social construction of
dependency within the dominant paradigm defines individual dependency
within wage-labour or family relationships as independence but state welfare
is seen as dependency (Dean and Taylor-Gooby, 1992; see also Chapter Ten of
this book). Interviewees did not share this view. Interviewees expressed clearly
their sense of relationships as meaning love and interdependence, but the research
also demonstrated some examples of the family as meaning dependence. For
example, some interviewees questioned the involvement of grandparents in
childcare. As Janardan said of his mother- and father-in-law:

> They do help out, but they are retired. We don't want to burden them with
> childcare and burden them in their retirement. They've worked all their
> lives. They've brought up their children.

Indeed, dependency on parents, despite reaching adulthood, is felt by those in such a situation to be wrong, compromising independence and adult status (Finch and Mason, 1993).

Like the experience of family, the experience of community can mean dependency, which threatens people's sense of self-worth. As Ray said:

> There's a few friendly people around here. I've got a few friends around here so I can phone them and they'll be down.... I can't iron me own clothes ... I have to wait for someone to come who can iron, to do me ironing for me. Till somebody's in a good mood.

Sheila, who was in receipt of income support, welcomed help from her friends because of her poverty, but the experience was a contradictory one:

> I've got two good friends. They help me out a bit. But that makes me feel awful as well. I'm not that way.... It makes me feel awful. It's not a lot but it's a help. A fiver. Something like that. If I see them, they say 'Here's a fiver'; [I say] 'No, no'; [they say] 'Go on, take it'. That sort of thing. I've never been like this in my life. I feel a bit second class. A second class person. I really do.

Yet again, the fact that the interviewees here had failed in their obligation to pay local taxation did not mean that they experienced family and community differently to respondents in other studies. Like the members of Dean and Rogers'core sample' in Chapter Four of this book, they exhibited ambivalence about the nature of dependency. In the specific context of familial or community-based dependency and obligation, issues of dependence and independence are highly complex with people wishing to avoid being 'beholden' or 'too dependent' (Finch and Mason, 1993), and there being a need for both the giver and receiver to maintain independence and equality (Kempson et al, 1994). So, just as with other studies, the research demonstrated that the experience of family and community can be marked not by independence nor interdependence but by a dependency that undermines people's self-worth. Interviewees did not express discourses different to people in other studies. Rather, their experience of family and community, as in other studies, challenged the view of the dominant paradigm.

Obscuring social relations

Responsibility as care: citizenship and gender

The final point to consider is that the research demonstrated that responsibility is primarily expressed as care and, because responsibility for care overwhelmingly lies with women, this has specific implications for citizenship and gender. On the face of it, New Labour policies such as the National Childcare Strategy offer some acknowledgement of this, but there is a fundamental tension between New Labour's recognition of the importance of care and the political privileging of paid work (Williams, 2001). While the state's provision of childcare may expand, the public provision of childcare does not strike out the advantage given to men by the domestic division of labour (Lister, 1997) and New Labour certainly does not address the zero-sum politics of the distribution of time and power between men and women (Lister, 2001). Communitarians such as Etzioni (1995) may refer to the need for the involvement of men in childcare, but family-friendly policies are almost invariably seen as mother-friendly policies (Burgess and Ruxton, 1998). The state's real effort, as demonstrated by the creation of the Child Support Agency, is in making men contribute financially to the upbringing of their children through paying maintenance to former partners. As Garnham and Knights (1994) argue, what this is really about is the government's concern with the number of lone parents on benefit and the desire to reduce social security expenditure. It is not about addressing domestic and care responsibilities.

While childcare was the main form of responsibility identified in the research, the study also provided an example of a woman giving up paid care work to care (unpaid) for her mother, which raises the broader issue of community care. As Nora explained:

> I was a [paid] carer, a home help. I stopped to look after my mum. She had emphysema. She was poorly for a long, long time. I thought the best thing to do was come in and look after her myself.

The caring work that Nora did remained much the same, although the hours she dedicated to caring for her mother were greater than the paid work she had done. What changed was the status of that work. Rather than achieving social rights and the public status of citizenship, Nora, in taking responsibility for care within the family, disappeared into the private sphere of the home. At a general level, inadequately financed community care policies mean that responsibility for care is transferred to families, neighbours, friends and volunteers (Clarke et al, 1987). More specifically, community care assumes that the family has prime responsibility for the care of its own members and takes for granted the role of women as primary carers (Walker, 1982). As Wilson (1982) argues, community becomes an ideological portmanteau word for a reactionary, conservative ideology that oppresses women by silently confining them to the private sphere without so much as even mentioning them.

Thus, an idealised emphasis on family and community obscures rather than illuminates our understanding of the reality of the experience of family and community. The reality is that in contemporary society women face what Lister (1996) describes as the triple burden of childcare, domestic labour and paid work, and possibly the fourth demand of adult care. Rather than a simple emphasis on responsibility there is a need for an 'ethics of care' (Williams, 2001; see also Chapter Two of this book). This would include consideration of care as a practice invoking different experiences and multiple relations of power; recognition of the challenge of the disability movement to the assumed dependency of the 'cared-for' in care relations; and, with increasing migration, transnational familial obligations. The research, therefore, leads to a discussion of issues very different to those given centrality in the dominant paradigm.

The question this begs is, 'Why are family and community emphasised so heavily?' To make sense of the contradiction between the idealised accounts of the dominant paradigm and the reality of the experience of responsibility in families and communities means stepping back from the immediate debate about responsibility, and instead setting citizenship, family and community within a broader context of social relations and changes in the political economy.

Family, community and social relations

Finch and Mason (1993) argue that a line has to be drawn somewhere between the responsibilities of the state and responsibilities to be met by families (and the same could be said with regard to community). The Victorian Poor Law expressed this clearly, specifying financial responsibilities for different categories of relatives. The more contemporary emphasis on responsibility, family and community may not be as codified as this, but most certainly the 1980s saw a resetting of the boundaries of responsibility accepted by the state. At a general level, the rhetoric of responsibility justified the assault on welfare by Conservative governments, and was more specifically used in relation to social policies shifting the burden of care for elderly people away from the state, along with the withdrawal of welfare support for young adults.

So, the emphasis on family and community should not be located solely in the context of New Labour governments since 1997 but also within more fundamental shifts in the political economy, beginning in the 1980s. As Jessop (2002) argues in the context of what he describes as the transition from a Keynesian welfare state to a Schumpeterian workfare (or competition) state, the 'rollback' of the welfare state displaced the burden of adjustment onto the family and networks and solidarities of civil society. That shifts in the political economy placed new responsibilities onto families is also acknowledged by Esping-Andersen (1999). Indeed, as Levitas (1998) argues, the New Right project of the 1980s is widely misunderstood as exclusively neoliberal, whereas there were in fact two apparently contradictory, but actually symbiotic, strands of neoliberalism and neo-conservatism. Neoliberalism underpinned deregulation of the market, privatisation, and growing inequalities. The neo-conservative element was concerned with order, the family, nation and morality, using the state to uphold the conditions required for the operation of the market, what Gamble (1994) characterises as the free economy and the strong state. Thus, the emphasis on responsibility, family and community can be seen as integral to the New Right project of the 1980s.

With regard to New Labour, communitarianism's emphasis on responsibility in the family and community is appealing because it offers an alternative both to destructive free market individualism and 'expensive' social democratic welfarism (Smith, 1997). New Labour's calls to rebuild communities and for a return to family values address the obvious realities of increasing poverty among families and social disintegration within poor communities, without requiring social justice through radically redistributive policies. Responsibility for the fracturing of society is located not in the privatisation and inequitable programmes of recent years, nor in government policies and deregulated free markets, but in the communities and families that suffered most from these policies. As Lister (2001) argues, the danger with New Labour's locally-based regeneration initiatives is that problems are constructed as lying within deprived neighbourhoods and with those who live in them. Just as welfare-to-work policies tend to obscure the structural causes of unemployment (see Chapters Seven and Eight of this book), so neighbourhood regeneration policies divert attention from the need for structural change.

An idealised emphasis on family and community, therefore, obscures not only our understanding of the reality of the experience of family and community, but also the fundamental shift in the political economy that has taken place and the redrawing of the nexus of responsibilities between the state, family and community. Emphasising the importance of family and community, and asserting a contemporary deficit of responsibility, obscures the state's erosion of social rights and explicit rejection of collective responsibilities for which under the Keynesian welfare state there was at least some implicit acceptance.

Conclusion

The research began from the premise that a study of citizens guilty of civic irresponsibility may provide evidence of a broader deficit of responsibility, particularly in relation to family and community, thereby supporting what has been described as the dominant paradigm's assertion of a need for emphasis on family and community. The research did not, however, find a deficit of responsibility in relation to family and community. Interviewees' expression of responsibility in family and community was not marked by a differentiated discourse rejecting responsibility, but was consistent with other studies. More than this, the experience of family and community not merely failed to provide evidence of a deficit of responsibility; rather, it demonstrated a reality very different to idealised accounts. It is in this way that an uncritical emphasis on family and community obscures our understanding of people's experience.

What began with an interest in a rather particular sample of 'irresponsible citizens' in fact led to much more general issues about citizenship, and where the 'line' is drawn between the responsibilities of the state, family and community. Since the 1980s, this line has been redrawn, with responsibility emphasised and rights diminished. To refer to the research, a more plausible conception of citizenship would not necessarily be one that simply sought to move the balance between rights and responsibilities a little more in favour of the former. The research points to more fundamental issues of poverty and dependency, and care and gender. This demands attention to notions of an ethics of care as referred to above, and the need for a reappropriation of citizenship to address deeper bases of social power (Taylor, 1996). Such a radical and transformative conception of citizenship, as opposed to idealised images of family and community, is one that would resonate with the participants in this study (and others), speaking to their experience and providing the basis for an alternative to the dominant paradigm.

References

Andersen, H., Munck, R., Fagan, C., Goldson, B., Hall, D., Lansley, J., Novack, T., Melville, R. and Ben-Tovim, G. (1999) *Neighbourhood images in Liverpool: 'It's all down to the people'*, York: Joseph Rowntree Foundation.

Barrett, M. and McIntosh, M. (1982) *The anti-social family*, London: Verso Editions/ NLB.

Blair, T. (1998) *The third way*, London: Fabian Society.

Blair T. (2000) 'The new givers', *The Guardian*, 1 March.

Burgess A. and Ruxton, S. (1998) 'Men and their children', in J. Franklin (ed) *Social policy and social justice*, Cambridge: Polity Press.

Carpenter, M. (1994) *Normality is hard work*, London: Lawrence & Wishart.

Cattell, V. and Evans, M. (1999) *Neighbourhood images in East London: Social capital and social networks on two east London estates*, York: Joseph Rowntree Foundation.

Clarke, J., Cochrane, A. and Smart, C. (1987) *Ideologies of welfare*, London: Routledge.

Clarke, J., Gewirtz, S. and McLaughlin, E. (2000) 'Reinventing the welfare state', in J. Clarke, S. Gewirtz and E. McLaughlin (eds) *New managerialism, new welfare?*, London: Sage Publications.

Dean, H. (1999) 'Citizenship', in M. Powell (ed) *New Labour, new welfare state?*, Bristol: The Policy Press.

Dean, H. (2002) *Welfare rights and social policy*, Harlow: Prentice Hall.

Dean, H. with Melrose, M. (1999) *Poverty, riches and social citizenship*, Basingstoke: Macmillan.

Dean, H. and Taylor-Gooby, P. (1992) *Dependency culture: The explosion of a myth*, Hemel Hempstead: Harvester Wheatsheaf.

Dennis, N. (1997) *Families without fatherhood*, London: IEA Health and Welfare Unit.

Driver, S. and Martell, L. (2002) 'New Labour, work and the family', *Social Policy and Administration*, vol 36, no 1, pp 46-61.

Duerr Berrick, J. (2002) 'Marriage, motherhood and other social conventions: welfare reform and the politics of enforced morality', Plenary paper presented at European Social Policy Research Network Conference 'Social Values, Social Policies', Tilburg, 29-31 August.

Dwyer, P. (1998) 'Conditional citizens? Welfare rights and responsibilities in the late 1990s', *Critical Social Policy*, vol 18, no 4, pp 493-517.

Dwyer, P. (2000) *Welfare rights and responsibilities*, Bristol: The Policy Press.

Esping-Andersen, G. (1999) *The social foundations of post-industrial economies*, Oxford: Oxford University Press.

Etzioni, A. (1995) *The spirit of community: Rights, responsibilities and the communitarian agenda*, London: Fontana Press.

Fairclough, N. (2002) *New Labour, new language*, London: Routledge.

Finch, J. (1996) 'Family responsibilities and rights', in M. Bulmer and A.M. Rees (eds) *Citizenship today*, London: UCL Press.

Finch, J. and Mason, J. (1993) *Negotiating family responsibilities*, London: Routledge.

Forrest, R. and Kearns, A. (1999) *Joined-up places? Social cohesion and neighbourhood regeneration*, York: Joseph Rowntree Foundation.

Gamble, A. (1994) *The free economy and the strong state* (2nd edn), Basingstoke: Macmillan.

Garnham, A. and Knights, E. (1994) *Putting the Treasury first: The truth about child support*, London: CPAG.

Giddens, A. (1994) *Beyond left and right*, Cambridge: Polity Press.

Giddens, A. (1998) *The third way*, Cambridge: Polity Press.

Gittins, D. (1993) *The family in question: Changing households and familiar ideologies* (2nd edn), Basingstoke: Macmillan.

Goode, J., Callender, C. and Lister, R. (1998) *Purse or wallet? Gender inequalities and income distribution within families on benefits*, London: Policy Studies Institute.

Home Office (1998) *Supporting families*, London: The Stationery Office.

Jessop, B. (2002) *The future of the capitalist state*, Cambridge: Polity Press.

Johnson, N. (1999) 'The personal social services and community care', in M. Powell (ed) *New Labour, new welfare state?*, Bristol: The Policy Press.

Jordan, B. (1998) *The new politics of welfare*, London: Sage Publications.

Jordan, B. with Jordan, C. (2000) *Social work and the Third Way: Tough love as social policy*, London: Sage Publications.

Kempson, E., Bryson, A. and Rowlingson, K. (1994) *Hard times?*, London: Policy Studies Institute.

Lasch, C. (1995) *Haven in a heartless world*, London: Norton.

Levitas, R. (1998) *The inclusive society*, Basingstoke: Macmillan.

Lister, R. (1990) *The exclusive society*, London: Child Poverty Action Group.

Lister, R. (1996) 'Citizenship engendered', in D. Taylor (ed) *Critical social policy: A reader*, London: Sage Publications.

Lister, R. (1997) *Citizenship: Feminist perspectives*, Basingstoke: Macmillan.

Lister, R. (2001) 'New Labour: a study in ambiguity from a position of ambivalence', *Critical Social Policy*, vol 21, no 4, pp 425-47.

MacKian, S. (1998) 'The citizen's new clothes: care in a Welsh community', *Critical Social Policy*, vol 18, no 1, pp 27-50.

Marshall, T.H. (1963) 'Citizenship and social class', in T.H. Marshall *Sociology at the Crossroads and other essays*, London: Heinemann.

Mead, L.M. (1986) *Beyond entitlement: The social obligations of citizenship*, New York, NY: The Free Press.

Middleton, S., Ashworth, K. and Braithwaite, I. (1997) *Small fortunes: Spending on children, childhood poverty and parental sacrifice*, York: Joseph Rowntree Foundation.

Mooney, A. and Statham, J. with Simon, A. (2002) *The pivot generation: Informal care and work after 50*, Bristol/York: The Policy Press/Joseph Rowntree Foundation.

Murray, C. (1994) *Underclass: The crisis deepens*, London: IEA Health and Welfare Unit in association with *The Sunday Times*.

Murray, C. (1996) 'The emerging British underclass', in R. Lister (ed) *Charles Murray and the underclass: The developing debate*, London: IEA Health and Welfare Unit.

National Statistics (2001) *Social Trends*, no 31, London: The Stationery Office.

Orton, M. (2002) 'Why do people have council tax debts? – Citizenship, responsibility and poverty', Paper presented at the Social Policy Association Conference 'Localities, Regeneration and Welfare', University of Teeside, 16-18 July.

Silva, E.B. and Smart, C. (1999) 'The "new" practices and politics of family life', in E.B. Silva and C. Smart (eds) *The new family?*, London: Sage Publications.

Smith, J. (1997) 'The ideology of "family and community": New Labour abandons the welfare state', *Socialist Register*, pp 176-96.

Standing, G. (2002) *Beyond the new paternalism*, London: Verso.

Taylor, D. (1996) 'Citizenship and social power', in D. Taylor (ed) *Critical social policy: A reader*, London: Sage Publications.

Volger, C. (1994) 'Money in the household', in A. Anderson, F. Bechhofer and J. Gershuny (eds) *The social and political economy of the household*, Oxford: Oxford University Press.

Walker, A. (1982) 'The meaning and social division of community care', in A. Walker (ed) *Community care*, Oxford: Blackwell.

Wheelock, J. and Jones, K. (2002) '"Grandparents are the next best thing": informal childcare for working parents in urban Britain', *Journal of Social Policy*, vol 31, no 3, pp 441-63.

Williams, F. (1989) *Social policy: A critical introduction*, Cambridge: Polity Press.

Williams, F. (2001) 'In and beyond New Labour: towards a new political ethics of care', *Critical Social Policy*, vol 21, no 4, pp 467-93.

Wilson, E. (1982) 'Women, the "community" and the "family"', in A. Walker (ed) *Community care*, Oxford: Blackwell.

Wilson, W.J. (1994) 'Citizenship and the inner-city ghetto poor', in B. van Steenbergen (ed) *The condition of citizenship*, London: Sage Publications.

Wood, M. and Vamplew, C. (1999) *Neighbourhood images of Teeside: Regeneration or decline?*, York: Joseph Rowntree Foundation.

Part Four
Conclusion

TEN

Reconceptualising dependency, responsibility and rights

Hartley Dean

This book demonstrates the ways in which dependency, responsibility and rights are connected. Part One argued that any concept of rights capable of encompassing rights to social welfare must be premised on a celebration of human *inter*dependency and an ethical concept of social responsibility: it requires a politics of needs interpretation and an ethic of *co*responsibility. Embracing human interdependency means rethinking the context in which we can, nonetheless, demand autonomy as human beings. Autonomy is not the same as self-sufficiency. Conceptualising social responsibility means transcending ethically constrained notions of duty, obligation or obedience so as to bring moral sensibility to bear upon the ethics of the public sphere.

Part Two recounted findings from recent empirical research concerning popular and welfare provider discourses. It shows that such discourses can recognise that interdependency is an unavoidable feature of the human life course and that certain kinds of rights do attach to people by virtue of their humanity. But, insofar that such discourses tend to construe responsibility in essentially individualistic ways, they do not generally translate a recognition of interdependency into an acceptance of universal social or welfare rights. Indeed, welfare providers may be especially hostile to unconditional rights to welfare.

Part Three focused primarily on the perspectives of welfare service users: the way they negotiate their dependency on the state, the nature of the disciplines to which they are subject and the ways in which they understand their individual responsibilities. Individuals and households in welfare state societies are all to some extent dependent on the state and all are involved in strategies by which to advance their well-being. Yet, while certain of them are targeted by state interventions designed to construct them as responsible labour market participants, even those who might be adjudged irresponsible insofar that they have failed to contribute through local taxes quite clearly have their own standards and ideas about responsibility that are independent of the state's requirements.

This final chapter aims to bring together some of the several arguments that have been developed so far. It proposes, first, to amplify the argument that human relationships and the interdependency they entail are good in and of themselves; that 'third way' notions of responsibility are ethically deficient; and that prevailing concepts of rights remain fundamentally impoverished. It concludes by returning to the theme I began to address in Chapter One and to make the case for a human rights approach to social welfare.

Dependency

One of the points repeatedly made throughout this book is that *inter*dependency is an essential feature of the human life course and the human condition. One might argue that it is constitutive of our humanity and the achievement of human identity. This is neither new nor radical. It is captured, for example, in the timeless aphorism attributed to the Xhosa people of South Africa – "A person is a person through other persons" (see du Boulay, 1988, p 114). Personhood is founded in and through dependency on other persons.

Another of the points that has been made in several chapters relates to the nature of the 'third way' political project and the way this problematises human interdependency. In the event, the 'third way' is not necessarily distinctive. I have argued elsewhere (for example, Dean and Taylor-Gooby, 1992, chs 2, 6; Dean and Thompson, 1996) that there is a tendency across the conventional political spectrum to 'fetishise' dependency. The notion of 'fetishism' on which I draw is that applied by Marx (1887) to characterise the ideological distortions peculiar to capitalist social and economic relations. Insofar that Marxist epistemology has been largely eclipsed by cultural ontology (for example, Clarke, 1999), it is a notion that has fallen out of academic fashion. It remains pertinent, however, first, because of its heuristic power; and second, because it connects (I would contend) as much with ontological aspects of human identity as with structurally determined, or 'categorical', aspects (see Taylor, 1998).

The original Marxist premise was that the process by which surplus value is extracted from wage labour and by which the products of labour are both alienated from their producers as commodities and exchanged between supposedly autonomous subjects had been rendered 'fantastic'. Seen through capitalism's *camera obscura*, commodities become socialised, while social life becomes commodified. It is only through 'fetishised' or 'surface' categories and definitions – such as wages and prices – that this distorted reality can be made to appear perversely natural. Our everyday understanding of the 'value' of the work we do and the goods we consume is such as to conceal the fundamentally exploitative nature of wage labour and the system of commodity production. Nonetheless, recent analyses of the development of welfare state regimes (Esping-Andersen, 1990, 1999) and associated critiques and developments of those analyses (Langan and Ostner, 1991; Lewis, 1992) have emphasised that state welfare has the potential not only to de-commodify labour power (by allowing people access to healthcare, education and limited income security independently of the labour market), but also, for example, to de-familialise it (because such provision may or may not reduce or limit dependency within the ideologically constructed family). Perversely, however, rather than the welfare state being seen as a means of achieving independence (for example, from exploitative employment or from abusive or oppressive family relationships), dependency on the state by unemployed people and lone parents can be highly stigmatising. Evidence from previous research (Dean and Taylor-Gooby, 1992) and from that reported in the preceding chapters of this book all suggests that, while dependency on employers for the means of subsistence and upon families for care and support are made to appear 'natural', if not indeed as a form of 'independence', dependency on the state – particularly for cash benefits – tends to be uniquely visible and especially problematic. People's understanding of the relations of power and dependency under which capitalist economic relations are sustained is fetishised not only because the exploitative nature of wage labour is largely denied, but also because the sustaining potential of collective interdependency is similarly obscured.

'Work', narrowly construed as wage labour, is seldom thought of in terms of the dependency of the employee on her employer. On the contrary, this form of dependency is celebrated within political and popular discourse alike. However, other forms of dependency are regarded with caution. We sought to illustrate in Chapter Four how, in capitalist democracies, dependency is something that people seek, by and large, to minimise, if not avoid. Working-age adults aspire to be independent subjects, although they will usually acknowledge that they have experienced periods of dependency in the past and that they will in all probability experience dependency in the future. Dependency, however, is something that evokes negative feelings. The paradox we observed in our research was that those who most vociferously denied their interdependency were those who most strongly asserted the importance of their own dependability for others. This echoes findings from earlier research in which it was observed that an eventuality that made people especially angry was when their ability to be responsible for those (especially children) who depended on them was threatened or undermined (Dean and Taylor-Gooby, 1992, pp 100-2). In Chapter Nine, Michael Orton demonstrated that prevailing political discourses tend to obscure the ways in which dependency and responsibility in families and communities are negotiated in practice (see Finch and Mason, 1993). Especially revealing is the quotation from Sheila (p 183 above), where she says how awful it made her feel to be on the receiving end of a friend's generosity: it made her feel "a bit second class". It is important to be dependable, but to be dependent is to be 'a bit second class'. It is as if only one side of our collective and generational interdependency is clearly visible.

What Marx identified as 'commodity fetishism' is clearly implicated in this distortion. Marxist writers (for example, Pashukanis, 1988) have demonstrated how our notions of justice and equity are similarly distorted. Human beings are constituted by capitalism as proprietors engaged in bilateral exchanges of commodities (including labour power and subsistence goods) in the marketplace. Our notions of justice and equity are constituted by the understandings of 'value' and 'equivalence' that inform such market transactions. They are fetishised constructs in the sense that they obscure our understanding of human well-being and social relationships. They obscure the sense in which the primary value of things derives from their usefulness, while fairness has to do with relationships between people, not things. The ethic of care explained and espoused in Chapter Two by Kathryn Ellis is a challenge to the commodity fetishism that denies the realities of human dependencies and relationships. Ellis's chapter sought to demonstrate the tensions between an ethic of care, on the one hand, and the principles of justice and equity on the other. Nonetheless, writers such as Clement (1998) and Friedman (1993) indicate that for an ethic of care to embrace the interdependency of strangers as well as intimates it may need to call upon the justice and equity principles in order to muster the impartiality and the rules by which to accord recognition and respect to the dependency of distant others.

It may be, however, that recognition and respect require a sense of solidarity rather than (mere) impartiality or an a priori set of rules. It was a younger Karl Marx (1845) who had deplored what he regarded as the self-alienation of the members of civil society from their own 'social humanity'. Insofar that 'work' may be construed as that which defines human beings as active subjects in nature, the labour by which commodities are produced is an alienated form of work. The purposive human activity that constitutes work can range from introspective acts of self-expression (for example, Fischer, 1963) to the provision of care for others. Our 'social humanity', as I understand it, rests upon the way that human beings work to sustain each other in their interdependency.

Responsibility

Several chapters in this book have drawn attention to the centrality of responsibility as a term within the discourse of the 'third way'.

In the British context, there has been a quite explicit attempt by New Labour to reconstruct understandings of responsibility. My emphasis in the preceding section on the construction of 'work' as paid employment needs now to be considered in the context of the political discourse of New Labour, in which 'work' is firmly connected to responsibility. This may be illustrated if one takes, for example, the introductions to the Labour Party's manifestos from the 1997 and 2001 General Elections. In the 1997 manifesto, Tony Blair begins with an ostensibly solidaristic assertion that "I want a Britain that is one nation, with shared values and purpose, where merit comes before privilege, run for the many not the few". However, the nature of the governance that is envisaged is then expressed in explicitly contractarian terms: "This is the purpose of the bond of trust I set out ... in which ten specific commitments are put before you.... They are our covenant with you". And then it is made clear that a New Labour government "will govern in the interest of the many, the broad majority of people who work hard, play by the rules [and] pay their dues" (Labour Party, 1997, p 1). To count among 'the many' for whom New Labour governs, one must be hard working and complaisant. In his introduction to the 2001 manifesto, Tony Blair once again offers "to refashion the welfare state on the basis of rights and responsibilities, with people helped to help themselves, not just given handouts", but this time there is a clear implication that, while a New Labour government will extend opportunity, responsibility rests upon "hard-working families":

> My passion is to continue the modernisation of Britain in favour of hard-working families, so that all our children ... have an equal chance to benefit from the opportunities our country has to offer ... millions of hard-working families want, need and deserve more. That means more change in a second term, not less – to extend opportunity for all. (Labour Party, 2001, p 3)

By constituting the hard-working family, rather than the self-sufficient individual, as the central social and political actor, New Labour acknowledges one element of human interdependency, but at the same time seeks to contain it by placing responsibility within families. People should sustain themselves within families by accepting opportunities for (potentially demanding) paid employment. Responsibility is constructed primarily as an individual or familial matter. And we have seen in Chapter Four that this appears to resonate with currently prevailing popular discourses.

In Chapter Three, Shane Doheny argued that such an approach is founded more in morality than ethics. In ordinary English usage, 'morality' and 'ethics' have become virtually synonymous. For present purposes, however, we are distinguishing ethics from moral *codes* on the one hand (insofar that ethics reflect the values that inform a social *ethos*), and from *customary* morality on the other (insofar that I understand ethics to entail an element of reflexivity). In reality, ethics and morality exist in dialectical relationship each with the other and the distinction can prove elusive. Systemic ethical values promulgated through secular or religious doctrine will inform moral norms from the top-down (and may be perpetuated as ossified customs), while moral norms forged through social change and hegemonic struggle will inform ethical values from the bottom-up (and may be perpetuated as reflexive ideals). The 'hard-working family' is a moral rather than an ethical construction. Insofar that there is an ethical element to 'third way' conceptions of responsibility, it is to be found in the fundamentally restrictive, individualistic ethical techniques of the self promoted through welfare-to-work policies and the encouragement of prudential self-provisioning (see Rose, 1996; see also Chapter Eight of this book). In the event, the ethic imposed upon jobseekers by the British welfare-to-work regime, as Rogers demonstrates in Chapter Eight, is hardly 'moral' in that it encourages jobseekers to use tricks, verging on deception, in order to secure employment.

Such issues of morality and ethics bear most crucially upon questions concerning the motivation of both welfare providers and welfare recipients. Le Grand (1997, 2003) has argued that the marketisation of welfare provision reflects an assumption on the part of policy makers that welfare providers behave as instrumental 'knaves', rather than altruistic 'knights', while welfare recipients, instead of being passive 'pawns', must liberate themselves to become autonomous 'queens'. By contrast, Chapter Seven clearly demonstrates that welfare recipients are not passive 'pawns' at all, since they clearly do exercise agency. Dwyer's analysis in that chapter demonstrates that such agency is problematised within 'third way' political discourse: while citizens are enjoined to become responsible risk takers, welfare recipients may be characterised as irresponsible cheats.

There is a connection to be made here with Doheny's exploration in Chapter Three of the different kinds of citizen that are implicitly constructed through governmental press releases. The citizen as responsible risk taker equates with the citizen as heroic consumer, who seeks out the benefits on offer from instrumentally motivated, but efficient, welfare entrepreneurs. The citizen who wilfully plays the odds to cheat the system equates with the citizen as recalcitrant or disobedient subject, who is supposed to undermine the authority of an overburdened welfare system. However, Doheny also identifies the passive citizen, who has to be cajoled into risk taking and the 'good citizen' who is, as it were, a responsible but unreconstructed subject, reluctant to detach her/himself from the ministrations of altruistically motivated but inefficient state systems.

In practice, such distinctions cannot necessarily be empirically sustained. In Chapter Seven, Dwyer demonstrates the extent to which even the relatively affluent and highly mobile middle-classes may feel able quite legitimately to maximise what they can obtain through state welfare systems. The survival strategies that most people pursue entail an element of 'bet hedging'. Insofar that people are for the most part risk-averse, they are likely to cling on (in part at least) to the kind of solidaristic moral repertoires that value collective welfare provision (see Dean, 1999). What the evidence recounted in Part Two suggests, however, is that while collective provision is valued, this tends not to be translated into solidaristic interpretations of responsibility. Such thinking is of course explicitly *discouraged* by the 'third way'.

Rights

I have already in Chapter One set out the case for saying that social or welfare rights are under threat. On the one hand, social rights have always remained subordinate to civil and political rights. On the other, the capacity of governments to sustain social rights is compromised by processes associated with globalisation.

In the British context, the continuing shift towards selectivity and means testing means that certain rights have become more conditional in nature. Continuing changes to the welfare mix mean that certain aspects of social rights have been 'privatised'. It is not only that certain kinds of welfare provision have been transferred from the public to either the private or not-for-profit voluntary sector; rather, changes in the fundamental nature of public service provision have reconstituted the citizen as a consumer or 'customer' whose rights to choose and to complain about welfare services are akin to civil rather than social rights (Dean, 2002). Where, as in the case of community care policy, services have transferred to the informal sector, it could be argued that rights have been 'informalised': aspects of the care that one can expect will be negotiated not by right but by social custom.

We have seen in Chapter Four that popular discourse is by no means inimical to the idea of inalienable rights, but it is heavily influenced on the one hand by scepticism about the enforceability and affordability of unconditional social rights, but perhaps more fundamentally by intolerance towards 'others' who might also rely upon such rights. I have suggested that it is the relative absence of a solidaristic ethic of responsibility that stands in the way of an unequivocal popular commitment to social rights. In Chapters Five and Six, we saw that welfare providers can be especially sceptical about rights, in case they should diminish the complaisance of clients/claimants. Social workers, although they were supportive of the idea of basic rights to welfare, were concerned that more extensive notions of rights might constrain their capacity for professional judgement. Benefits administrators adopted a rigidly 'blackletter' approach to claimants' rights and were anxious that more extensive notions of rights might constrain the administrative process.

It may well be that, across the developed world, social rights are now dismissed as relics of a bygone Keynesian era. In the meantime, in the developing world the language of human rights is being applied strategically to defend the struggles of new and indigenous social movements; as a means of asserting rights to self-determination (for example, van Genugten and Perez-Bustillo, 2001). However, this does not necessarily mean that social rights are being embraced as a substantive component of human rights. This appears to be so sometimes because of the priority that is given in such struggles to civil and political rights, and sometimes because their association with the dirigisme of the capitalist state taints social rights.

Human rights lawyers will argue that insinuating a human rights culture throughout the institutions by which civil rights are regulated and upheld will ensure greater respect for social equality (for example, Massa Arzabe, 2001). It is assumed that the solidaristic gloss of human rights discourse can mediate the tension between liberty and equality. The emphasis placed by human rights instruments on the principle of human 'dignity' is seized upon as a rhetorical defence or argument for policies to combat poverty. It must be remembered, however, that all too often peoples who experience poverty do so with great 'dignity'. To achieve effective social rights it may be necessary that the poor abandon dignified acquiescence and refuse to suffer in silence! Emancipation entails political struggle.

Other commentators seek alternatives to the conventional assumptions of social development discourse (for example, Crush, 1995). Escobar (1995, p 209) suggests that, for many scholars in or of the developing world:

> The 'old' is often yoked to analyses of modernisation or dependency; to politics centred around traditional actors like parties, vanguards, and the

> working class who struggle for the control of the State.... The 'new', by
> contrast, is invoked in analyses based not on structures but on social actors;
> the promotion of democratic, egalitarian and participatory styles of politics.

Alternatives to development are to be found, it is argued, not by engagement with the state, but through new social movements: through a subaltern political domain or through parallel networks of power. It has been claimed that new social movements – including urban popular movements, religious communities, peasant mobilisations, new types of workers' organisations and novel forms of popular protest – can contribute to "constructing new social orders, propitiating new models of development and promoting the emergence of new utopias" (Colderon, cited in Escobar, 1995, pp 218-19). Yet, despite the concerns of new social movements with issues of social justice and human rights, their axiomatic preoccupation is with informal strategies and action, rather than with the discredited formal apparatuses of the state.

The relationship between individual rights and social movements has been investigated empirically by Foweraker and Landman (1997) who have conducted a comparative analysis of mobilisation against authoritarian rule during the latter half of the 20th century, in Brazil, Chile, Mexico and Spain. Their data tend to indicate that, in practice, labour movement activity in pursuit of citizenship rights tended to precede and to be greater in scope than social movement activity. The risk, so far as these authors are concerned, is that the class-based demands of labour can lead too easily to the kind of state-corporatism that is regarded as inimical to liberal democracy, but in this context, they claim, the collective demands of social movements tend to shift over time from economic and material (or 'social welfare') rights to civil and political rights. The empirical evidence, therefore, tends to confirm that new social movements, while engaging with the human rights agenda, do not necessarily situate demands for social rights as a part of this process. The implication is that, although it may be mobilised in radically different ways and for quite different purposes, the human rights agenda can be as contractarian or liberal-individualist in its interpretation in the developing as in the developed world.

The issue, therefore, is whether and how it might be possible to re-establish and invigorate social rights as a component of human rights. In Chapter One of this book, I argued in abstract terms for the concept of an 'ethical state' as a precondition for such a development. In the final section of this book, however, I want to return to theorise the relationship of rights to dependency, on the one hand, and responsibility, on the other.

Towards a human rights approach to welfare

I would accept, with Campbell (1999, p 25), that the "content, form and valence of human rights are inherently controversial", and that, therefore, "a culture of rights may be political rather than legal in its nature". More fundamentally, I would argue that rights represent a mode of discursive struggle. Rights provide a medium through which demands may be framed and concessions secured. Ultimately, rights are negotiated, not determinate; they are constitutive of our personhood, not contingent upon it. It is through rights that we can give expression to our needs, on the one hand, and our capabilities, on the other. Although it is a facile and reductionist representation of the argument that follows, I have attempted to outline diagrammatically the conceptual connections that I am seeking to build (Figure 10.1).

Personhood

The primary concern of this book is with welfare rights (broadly conceived). The idea that welfare rights may be counted as human rights is not without its supporters. Griffin has argued that "human rights are best seen as protections of one's human standing" – "one's *personhood*, as one might put it"; and on this premise, that human rights therefore include "not only autonomy and liberty but also *minimum material provision* – that is some sort of right to welfare" (2000, p 29, emphases in original). Here, Griffin is disagreeing with those who would claim that autonomy and liberty are the constituents of personhood, whereas minimum provision is only a necessary condition of it. The right to life – that is, constituted as a civil not a social right, but from which rights to welfare must surely follow – is no less and no more than a necessary condition of personhood, and any sustainable or practical conception of human rights must be broad enough to encompass the things that make personhood possible: they must protect life itself as well as its idealised form. Griffin does not go so far as to argue that a right to welfare (or to well-being) can itself be constitutive of personhood, rather than a mere condition for it. The first part of the argument

Figure 10.1: Constituting personhood through rights

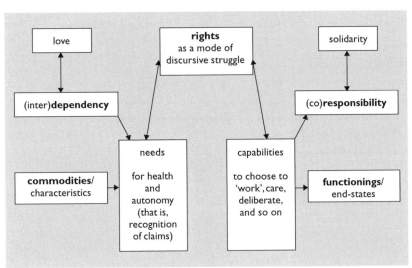

that I develop here is that, through Amartya Sen's concept of 'capabilities' (as I interpret them), we have a notion that can capture the sense in which a right to welfare does indeed constitute, rather than potentiate, personhood.

Griffin also addresses the idea that human rights should reflect no more and no less than the responsibilities every human being owes to every other human being. Opponents of welfare rights claim that no one person can have ethical responsibility for the welfare needs of every other person on the planet. Griffin, in effect, says they may. Were any adult able, without risk to her/himself, to rescue a drowning child we might accept that she would have a responsibility to do so if, by accident of circumstance, s/he were the only person in a position to effect such a rescue. The point is that "there are some forms of aid that anyone able to give them owes to anyone in need of them – whether or not the two agents are related as government and citizen" (2000, p 34). While there is on the one hand a resonance here with the ideals of 19th-century anarchists, such as William Godwin, who asserted the right to the *individual* assistance of one's neighbour (see Marshall, 1993, p 205), Griffin expressly permits the idea that it is through *collective* provision that the responsibilities of all towards all can be met. Providing for essential welfare needs need not be left to accident. The welfare state enables us to give to strangers (see Titmuss, 1970). Those who resent the intrusion of the state into the moral equation might complain, with Ignatieff (1994, p 141), that:

> We think of belonging in moral terms as direct impingement on the lives of others: fraternity implies the closeness of brothers. Yet the moral relations that exist between my income and the needs of the stranger at my door pass through the arteries of the state.

However, the second part of my argument returns to Axel Honneth's claim (see my interpretation in Chapter One of this book) that rights must rest upon the recognition of one human being by another. Such recognition does not require intimacy. It is no more fantastic to accept that a stranger has a right to deny me goods that I might need because she claims superior title through ownership of such goods than to suppose she has a right to demand help from me because she claims needs that I (whether personally or through my participation in a collective process) can meet. If, under capitalism, we have come to recognise each other as proprietors (whether we possess anything or not) we can surely come to recognise each other as persons (whether we know each other or not).

Capabilities

We come firstly, therefore, to the concept of capabilities and the relationship between capabilities and needs. Sen (1984, 1985) draws an important distinction between the space of *capabilities* – by which he means the capacity and the freedom of the individual to choose and to act – and:

- the space of *commodities* (the goods, services or other resources to which people have access), on the one hand, and the essential characteristics of those commodities (the properties which define their purpose or utility);
- and, on the other hand, the space of *functionings* (the range of activities that human beings may achieve) and subjective end states (the happiness or sense of well-being that are the final outcome).

Capabilities, therefore, represent the essential fulcrum between primary resources and human achievements; or between welfare inputs and welfare outputs. Equal inputs do not necessarily give rise to equal outputs because human capabilities may be constrained. The utility of particular commodities and the well-being that results from particular functioning are determined and mediated by a host of socioeconomic, cultural-historical and geographical-climatic factors. Capabilities are constitutive of the person in a way that neither commodities nor functionings can be, since they relate to the ability of a particular individual in a particular social context freely to determine how she lives her life. A slave might be adequately provided for in the space of commodities and might acquire and exercise useful skills in the space of functionings, but s/he would still be impoverished in the space of capabilities. For this reason human capabilities should not be conflated with human capital: investment in a person's health and in their skills may produce a return that will benefit both the welfare of the individual and the productivity of the economy. But if such an investment is in any way imposed, it does not enhance human capabilities.

However, Sen is notoriously reluctant to define or to list specifically what human capabilities are or should be. In Sen's sense of the term (as I grasp it), capabilities represent the sum of a person's actually achievable potential and, strictly speaking, are particular, not universal.

In contrast, the theory of human need developed by Doyal and Gough (1991) is premised on the idea that it is possible to establish universal criteria for the satisfaction of human beings' most fundamental needs for health and autonomy. However, while identifying autonomy as a basic human need there is a sense in which the approach tends to conflate the space of capabilities (in which human subjects must be free to exercise substantive choice) with the space of actual human functionings through which people may ultimately achieve their 'ontological identity' (Taylor, 1998), but in which choices can in practice be constrained and needs will be contested.

There are aspects of the human-needs approach that are less individualistic in orientation than Sen's original capabilities approach. It is concerned with emancipation and the 'societal preconditions' for optimising need-satisfaction (Doyal and Gough, 1991). This chimes with Nussbaum's (2000) reinterpretation of the capabilities approach, which develops the concept of 'combined capabilities', where individual capabilities are facilitated by suitable institutional conditions. Nussbaum also goes further than Sen in generating a list of what individual capabilities might consist of, a list that encompasses not only life itself, bodily health and bodily integrity, but such things as emotions and affiliations. It could as easily be construed as a list of rights, or, for example, as a list of the kind of items that Williams (1999) identifies as "good enough principles of welfare".

For my own part, I wish to identify a set of three capabilities that should, to my mind, be construed as contributing to the sum of human capabilities: the capability for work, care and deliberation. Following the discussion earlier in this chapter, it should be clear that by the capability to work I mean far more than the capacity for wage labour, but for all kinds of freely chosen productive or expressive human activity. By the capability for care, I am referring to the capacity and the freedom to give and receive effective care in the context of supportive, satisfying and non-coercive human relationships. By the capability for deliberation, I am referring to the ability freely and effectively to engage in mutually constituted discursive processes – both informal and formal – through which human needs can be identified and resources to meet needs can be negotiated: it is upon this capability that a 'politics of need interpretation' would depend (Fraser, 1985; see also Chapter One of this book).

What the capabilities approach and the human needs approach have in common is that they are mutually dependent on rights as an ethical device; that is, as a mode of discursive negotiation or struggle. Rights provide the medium through which definitions of need can be translated into normative standards, and therefore capabilities. Conversely, rights provide a means of interpreting capabilities in terms of substantive needs. Insofar that there is a conceptual 'black box' at the ethical and normative heart of the process by which human beings translate what Sen calls commodities into functionings, I would suggest we need to understand the role that rights play in mediating needs and capabilities.

Recognition

Second, we turn again to Honneth (1995) and his contention that rights require the recognition of the subject's ethical capacity to make claims. When we translate needs into claims (see Spicker, 1993) it is through rights that we may seek and achieve recognition. For Honneth (1995, p 92), "the reproduction of social life is governed by the imperative of mutual recognition" and he identifies three modes of intersubjective recognition: in addition to rights, there are love and solidarity. All human beings need love and all are capable of solidarity.

Love provides the emotional substance of our more intimate relations of dependency. It is through caring for each other that we come to recognise, accommodate and respect each other as needy creatures. Honneth, drawing on Hegel's social philosophy and Mead's social psychology, contends that love entails discovering and being oneself in and through another: love is necessary for self-identity. Solidarity provides the basis on which to apprehend our shared responsibilities for strangers. It is through the sharing of ethical goals and cultural understandings with other members of a social group that we come to recognise, accommodate and respect each other as creatures defined through difference. Honneth contends that solidarity entails establishing one's traits and abilities through collective identity: solidarity is necessary for self-esteem.

For Honneth rights entail cognitive respect. It is through rights that we come to recognise each other – not merely as proprietors – but as bearers of that universal capacity which characterises human beings. There is a certain affinity, I would suggest, between this idea of a universal constitutive capacity and Sen's notion of capabilities. There is also a more explicit affinity with Kant's categorical imperative, insofar that it is through rights, Honneth supposes, that we come to recognise each other as we would ourselves wish to be recognised: rights are necessary for self-respect. Honneth's argument is that all three modes of recognition are the subject of conflict and struggle. My own argument, however, is that it is rights as a mode of discursive struggle – or rather the nexus of our rights, capabilities and needs – that provide a pivotal link between love and solidarity; between the ways we come to recognise and negotiate our interdependency and the ways in which we might establish cooperative forms of responsibility; between the welfare of intimates and that of strangers. It is an attempt to engage with calls – including, for example, those by Dwyer and Orton in their respective contributions to this book (Chapters Seven and Nine) – for a new way of thinking about dependency, responsibility and the rights of citizenship. The model I have outlined (and more or less crudely represented in Figure 10.1) provides, on the one hand, a logical heuristic analysis, and thereby offers an ethical framework. On the other hand, it is also a normative argument and therefore represents a moral framework. The question must be: 'Is it – literally speaking – 'sensible'?'

Conclusion

There is evidence that over the past quarter of a century people in Britain have come to see personal relationships "less in terms of social responsibilities and obligations and more in terms of personal resources and fulfilment" (Ferri et al, 2003, p 303), while trade union membership – that most traditional badge of class solidarity – has almost halved (Machin, 2000). It has been suggested that we live increasingly in an amoral, 'post-emotional' age (for example, Rodger, 2000, ch 7), in which people's emotional responses have ceased to be authentic and their goals are informed by a self-centred form of survivalism. Britain's National Lottery, instituted in 1994, captures the sense in which a shallow, residual kind of caring for others though support for 'good causes' is married to a self-preoccupied desire for personal wealth through the chance of winning the jackpot. However, the evidence presented in previous chapters (most particularly those comprising Part Two of this book) would not entirely support such a sweepingly pessimistic conclusion. We have seen that people are conscious by and large of their own dependency on others and they are prepared to acknowledge that others should have at least certain kinds of rights, but the sphere within which they apprehend the nature of responsibility does indeed tend to be narrowly construed, their support for dependency on the state tends to be qualified and their commitment to universal welfare rights remains weak.

Our evidence tends to support findings from previous research (Dean, 1999) that popular discourse is flexible, rich and complex. It embodies mixtures of repertoires that would probably be capable, depending on the circumstances, of responding to hegemonic shifts in favour of a demystification of dependency, solidaristic forms of responsibility, and a more extensive appreciation of welfare rights. The principal obstacles to this, however, lie in the hostility that welfare providers and 'third way' ideologues seem to have to a rights based approach.

It will be clear from Chapters Five and Six that, although they may be welfare providers, the discourses of social workers and benefits administrators are not so very different from popular discourses. Social workers and benefits administrators are, as might be expected, rather more inclined than the public they serve to be committed to the provision of welfare and to the public service ethic. However, their respective commitments to professional autonomy and to administrative process tended to preclude an acceptance of a universalistic approach to welfare rights. Their own roles and their authority are constructed in relation to the needs of their clients or claimants, and responsible or 'good' clients or claimants should, by implication, be if not passive, then at least cooperative or compliant. The identity that is conferred upon social workers and benefits administrators by the roles they fulfil can be threatened when clients and claimants make demands based on rights. The bigger problem, however, lies with the essentially contractarian nature of the 'third way' political consensus and its hegemonic grip around questions of dependency, responsibility and rights. It is a consensus that problematises dependency, restricts responsibility and marginalises rights. I wish to advance four suggestions:

1. *A new theoretical project is required by which more fully to articulate the sociological conception of social rights with the emergent international human rights agenda.* In the past social rights have been dismissed as a dangerous fiction – from the right of the ideological spectrum, because they are an infringement of property based rights; and from the left, because they mask the exploitative nature of class relations. In an era of globalisation, however, social rights may now become either an ineffectual anachronism within the discourse of human rights, or a concept that can perhaps effectively challenge capitalism's globalising tendencies by providing the medium through which needs may be articulated and demands framed at the local level. Critical to this theoretical project, I believe, is our conception of ethics on the one hand, and the role of the state on the other.

2. *It is necessary, for such a project to have real consequences, to engage critically with the language of human rights instruments and with their legal meanings and consequences.* A new socio-legal project is required in order to move the discourse of human rights into the arena of enforceable social rights. A dialogue is required between social scientists with an interest in welfare reform and the

kind of lawyers who seek to extend constitutional law and human rights in the cause of social justice (see Hunt, 1990; Bowring, 2002).

3. *A political project is required to extend the commitment to social rights as human rights.* In the European context, this means strengthening and building upon such instruments as the revised Social Charter of the Council of Europe and the Charter of Fundamental Rights of the European Union. At the very least, more European nations should be persuaded to ratify the former, and greater specificity and power should be accorded to the latter.

4. *It is important that the people who interpret and implement social policies at street level should have the opportunity to debate such issues and to consider to what extent a human rights approach to welfare might present not a threat to their professional autonomy or administrative authority, but an opportunity to be more effective as advocates for the rights of the citizens they serve.* There is scope here within several professions and, potentially, a role for those involved in the training and education of welfare providers.

It is still possible to foster a solidaristic, rather than a contractarian, understanding of human rights, an understanding that connects personal dependency with shared responsibility through a commitment to human welfare.

References

Bowring, W. (2001) 'Forbidden relations? The UK's discourse of human rights and the struggle for social justice', Inaugural Professorial Lecture, University of North London, 30 January.

Campbell, T. (1999) 'Human rights: a culture of controversy', *Journal of Law and Society*, vol 26, no 1, pp 6-26.

Clarke, J. (1999) 'Coming to terms with culture', in H. Dean and R. Woods (eds) *Social Policy Review 11*, Luton: Social Policy Association.

Clement, G. (1998) *Care, autonomy and justice: Feminism and the ethic of care*, Boulder, CO: Westview Press.

Crush, J. (ed) (1995) *The power of development*, London: Routledge.

Dean, H. (2002) *Welfare rights and social policy*, Harlow: Prentice Hall.

Dean, H. and Taylor-Gooby, P. (1992) *Dependency culture: The explosion of a myth*, Hemel Hempstead: Harvester Wheatsheaf.

Dean, H. and Thompson, D. (1996) 'Fetishising the family: constructing the informal carer', in H. Jones and J. Millar (eds) *The politics of the family*, Aldershot: Avebury.

Dean, H. with Melrose, M. (1999) *Poverty, riches and social citizenship*, Basingstoke: Macmillan.

Doyal, L. and Gough, I. (1991) *A theory of human need*, Basingstoke: Macmillan.

Du Boulay, S. (1988) *Tutu: Voice of the voiceless*, London: Hodder and Stoughton.

Escobar, A. (1995) 'Imagining a post-development era', in J. Crush (ed) *The power of development*, London: Routledge.

Esping-Andersen, G. (1990) *The three worlds of welfare capitalism*, Cambridge: Polity.

Esping-Andersen, G. (1999) *Social foundations of post-industrial economies*, Oxford: Oxford University Press.

Ferri, E., Bynner, J. and Walsworth, M. (2003) *Changing Britain, changing lives: Three generations at the turn of the century*, London: Institute of Education.

Finch, J. and Mason, J. (1993) *Negotiating family responsibilities*, London: Routledge.

Fischer, E. (1963) *The necessity of art: A Marxist approach*, Harmondsworth: Penguin.

Foweraker, J. and Landman, T. (1997) *Citizenship rights and social movements: A comparative and statistical analysis*, Oxford: Oxford University Press.

Fraser, N. (1989) *Unruly practices*, Cambridge: Polity.

Friedman, M. (1993) 'Beyond caring: the de-moralisation of gender', in M. Larabee (ed) *An ethic of care: Feminist and interdisciplinary perspectives*, New York, NY: Routledge.

Griffin, J. (2000) 'Welfare rights', *The Journal of Ethics*, vol 4, pp 27-43.

Honneth, A. (1995) *The struggle for recognition: The moral grammar of social conflicts*, Cambridge: Polity.

Hunt, A. (1990) 'Rights and social movements: counter-hegemonic strategies', *Journal of Law and Society*, vol 17, no 3, pp 309-28.

Ignatieff, M. (1984) *The needs of strangers*, London: Chatto and Windus.

Langan, M. and Ostner, I. (1991) 'Gender and welfare: towards a comparative framework', in G. Room (ed) *Towards a European welfare state*, Bristol: SAUS Publications.

LeGrand, J. (1997) 'Knights, knaves or pawns? Human behaviour and social policy', *Journal of Social Policy*, vol 26, no 2, pp 149-69.

LeGrand, J. (2003) *Motivation, agency and public policy: Of knights and knaves, pawns and queens*, Oxford: Oxford University Press.

Lewis, J. (1992) 'Gender and the development of welfare regimes', *Journal of European Social Policy*, vol 2, no 3, pp 159-73.

Machin, S. (2000) 'How are the mighty fallen: what accounts for the dramatic decline of unions in Britain?', *CentrePiece*, vol 5, no 2, pp 28-30.

Marshall, P. (1993) *Demanding the impossible: A history of anarchism*, London: Fontana.

Marx, K. (1845) 'Thesis on Fuerbach', in *Marx-Engels Gesamtausgabe*, vol 1.5, translated extract in T. Bottomore and M. Rubel (1963) *Karl Marx: Selected writings in sociology and social philosophy*, Harmondsworth: Penguin.

Marx, K. (1887) *Capital*, vol 1 (1970 edn), London: Lawrence and Wishart.

Massa Arzabe, P. (2001) 'Human rights: a new paradigm', in W. van Genugten and C. Perez-Bustillo (eds) *The poverty of rights: Human rights and the elimination of poverty*, London: CROP/Zed Books.

Nussbaum, M. (2000) *Women and human development: The capabilities approach*, Cambridge: Cambridge University Press.

Pashukanis, E. (1988) *A general theory of law and Marxism*, London: Ink Links.

Rodger, J. (2000) *From a welfare state to a welfare society*, Basingstoke: Macmillan.

Rose, N. (1996) 'The death of the social?', *Economy and Society*, vol 25, no 3, pp 327-56.

Sen, A. (1984) *Resources values and development*, Oxford: Blackwell.

Sen, A. (1985) *Commodities and capabilities*, Amsterdam: Elsevier.

Spicker, P. (1993) 'Needs as claims', *Social Policy and Administration*, vol 27, no 1, pp 7-17.

Taylor, D. (1998) 'Social identity and social policy: engagements with postmodern theory', *Journal of Social Policy*, vol 27, no 3, pp 329-50.

Titmuss, R. (1970) *The gift relationship*, London: Allen & Unwin.

van Genugten, W. and Perez-Bustillo, C. (eds) (2001) *The poverty of rights*, London: Zed Books.

Williams, F. (1999) 'Good-enough principles for welfare', *Journal of Social Policy*, vol 28, no 4, pp 667-87.

Index

Page references for figures and tables are in *italics*